PHYSICAL EDUCATION:
A MOVEMENT ORIENTATION

PHYSICAL EDUCATION:
A MOVEMENT ORIENTATION

SHEILA STANLEY, B.A., M.Sc.
Toronto Teachers' College

Toronto

McGRAW-HILL COMPANY OF CANADA LIMITED

Montreal
New York
St. Louis
San Francisco
London
Sydney
Johannesburg
Mexico
Panama

CREDITS

The author and publisher wish to extend their thanks to the Boards of Education for the various Boroughs for their splendid response and cooperation in providing photographs. To Etobicoke for the photographs on pages 2, 18, 59, 77, 167, 238, 244, 279; to North York for the photographs on pages 138, 196, 259, 290, 324, 325; to Scarborough for the photographs on pages 4, 41, 45, 85, 109, 131, 217, 230, 284, 313, 314; to Toronto for the photographs on pages 11, 17, 42, 90, 91, 199, 202, 272, 307. To the Vancouver School Board for the photographs on pages 105, 207, 208. To the Edmonton Public Schools for the photograph on page 215. To the Manchester School, Galt, Ontario for the artwork on pages 134, 135, 261, 268.

PHYSICAL EDUCATION: A MOVEMENT ORIENTATION

94988

Library of Congress Catalog Card No. 71-75772

34567890 M & B 69 876543210

Printed and bound in Canada.

ACKNOWLEDGMENTS

The author acknowledges with great appreciation the goodwill and support offered by colleagues in physical education in Ontario, other parts of Canada and in England. The generosity in allowing free access to picture collections is particularly appreciated. Miss Nora Chatwin and Miss Janette Vallance of the Ontario Department of Education; Mr. Bing Caswell, Mr. Ross Waters and Miss Brenda Beckett of the North York schools; Mr. Charles Prince and Mr. Arthur Webb of the Toronto schools; Mr. Lew Smith, Mr. Harry Mighton and Miss Elizabeth Adamson of the Scarborough schools; Mrs. Mary Liddell of the Etobicoke schools supplied many of the pictures. Mr. Stuart Bird and Miss Marion Irwin of the Edmonton schools, and Mr. Gordon Brandreth and Miss Flora Gillies of Vancouver were generous in their response to the author's request to have school systems from across Canada represented.

To Miss Patricia Bailey, thanks for the use of some of her pupils' art work.

To Mr. Ted West and Mr. R. Webster, thanks for their graciousness in contributing their special ability in action photography.

While the author must assume full responsibility for any errors in interpretation, judgment or presentation, she wishes to acknowledge the valuable assistance given by those who read the first drafts of some or all of the chapters, namely Miss Rose Hill, McMaster University, Hamilton; Miss Lisa Ullmann, The Laban Art of Movement Studio, Addlestone, England; and Miss Elsie Palmer, Physical Education Organizer for the County of Lancashire, England.

Lastly, the author recognizes the debt owed to her own teachers and to her colleagues, particularly Mrs. Mary Liddell of Etobicoke, who have participated in discussions, experimental lessons and programs in an effort to clarify the purpose, method and "the logic of movement." Thanks are also due to students and pupils who have willingly entered into participation in those early lessons.

TABLE OF CONTENTS

INTRODUCTION

PHYSICAL EDUCATION IN SCHOOLS

For some thirty years now the term "physical education" has been used to designate the curriculum followed in the school gymnasium and the school playing field. It has been regarded by Williams as education through the physical.[1][2] Teachers have realized that the term "physical training," as it was once called, narrowed the outlook and focussed attention on physiological outcomes such as joint flexibility, muscular strength and heart-lung capacity.

The term "physical education" indicates a widened outlook. As teachers have striven to educate the whole child by means of guided participation in physical activity, they have made use of vigorous movement to maintain and develop a physically efficient body mechanism. They have ushered the pupil through a carefully evaluated series of progressive stages toward the mastery of the various skills required for participation in team games, swimming, tumbling and gymnastic activities, and dance. They have made use of the demands of team participation to advance his ability to interact satisfactorily with his peers and his elders. They have been alert to recognize the emotional demands that are made upon the pupil and have endeavoured to keep these demands within the level of the maturity of the child. Teachers have also made use of the activity situations which demand an understanding of strategy, cause and effect, and knowledgeable use of the body as an instrument.

[1] Jesse F. Williams, "Education through the Physical," — *Journal of Higher Education,* Vol. 1, no. 5, The Ohio State University Press, Columbus, 1930, pp. 279-282.

[2] Jesse F. Williams, *The Principles of Physical Education*, Third Edition, W. B. Saunders and Co., Philadelphia, 1938.

Since the purpose has been "to educate through the physical," teachers have been mindful that this should be an opportunity available to all pupils. Therefore, in class instructional periods, they have chosen activities and methods which would permit all to participate and all to grow. Aware that some grow faster than others, teachers have arranged an intramural program in which all performers could participate if they were interested in doing so. In the high school program, it has also been customary to challenge the most talented players by means of competition against their counterparts in neighbouring schools.

However, progress has been geared to the average ability of the class. In spite of the best intentions of the teacher, the poor performers have lagged behind the general standard of the class, while the highly skilled pupils have never been really extended during the class lesson.

MOVEMENT EDUCATION IN SCHOOLS

Into this set of circumstances has come, in recent years, a change which is rooted in the philosophy and principles of movement which have been postulated by Rudolf Laban. These principles have evolved empirically and they stem from a long and detailed study of the movements of men and women in the pursuit of everyday activities at work and in recreation, as well as a study of the highly skilled artistry of movement on the stage.

Teachers enrolled in classes conducted by Laban or his associates began to see in his work, concepts which could be applied with advantage to the physical education work in their own schools.

It is the application of these principles to physical education with the philosophy underlying them that this text purposes to present.

ONE

THE NATURE OF THE CHILD AND ITS EFFECT UPON THE MOVEMENT PROGRAM

Teachers are teachers of children rather than teachers of physical education, English or mathematics. This does not mean that they need to know very little about physical education, English or mathematics. On the contrary, they must be thoroughly familiar with their particular body of knowledge in order that they may use it in all its manifold aspects in the service of their pupils' growth and development. This does mean, however, that teachers must make use of their understanding of children as they move through the various stages of growth and development.

A brief presentation of the characteristics of children, which are especially significant to procedures in physical education, may be helpful at this point. Further details may be obtained by reading the material listed in the references.

Children:

- vary in body build

Some have a relatively large skeletal frame, while others appear to be small and delicate. Some tend to be lean and muscular; others carry a relatively greater proportion of fatty tissue. There is a wide range of heights at any given age.

- vary in temperament

Some are placid, even lethargic; others are nervous, energetic and highstrung. Some, even at an early age, take matters lightly, seem secure in their world and bring a sense of humour to the situation. Others are less secure, worry, try too hard to succeed and bring an intensity of spirit into all they do.

- vary in family background

Some have been overprotected at home. Their sense of independence and adventure has been curtailed. They may have become overcautious or, as a reaction to undue surveillance, aggressive and reckless. In contrast, some have had little guidance from their families; therefore they may be

Children vary in body build.

rash and without powers of concentration. Alternatively, they may be seeking a status at school through various forms of attention-getting behaviour.

- vary in physical health

Some are robust, well-coordinated, generally free from colds and seemingly able to resist many of the health problems which beset their classmates. Others may be subject to frequent colds and susceptible to all the common childhood diseases. Some may be undernourished or lack sufficient rest and sleep. Some may be overweight, even at an early age. Occasionally, a small child will suffer from a defect such as poor eyesight or hearing, an orthopaedic malformation or a heart condition which will affect his physical performance. It is possible that some children will require a restricted activity program, or be excluded by their doctors from any participation.

The best teachers recognize, among other things, that pupils must be regarded as individuals who react to various situations in quite personal ways. Their responses are affected by inherited and environmental factors, and the teacher must seek to make allowances for these individual differences. Furthermore, good teachers will attempt to find the means for allowing each child to grow and develop towards his own greatest potential and in accordance with his own rhythm of growth.

CHARACTERISTICS OF CHILDREN DETERMINE THE CHOICE OF ACTIVITIES

Although it is important to recognize that the individuality of the pupil must be a guiding factor in the teacher's selection of method and activities, it must also be recognized that children develop in accordance with a fairly characteristic sequential pattern.[1] The individual child's pattern is a variation of the general pattern. Hence it is helpful to identify the characteristics of children in the different levels of the elementary school. The general characteristics discussed here are those which have a particular bearing on the physical education program.

KINDERGARTEN CHILDREN

They are topheavy, and, therefore, have difficulty in retaining their upright posture in times of stress. When five-year-olds run, it is easy to observe their unsteadiness. They have difficulty in stopping suddenly and in dodging. They will often choose to work close to the floor. They have difficulty in upward jumps and rarely land in other than a sort of collapse on the floor. They have a great deal of energy but little stamina. They tend to work with great speed and force. Occasionally some dawdle, but in the main a child working at a slow pace should be watched to determine the reason behind this type of action. From a psychological point of view they are at the egocentric stage. That is to say, they can interpret the world only in the light of their own relatively limited experiences. Thus they think in terms of "ME doing this — or that." Physically, they throw their "whole selves" into an activity. It is not natural for them to isolate movements. For example, if they happen to be doing a movement which is basically an arm action, their whole bodies will be engaged in accompanying actions.

The lack of physical maturity described above which pertains to balance is clearly observed in gymnastic work. However, they can be very inventive in locomotor activities, using many variations of running, hopping, crawling, creeping and rolling. Skipping, either as a form of locomotion or as a rope skill is a coordination which develops slowly for many children, particularly for boys. However, young children can grip, climb, hang, pull, push, and roll like a log. When they roll over they tend to lose the curled shape of the body at the conclusion of the action and slap their feet and even their hips on the ground. Some have discovered ways of inverting themselves, probably in an attempt to stand on their heads. Most of them are interested in experiencing the sensation of being fairly high off the ground, as on a balance bench, and many enjoy the sensation of jumping down from a height of two or three feet.

[1] Camilla Brown and Rosalind Cassidy, *Theory in Physical Education*, Lea and Febiger, Philadelphia, 1963, p. 59.

"Me, doing my own thing."

Kindergarten children are highly imaginative and have a keen imitative sense. They are quick to respond to descriptive words such as "scoot," "whirl," "twist." Similarly they respond to words charged with dramatic content such as "sneak," "slither," "chase." These characteristics are particularly noticeable in their dances, and also in their responses to drama, and games with a dramatic element.

They react to strong rhythmic music, and sounds from percussion instruments provide simple stimuli which elicit very sensitive responses. Their dances will reveal these influences. For example, Scottish Country Dance music will often bring forth the correct "skip-change-of-step."

The skills which are associated with ball games depend upon the establishment of the hand-eye and foot-eye coordinations which develop in accordance with the child's personal pattern of maturation. Generally speaking, the five-year-old has difficulty in catching. Throwing, bowling and bouncing are also hard to control. Kicking a stationary ball is much easier than kicking a moving one. At this stage, large (seven-inch diameter) and fairly light balls are more suitable than small ones.

Kindergarten children have a great appreciation of fun and enter wholeheartedly into games that are simple enough for them to comprehend. Their egocentric nature and their often meticulous interpretation of rules and exaggerated concern for fairness, however, make it difficult for them to cope with a highly competitive game. Their desire to participate personally in most games, together with their characteristic energy, make it prudent to use games in which all are actively participating all the time. As a result, chasing games are particularly valuable. It is the joy of doing that appeals at this age; not the joy of winning.

PRIMARY CHILDREN (SIX-, SEVEN-, EIGHT-YEAR-OLDS)

A span of three years necessarily includes a variety of different levels of growth and development among the children involved. During this period each individual child passes through marked changes in his own development. A consideration of the characteristics of children in the early grades is useful primarily to alert the teacher to what he may expect to recognize as levels of development attained by one child during the progress of a year in his classroom. It may also guide him in his effort to compare the relative stages attained by one child as compared to another within the class. It will be necessary for the teacher to attempt to plot the individual's position on a continuum of developmental stages.

Six-year-olds and, to a less frequent extent, seven- and eight-year-olds, are still egocentric in nature and, therefore, interested in being personally active. They are not prepared to sacrifice activity for team goals. The more mature children will, however, show signs of enjoying group activity if the size of the group remains small. Two, three, or four members make a satisfactory group. It is clearly noticeable that, as children become older, they become physically more skilful. The body proportions facilitate better balance. The neuro-muscular system improves, the eyesight becomes mature, and difficult hand-eye coordination becomes possible. The coordinations required in skipping, hopping, kicking, throwing, and rolling should have developed at this stage. However, some boys may be unable to skip or hop as yet, while some girls experience difficulty in throwing. Their most frequent approach to an activity is still likely to be with the whole body, but they are increasingly aware of the specific functions of various parts of the body in a given movement. They are still likely to stay close to the ground in an unfamiliar and insecure situation, but by eight they are capable of elevation and can rejoice in the exhilaration of running, jumping and landing. Their interest in inverted positions such as handstands, headstands, and cartwheels becomes more evident but rolls and various forms of crawling are still enjoyed. When attempting landings from a height, they may, in the beginning, be satisfied with a simple jump; but as they get older they will tend to add the thrill of a speedy take-off, a high flight, or a trick during the course of the flight. Manoeuvres on climbing apparatus become more complicated. At an early age they may be satisfied to climb to a height, survey the space below and climb down, but as their confidence and skills develop they may hang upside down or travel horizontally at a chosen height. By Grade Three, their work on the floor or on mats is likely to show a strong, speedy approach but it is unlikely that they will think at all about its termination.

At six, chasing games which embrace a dramatic element will be very much enjoyed. Each child, however, will covet the "It" position and will often manoeuvre to be caught, if, by being caught, he may become "It." This may be regarded as a rudimentary form of strategy. The teacher must find ways of directing it into acceptable channels without destroying the design. Eight-year-olds continue to enjoy chasing and tag games, but much more for the elements of the chase than for the dramatic content. Therefore, these children in their games lesson need good spaces for running, simple, well-defined rules and the firm whistle of the referee.

Balls have an immense fascination for children and should be provided in a variety of sizes and weights in the primary grades. Each six-year-old child should have one to himself and be allowed to work very freely with it. The teacher should know that children's experiences of throwing and catching with a small ball are remotely related to their participation in softball at a later date. Similarly, their experiences of throwing and catching with a ten-inch ball are remotely related to their participation in basketball when they are older. With this insight, the teacher will appreciate the need to give young children ample opportunity to play freely with a variety of balls. Bats of various sorts, ranging from table tennis paddles to plastic models of softball bats should also be available. As has been stated earlier, eyesight and hand-eye coordination are still maturing at this stage. Some children will be able to toss, but not to catch. Some may be able to bounce and not to catch. Many will choose to kick or roll the ball and then chase it. Some, especially some of the eight-year-olds, will be quite facile in their use of balls and they may be able to use them in a game situation involving three or four players.

Children in the primary grades are ready to enjoy simple dances and singing games. The latter form part of the birthright of every child and therefore should be included in some stage of the curriculum. Six-year-olds can respond to music which has a well-defined rhythm and a simple, repetitive melody. Eight-year-olds have matured to the point where they can respond to more difficult rhythm and subtler melodies. Music tends, however, to be restrictive, whereas, the use of percussion as a stimulus to movement is especially fruitful. The egocentric tendencies of this age group will be manifest in the pupils' satisfaction in working alone and in the tendency to throw the whole body into dance movements. As they proceed through the grades there is a decrease in egocentricity and an increasing number of pupils will choose to dance with a partner and some may even choose to dance with two or three others. At first these pupils will respond well to ideas stemming from the use of the whole body. Later, they will find great interest in making specific parts of the body prominent in their dance. For example, they may do a "knees" dance and, when it is done, find that they have a "Clown Dance" or a "Rubber Man" or a "Sailor Dance." Their concept of dance is rudimentary. In its early stages, it is not likely to have any form. It will tend to be a string of different movements in the same way that their paragraphs tend to be a string of different facts, and their art work strange assortments of colour. It might, however, be a continuous repetition of a movement motif that fascinates them. This roughly parallels the appearance of "symbols" in their art work. To the teacher, their efforts may appear as "dancing" rather than as "a dance." Sometimes, they will veer off into gymnastic stunts or they may find themselves involved in dramatic play. If either of these attitudes become dominant in their work they will cease to be dancing and will, for the time being, be doing gymnastics or drama.

JUNIORS (NINE-, TEN-, ELEVEN-YEAR OLDS)

It has been pointed out earlier that the individual may be located with respect to certain characteristics at particular points of development in a continuum of stages leading toward maturity. In some respects, individuals in the middle grades will show behaviour or skill patterns which are generally characteristic of pupils in Grade Three or even Grade Two. These same individuals, or others within their group, may display other characteristics more often found in the early teenage group. Teachers, however, have learned to expect certain reactions from children in the middle grades.

Physically, they are at a very adroit stage. They have increased in height; their legs are relatively long; their hips are relatively small; and the upper part of their body is in good proportion to their total skeletal structure. Thus, they have good balance, are agile, and have great bodily flexibility. This is, however, a time when there is likely to be a great variation of height and weight among the individual members of a class.

Children of this age generally have plenty of energy and enjoy doing physically demanding things. Their endurance, however, is still not long-lasting and they tend to relax or flop between periods of high exertion.

Psychologically, this age group is more social in outlook. They are in the "gang" stage and develop strong attachments to others which may last for some time or which may terminate suddenly. They are very intense about rules, fair play, the role of leader, and the rotation of turns. Winning and losing is of immense immediate importance and is very closely attached to their image of personal success and self-value.

Boys and girls have separate interests which may cause friction between the sexes. There is a general protestation of contempt for the opposite sex, yet there is a great notice given to any alliance between individuals of the opposite sex. Boys tend to be highly and fiercely competitive. They are out to win; take pleasure in showing off; need recognition as individuals and leaders. The girls also are often fiercely competitive and take pleasure in winning. In general, though, they are less competitive than boys, and if there has been no previous conditioning, this can be seen in early partner work in games. In these circumstances they tend to cooperate with each other rather than to compete. However, they are often very "managing" and seemingly waste a lot of time organizing groups of other girls and "bossing" their followers. They talk and argue a lot and are often more involved in this than in physical activity. In the case of both boys and girls a firm adult hand is needed. An arbitrator can help to guide their thinking when conflicts arise.

Observation of children of this age seems to indicate that the stage of physical growth of the individual is the determining factor in respect to what they attempt and accomplish in "gymnastic type" activities. Those who are slim and well-proportioned skeletally can perform stunts and activities of great difficulty with a very high degree of skill — flexibility in joints and ligaments facilitates this. However, activities requiring strength and stamina come less easily. For this reason, pupils will be seen to use a high proportion of activities based on flexibility, and to move experimentally towards activities which demand strength and stamina. Teachers should be aware of this and understand the reason for it. They should help the pupils to understand the situation and to be prepared to use their strength and stamina as they find it developing. This means, also, that teachers should be alert to recognize situations which they can use for effort training in accordance with Laban's concept of effort.[2] (Laban's concepts will be outlined in Chapter Four.)

Children of ages nine to eleven are very much aware of what adults are doing. They are, therefore, very desirous of playing adult games in the appropriate season. This means that there is an expectation of football in fall, hockey and basketball in winter, softball or hardball and possibly track and field in spring. The precise interest is determined by adult leagues in each community and by television and newspaper emphases. This interest is in some ways unfortunate and puts undue pressure on the school. The chief difficulty is that the professional leagues are big business, designed for the cream of adult talent, working under the best coaching talent and under rules designed to promote spectator interest. It is easy to understand how the young pupils' aspirations can become attached to such goals, but it is also easy for the teacher to see that the situation must be faced realistically.

Physical education is given two to three thirty-minute periods per week in most school systems. It is the responsibility of the teacher to use the time for the educational advancement of all members of the class. This poses a difficult organizational problem. The question to be solved

---

[2] Rudolf Laban and F. C. Lawrence, *Effort*, Macdonald and Evans, London, 1947, pp. 18-34.

is: Can there be a place for team games in the thirty-minute period? How should the time be utilized? The most usual answer is to provide a good basis for games play. Good ball handling is dependent upon the development of good hand-eye coordinations. Pupils of the ages of nine to eleven are ready for this. They should be given maximum opportunity to throw, catch, pass, bounce, kick, bat, aim, and retrieve balls under a wide variety of circumstances. These experiences may be more closely allied to specific games — softball, soccer, volleyball — than was the case in the primary grades. In most cases, the regulation balls used in the major games should be available in large quantities. The exception may be the basketball because it is usually too large and heavy for even the eleven-year-olds to handle properly. If pupils use it before they are big enough and strong enough to handle it easily, they may compensate for their weakness by using unsuitable techniques which may become habitual.

As skill increases competition is the natural development, for the able performer naturally wants to know "How good am I?" Games and contests, invented or adapted by the teacher or the pupils, are the natural outcome. This dovetails nicely with their psychological development which is toward a competitive outlook, an interest in group activities and membership in gangs.

Children of this age find tremendous enjoyment in running and jumping. Therefore chasing games are good fun for them and have the added advantage of familiarizing them with folklore. They represent a heritage of the race in the same way that folk dances and folk songs do. For both these reasons they should command a place in the education of this age group. Running and jumping contests — devised by teacher or pupils — are the beginnings of track and field contests. For this reason chasing games and running and jumping contests should have a place in each year's work.

Skating and swimming are not always feasible, but if and when they are, they should be made available to pupils of the junior division. Both are basic skills requiring much practice and adequate time to develop.

Underlining all games activity is the need to handle the body efficiently. To dodge, to change pace, to reach to retrieve a ball, to move into line with a ball, to bend to get under a ball, all these abilities are necessary to a good player. Children of age nine to eleven are mature enough to develop these body management skills, but they need help in establishing the correct form. They are at an age when they will concentrate and practise. They need the proper information and much encouragement.

As mentioned before (page 7) boys and girls have different interests, but because the best performers in the class will include both boys and girls, the mixed groups based on ability can work together with advantage. At other times, especially in competitive situations, the boys should compete with each other and so should the girls. Since there is a natural antagonism between the sexes, a deliberate pitting of one against the other in competition is not helpful and can, indeed, cause injuries and hurt feelings. The skills of social interaction are not well developed at this age and, therefore, the teacher needs to help pupils to develop tolerance and a sympathetic concern for other individuals.

These experiences of interaction can be carried over into dance. Although boys will rarely admit that they like to dance, they enjoy vigorous activity and lively rhythm. It will be necessary to underline the men's role in the folk dances and to give the boys the genuine feeling of the folk idiom. Girls enjoy the rhythm and dancing but, for the sake of the boys, they should not dominate the lessons.

For both boys and girls, creative dance, which is fostered in what is called "modern educational dance," may be a better medium than folk dance. In this form of dance the pupils learn to handle a basic movement material. They can be free to work out their own ideas in movement sequences and dances. These very often tend to be dramatic in content and there need be no taint of dainty "girlie stuff" in the composition. The movement can be as vigorous as they wish. It can even be grotesque if the theme requires that sort of movement. Dancing with percussion has a real fascination and can give expression to a wealth of ideas. Pupils of nine to eleven are alert to what is going on in the world around them. They need varied ways of expressing their ideas and interpretations. Dance can offer a very valuable outlet of expression and at the same time, through its form and rhythm, provide a discipline. To the extent that it is not competitive, it can meet the need for a counterbalance to their many situations of rivalry in life.

INTERMEDIATE CHILDREN (TWELVE-, THIRTEEN-, FOURTEEN-YEAR-OLDS)

Children of the intermediate grades, that is Grades Seven, Eight or Nine, are children of early adolescence. As in other ages, they mature in accordance with their own bodily rhythms and, therefore, a class of these children will include a wide range of individual differences. Stature, weights, endocrine development, intelligence, poise, interest, past experiences, home background will all contribute to the individuality of each member of the group.

Certain generalities may be made however. The girls tend to be taller than the boys and more mature socially. The girls are likely to be interested in boyfriends, dating and fashion. The boys may be somewhat interested in heterogeneous relationships, but they are more keenly interested in the "team" and in the group relationships and activities of other boys. Some girls are enthusiastic about sports and chafe under any restrictions which may suggest that such activities are not suitable for girls. Other girls are so intent upon dating and its attendant requirements that they feel marked irritation at the idea of participating in vigorous activity. However, if they conceive of such activity as making a contribution to their appearance or popularity they will participate enthusiastically.

The early adolescent pursues activities which are the current vogue.

Children of this age wish to pursue activities which they feel are the current vogue. They are influenced by the impact of professional sport and by the implications of what they see on television. Thus the school games program often reflects the seasonal changes in professional sport. Likewise, the dance program may be influenced by the currently popular music and the current social dance patterns.

Early adolescents are eager to assume responsibility, and, under guidance, are often very capable of entering into group planning and of handling many of their own activities. It is usual for them to show considerable enthusiasm in the initial stages, but to lose this interest before bringing their plans to fruition. It, therefore, becomes essential that the teacher stand behind them in their efforts, guiding, encouraging, evaluating, renewing interest and helping them to sustain their efforts until the job is done.

In these grades the differences in needs, interests and abilities between the boys and girls are radical enough to make it desirable to separate the classes for physical education and to have men and women teachers in charge of the respective programs. There are some activities, such as swimming, social dance, modern educational dance, volleyball, which, in the adult situation, are taken in unsegregated circumstances. If these are organized in schools on a coeducational basis the experience of planning and playing together can make a valuable contribution to the development of these pupils, particularly to their social maturity.

The needs of boys of this age can, in general, be identified as a need for strenuous physical activity, for a challenge to the best level of performance possible, for acceptance as a worthy member of the group, for a chance to sacrifice personal desires for a team goal, for a chance to stand up to reasonable stress (emotional, physical, ethical), for a chance to assume responsibility and to be held to account for it. These needs have dictated the selection of certain team games, gymnastic and track and field activities in the physical education programs for boys and should indicate the kinds of method used for teaching them.

Our social climate has made it difficult for men and boys to accept either folk dance or modern educational dance as curriculum material for boys. It has always been urged, on a theoretical basis, as giving another dimension to their education, namely that of expressive activity. In this field, it offers an experience related to drama, music and art. However, if it is taught with discernment, it can also compete on the basis of physical demands and skill requirements with many of the games or gymnastic activities. It is hoped that good training given in dance in the primary and junior grades will be continued in the intermediate grades by selecting activities which are challenging physically, mentally and emotionally for this age group of boys.

The needs of girls of this age are not unlike the needs of boys but the difference in physical capacity and in interest is sufficient to make it expedient to offer them a separate program.

The girls need guidance to help them develop a healthy attitude toward their menstrual period. It is necessary for them to regard this as a natural occurrence which can and should be integrated into the normal demands of their lives. It was once considered that women should avoid undue exercise and stress during their menstrual period. It is now considered that girls, with few exceptions, should participate in regular classes, but that individual reactions to extremes of competition during the menses should be given due consideration. However the latter are not those which would occur in the physical education lesson or even in interschool team play in most school systems. The physical education teacher of girls of Grades Seven to Nine may have a very important role to play in launching these girls into their adolescent period with good mental health habits related to the menstrual period. Proper attitudes established at this time will benefit them for the rest of their lives.

Apart from the pupils' activity needs in respect to menstruation, the range of their requirements include: an ability to move well and skilfully in a variety of situations, an ability to play a reasonable number of sports sufficiently well to receive pleasure from participation and to be accepted in leisure time activities as a participating member. Many girls want and need some strenuous activity. Many need self-fulfilment which may come from being a good or excellent player on a good team. Some girls need the experience of living up to a situation fraught with the rough and tumble of personal discomfort or sacrifice often found in a competitive game, a demanding gymnastic sequence or in swimming. Many need the joy that they find in dance activities — social, folk and modern educational dance — or the exhilaration of performing gymnastics or swimming with grace and virtuosity. Probably all girls need the security of being an accepted member of a group, measuring up to the group standards of physical performance and social intercourse.

These requirements indicate the suitability of selected experiences in team games, dance of different sorts, gymnastics and swimming. The particular basis for selecting the most helpful activities and the details of methods of teaching and of organization will be dealt with later.

In summary, it may be considered that the boys and girls of the intermediate grades can profit by specially selected programs. Within any group of boys or girls there will be a sufficient range of individual differences to indicate a need for considerable choice during the lesson. While the responsibility to provide for individual differences is recognized, it may also be recognized that self-indulgence may result from a misunderstanding of needs, and that the teacher may often have to interpret and identify suitably high standards of performance, integrity, personal sacrifice, and help the pupils acquire the needed motivation to reach satisfying goals.

TWO

THE TEACHING-LEARNING PROCESS

There are various ways that one may learn and, consequently, various ways by which one may be taught. The teacher is concerned that learning does, in fact, take place. However, it may be of greater significance that the teacher be concerned with *what* is being learned. Surprisingly, that which is being learned is rarely limited to a specific motor skill such as an underhand pitch, a polka step or a headstand. Learning is likely to embrace such additional things as attitudes, mental concepts, ethical standards and social reactions. Since learning is wide in its possible scope, the teacher's concern is with his ability to estimate the various forms of learning that are taking place, and with his aptitude in adjusting procedures to permit the greatest possible value to accrue from the experience.

Therefore it is necessary to examine some of the forms by which learning has traditionally taken place, and some which are supplanting the traditional methods because they provide a more valuable learning experience.

COMMON TEACHING-LEARNING PROCEDURES

LEARNING AS A RESPONSE TO COMMAND

"Class, with a jump, a-tten-tion! Running on the spot, with high knee raising, ready, be-gin!"

It is clear that the command is given and a specific response is expected. This is a modification of the kind of learning which took place in the dog in Pavlov's classic experiment. The teacher is likely to demonstrate the required action and then give the commands so that the pupils may emulate his performance. In the early stages of learning, the teacher may perform along with the class, thus providing a model for imitation. The response of the members of the class will be evaluated by the teacher. Those aspects of the performance which are acceptable will be *reinforced* by praise and approval. Those aspects which are unacceptable will be given *negative reinforcement*. The teacher's performance plus his cues for correction will act as a form of *guidance* in the learning process.[1] After a sufficient number of repetitions, the class may be expected to execute the activity without the benefit of a demonstration. The activity is considered to be "learned" when it can be quickly executed following the command and when the details of the execution conform to the demonstrated pattern.

It should be noted that the concise description of detail

1. running . . .
2. on the spot . . .
3. with high knee raising . . .

is given first. The timing is controlled by the cautionary word "ready," the thinking pause which follows, and the breaking of the executive word "begin" into two syllables, i.e. be—gin! The final syllable explodes into a starting signal.

It has been suggested that the teacher is concerned with estimating the forms of learning which are taking place in any given situation. It should, therefore, be worthwhile attempting to do just this for the situation discussed above. It is clear that greatest concern is placed on correct physical performance. As a result skill-learning takes place. An almost equal concern is placed upon an immediate response. This might be evaluated as an inculcation of discipline as evidenced by obedience to authority. When this response comes simultaneously from an entire class, there is the possibility that a feeling of membership in a group may be engendered. There is likely to be the experience of subjugating one's own desires and inclinations to the requirements of the group or of the situation. For various individuals, there are likely to be feelings of frustration, boredom and even resentment. To some there may be the pleasure of being released from the responsibility of decision making. The challenge to the thinking capacities tends to be limited to paying sufficient attention to hearing the cues, recognizing the required response and adjusting the timing.

The reader is invited to contemplate these and other forms of learning which may be found within the situation and to consider whether the experience might best be considered to be training or to be education.

LEARNING BY DEMONSTRATION, EXPLANATION AND PRACTICE

"We are going to play 'Volleyball Keep-up.' You need to use the high volley. Watch this. Notice that you line up with the flight of the ball. Where is the ball when you hit it? Notice the use of the hands. What part makes contact in the volley? Right . . . Now each team of four start your game. See how many times you can volley it before it touches the floor."

[1] John M. Stephens, *The Psychology of Classroom Learning*, Holt, Rinehart and Winston, Inc., New York, 1966, pp. 121-122 and pp. 125-126.

Some of the significant features of the situation are:

- A need has been established.
- The skill will be used in a game context.
- The details being presented have been selected from many possible ones because the teacher is aware that pupils can concentrate on only one or two features at a time.
- The child's mental processes are engaged.
- More than one sense — seeing, hearing — has been used.
- The learner has been put into the activity very quickly.
- There is a possibility of achieving a feeling of success.

It is presumed that this situation[2] offers a starting point from which coaching, correction and reinforcement will proceed.

Note also:

- Who sets the situation?
- Who demonstrates?
- Who foresees points of difficulty in the coming skill situation?
- Who controls the time spent on analysis?
- Who determines how many aspects of the skill are considered?
- To what extent are general concepts considered?

In the past, it has been usual that a pattern similar to the one outlined earlier has formed the basis of the teaching situation but instead of the details being derived through questioning, the teacher has offered a brief verbal analysis.

From the psychological point of view, the problem seems to be one of establishing insights[3] by showing the meaning or relationship in the new situations.

However, there are two possible routes to establishing insights. Recently, writers (Bruner, 1961[4]; Hendrix, 1961[5]) have proposed that the learner must discover principles and laws for himself before they can have genuine meaning for him. Other writers (Ausubel, 1961[6]) have supported the idea that it is helpful for the teacher to give some guidance to the pupil as he attempts to attain insights into the task at hand. In other words, the teacher offers ready-made insights. Present literature seems to indicate that some help in establishing insights is an advantage, but that too much guidance and direction is detrimental.

[2] *Ibid.* pp. 147-150.

[3] *Ibid.* p. 158.

[4] J. S. Bruner, "The Act of Discovery," *Harvard Educational Review*, vol. 31, no. 1, Harvard University Press, Cambridge, Mass., 1961, pp. 21-32.

[5] Gertrude Hendrix, "Learning by Discovery," *The Mathematics Teacher*, vol. 54, no. 5, National Council of Teachers of Mathematics, Washington, D.C., 1961, pp. 290-299.

[6] D. P. Ausubel, *The Psychology of Meaningful Verbal Learning; An Introduction to School Learning*, Grune and Stratton, Inc., New York, 1963, pp. 170-172.

"Find as many ways as possible to move across the floor. Good. Now go across using feet and hands. Find another way to use feet and hands. Find another way. Use your feet and one hand. Use your feet and hands and find ways of going high and low."

This is a relatively new approach which some teachers are using to facilitate movement experiences.

Some of the significant features are:

- There is a high degree of pupil participation. In most cases all the pupils are active.
- The teacher sets the problem.
- The pupil invents a response.
- The teacher controls the time given to each problem.
- The stress is on what is done rather than how it is done or why it is done.

"Move with tummy upward."
The teacher controls timing; also extent of invention.

Careful consideration of this process seems to suggest that it is closely related to the response-to-command situation of yesteryear. However, in this case, the command is to invent within the limitation set by the problem. This is at least one step ahead of the response-to-command situation in the contribution expected from the learner. However, the invention of movement actions within certain limitations may be equated with the acquisition of facts in a verbal situation. For example in a language lesson, the teacher may be dealing with the word "worry" and might ask for an adjective derived from this word. Answer: "worrisome." "Good! Can you think of a noun?" Answer: "worrier." "Right! Use 'worry' in a sentence. Find two words which rhyme with 'worry'." The parallel between the action tasks and the verbal tasks is obvious. In both, the value of the learning experience is inferior to that which demands conceptual thinking. The latter can receive attention if the discovery process is used.

LEARNING BY THE DISCOVERY PROCESS

A number of children are working on tumbling mats while others are busy on climbers, benches and boxes. Those on the mats are making assorted attempts to roll or to balance on the head. The teacher observes the general situation and notes that there is a need to upgrade the standard of performance which is suffering because the pupils are unaware of the effect of the shaping of the body upon the roll and upon the balance.

Teacher observes the results of exploration, e.g. some have legs stretched upward.

Having determined the problem, the teacher may help the pupils to become aware of the *principle* involved by having the whole class observe several selected pupils in action. The teacher must select pupils whose performances will illustrate the *principle* to be classified. The observations should be made specific by the question the teacher poses before the pupils show their work. For example, the challenge might be: "Watch the rolls and the headstands. Find out what body shape is used for rolling and what shape is used for balancing." Upon observing the performances, members of the class may suggest that rolls stem from a rounded body, while an elongated arch is characteristic of the balance. The teacher may have to help the observers by asking precise questions or, occasionally, by supplying the correct analysis. Certain details of the basic shapes may be observed and discussed, but as quickly as seems reasonable all performers should be allowed to work again with the problem of identifying the dominant shape which they find themselves using and experimenting with the effect of variations of that shape upon the execution of their stunt. Careful observation and analysis by the teacher of their resultant efforts will dictate the subsequent observations and discussions of the pupils.

It may be noted in passing that the discoveries initiated in the above process need not be limited to the performers on the mats, but may be used with benefit by those on the climber, benches or boxes, as long as the performer is free to identify his own use of body shape and to discover the effect of variations of it upon his performance. There may come a time when the assignment will demand the use of a particular body shape. The assessments and discoveries will then extend from this requirement. The details of methodology are discussed in Chapters Eight, Nine and Ten.

What learning process is taking place in the previously described situation?

- The situation arises from activities initiated by the pupils, although it may, in less favourable circumstances, arise in answer to a challenge posed by the teacher.
- The need for consideration of the problem is well established.
- The pupils have the opportunity to discover elements of cause and effect.
- They are able to examine contrasts.
- They are left free to apply the principle to their own work. At a later stage, they could observe the principle being applied in a wide variety of situations. Thus in a rather free fashion, they are allowed to experience the need to analyze a difficulty, decide upon a tentative solution, try out their hypothesis and see its adaption to varied situations. It will be noted that the teacher's role is to assist the learners rather than to dictate to them. It will also be noted that the level of concern is upon the principle of movement rather than merely upon a specific movement.

It might be suggested that the discovery process leads to conceptual thinking and that, if the principle is applied in many and varied situations by the pupils, it can become the basis for establishing a command of the abstract concept. To extend the example in this instance, the pupil may find that the rounded shape of the body is helpful in rolling forwards or backwards or even sideways in an egg roll. He may discover that if he overbalances while doing a headstand, the quick rounding of the body facilitates a smooth transfer of weight. He may discover other ways of rounding his body, as, for instance, arching sufficiently so that his stomach takes on the form of a rocker. From these extended experiences he may deduce that a rounded body shape can facilitate a transfer of body weight and that a transfer of body weight can bring about locomotion through space.

These concepts are more complicated forms of learning than are the invention of actions as responses to action tasks. The exercise of cause and effect judgements, the drawing of conclusions, the formulation of principles may be regarded as prime goals of learning.

USING THE SENSES IN THE TEACHING-LEARNING PROCESS

In the response-to-command form of learning, the action comes when the command is heard and interpreted by the performer. At an earlier stage in the process, the observation of a correctly executed demonstration was the model to be copied by the performer. Thus sight was a key sense in the acquisition of the movement skill. Similarly, in the problem-solving method, the pupils viewed two contrasting actions to assess the role of the shaping of the body. These two senses, hearing and seeing, and the sense of feeling can bear an examination as tools for learning.

HEARING

In the description of the response-to-command form of teaching it was noted that the command
- named the action: "running"
- named the variations required: "on the spot with high knee raising"
- gave a *thinking* pause: "ready"
- gave the executive signal: "begin!"

Many teachers are far too verbose in the gymnasium. It is very useful to acquire the skill of identifying action in a few words. Verbs, not unnaturally, often suffice in the gymnasium. "Sit" will quickly bring a class into a position of inactivity when such a situation is required.

In movement education[7] classes of the games, dance or gymnastic type, words have very specific meanings and the discerning teacher selects his words very precisely. "Travel about the whole room" gives the pupils free choice as to the form of locomotion (run, cartwheel, crawl) and the responsibility to move in pathways which are well placed in the space available (down a side, into the middle, past a corner).

"Run fast counterclockwise" allows very little freedom of choice.

[7] Movement education, see definition, Chapter Four, pp. 36-38.

"Everyone run around until I yell 'Stop' " is a verbal invitation to chaos which is chosen more often than not by an innocent, unaware student teacher. "Everyone" implies an unorganized mass; "run around" implies easy action without purpose; "yell" implies that the class will be so noisy and disorganized that the teacher will have to struggle to be heard.

In movement education classes, it will be necessary for the teacher and the pupils to acquire a "movement vocabulary" which may come as a response to the teacher's verbal instructions, challenges, comments or from attempts to describe in words a performer's actions.

This precise use of words is linked with an understanding of Laban's analysis of movement. Later chapters provide a fuller list of significant words. The purpose of these few paragraphs is to alert the reader to the fact that words have a very strong stimulus to movement and that much learning can be initiated by response to carefully chosen movement words.

It is necessary to stress that the modulations of voice and expression have a marked effect upon the performer's response. Suppose the teacher realizes that the children are landing with a thump. The action can be modified by controlling the absorption of body weight through the ankles, knees and hips. Very often the improvement in control can be achieved by listening to the landing. The teacher may set the stage by choice of descriptive vocabulary given in an appropriately quiet tone. "Run, *jump* and land softly, softly."

Dance, which is movement with a marked expressive quality, will be affected by the pupils' ability to respond to auditory cues. Listening, to voice, percussion, or music should be linked with the movement response.

Perhaps the brief survey given here will serve to encourage the teacher to experiment with the pupils' responses to auditory stimuli and to work toward enriching their mutual experiences.

SIGHT

As has been noted earlier, demonstrations have long been used as a means of teaching and learning. These can include the observation of the teacher, a pupil or a film. The observation has often been for the purpose of emulation or copying. Usually, the learner has been required to keep still and to mentally note the form of the action. The demonstration may be accompanied by a verbal analysis. The performance is then followed by the learner's attempt at emulation and this may be accompanied by the verbal coaching of the teacher.

There are at least two other forms of learning by observation. Firstly, incidental observation of the pupil's peers can result in his copying the movement or adapting it to his own purposes. This is a form of informal learning which probably provides greater results than adults realize.

Secondly, in modern movement classes, it has become customary to use observations as a well organized teaching technique. They are used less for copying or emulation than for analyzing the presence or function of a movement factor in a performance. For example, the teacher might have two pupils show how to jump and land. One might land with little noise. The other might land with a thump. The class might be able to see that the one who landed softly allowed the knees to bend as he came down, while the other jumper kept the knees straight. Following the observation interval, the class might return to their work to find out how they were using their knees.

So important is the use of observation in movement education classes, that the teacher will find it necessary to cultivate a personal ability to see specific movement elements in operation and to cultivate similar skill on the part of the pupils.

FEELING

We have all heard an embarrassed beginner exclaim, "Just a moment until I get the feel of the racquet." Such a beginner is recognizing the fact that habitual movement patterns are controlled to a considerable degree by the sensations sent to the brain by the proprioceptors located in the muscle fibres. These sense organs relay to the brain the tensions arising in the muscle fibres as they move a body part. Through the many repetitions used to establish any skill, the pupil learns to expect a pattern of feeling. Thus, for example, while running downstairs, the pupil *feels* the interval between the steps and if the last step should be raised by an upheaval of frost, he could miss his footing.

It is important to realize that the sense of kinesthetic feeling can be an aid in acquiring new coordinations. The performer should be alerted to feel the point at which he can release the ball for a two-hand underhand free throw in basketball. Similarly, he may be assisted in developing his coordination if he feels the rhythm of the hop, step and jump pattern in track and field or he feels the amount of arch in his handstand, or feels the centrifugal force in a body turn in dance.

LEARNING BY MENTAL APPLICATION

Recent research[8] has shown that time taken in thinking about a performance can increase the efficiency of a skill. Consequently, the teacher should frequently give the pupils a thinking task for the interval between physical education lessons. It is marvellous what responses will result if the teacher finishes a lesson by saying: "Next lesson we shall be working with the ball against the wall. You can be thinking of all the ways you can use your ball and the wall."

[8] J. K. Ewart Bagg, "The Effect of Mental and Physical Practice on Baseball Batting," unpublished thesis, University of California at Los Angeles, Los Angeles, 1966.

We learn when we need to learn. We learn best when we want to learn. These facts apply to children also. If the need and desire are felt by the child, he is ready to learn and he may set about solving his own problems or he may ask the teacher for the help he needs. The teacher's task is to get the pupil active, to assess the particular movement problem facing the child and to find a way to help the pupil to discover his own problem. Once the problem is identified, energy may be directed toward finding solutions. The solutions then have to be assessed. The performer must select the best solution and then repeat the performance with care to gain control of it. As mastery is achieved the skill may be tested in varied situations. The teacher needs to keep the motivation high through all these stages.

How can this be done?

There is no simple or foolproof formula for the teacher. However, teachers have found certain procedures helpful. There is the long term procedure of creating an atmosphere in the class which gives the pupils the confidence to use their own ideas. For example, it helps greatly if the teacher makes a point of accepting first attempts at legitimate efforts to answer a challenge. These first attempts are likely to be unsatisfactory to both the performer and the teacher if regarded as a finished product. However, they should be viewed as exploratory attempts from which can grow the modifications and refinements. Eventually they will turn into a satisfactory performance and the process of refinement will afford the all-important learning experience of trying many tentative solutions, of evaluating, rejecting, modifying and of finally accepting the movement. The teacher who can accept the first attempts as important beginning solutions will give quick approval or praise and thus reinforce the pupil's confidence and sense of worth. This climate of approval works wonders for growth and achievement. It forms a current and ongoing form of motivation for the pupil. If the teacher frequently circulates quite rapidly among the pupils dropping a word of approval to individuals, it is possible to give each pupil a sense of receiving individual attention. It is also possible for the teacher to have a good assessment of the work being done and to ask penetrating questions which will increase the pupil's awareness of movement.

The specific challenge presented to the pupil has a significant effect upon his motivation. Many teachers have successfully used the technique of making available selected equipment such as balls, ropes, hoops or mats, and allowing the pupils to work freely with their choice of the equipment for a few minutes at the beginning of the lesson. By watching what pupils choose to do under these circumstances, it may be possible to observe children already using a movement concept which can be the basis of the lesson of that day. For example, from the free work likely to be done with the equipment mentioned, it would be possible to find pupils using forward or backward directions; or working on the spot or travelling about the room; or stressing the use of feet and hands. By observing two pupils working in one of these movement categories, it would be reasonably easy to interest the entire class in concerning themselves with their own use of these elements. The point being made here is that the motivation is helped by the appeal to curiosity, the personal implication of the task and by the fact that the performer moves from the known (what he is doing) to the unknown (to the awareness of what he is doing and the modification of it).

It should be noted that the pupil is personally involved in the activity. It is his own performance which is under assessment and modification. This increases the possibility of high motivation.

It should also be noted that pupils of the primary grades will prefer to work alone, each with his own equipment. By the age of nine, ten and eleven, pupils, although they enjoy working alone and profit from it, gain added motivation from working in a partner or a group situation. It is likely that the teacher will find that pair work is particularly enjoyed by the twelve-, thirteen-, and fourteen-year-old.

It is of utmost importance that each child acquires the skill of observing and assessing the movement of his classmates. This skill can then be used as a teaching technique. For example, two children who are using contrasting directions in their movement may be observed. Before they perform, the class should be asked to find the difference in their performances. The fact that one child is moving backwards while the other moves sideways will provide a basis for each pupil to assess his own use of direction. This sequence of events is also likely to motivate each pupil to search out the use of other directions. However, the teacher must make such observation sessions very short because they can interfere with individual participation and cause frustration.

Most pupils respond to the challenge to perform at a high standard after the preliminary exploratory stage has been given due reign. Therefore, the teacher must judge when to require that pupils select a limited response and repeat it extensively, trying to achieve control, elegance, beauty and virtuosity. Pupils need to be reminded to check their performance for standards. Such questions as the following are useful for improving a performance:

- Do you have a clear starting and a clear finishing position?
- Can you repeat your work exactly?
- Do you know exactly what the different parts of your body are doing? Do you want straight knees? pointed toes? arched back? feet wide apart?
- Are the fast parts of your work really fast? Are the high parts really high?
- Make your performance very clear. If you intend to jump, really jump!
- Do you know how you join the different movements together?

Another form of motivation available to the teacher is that of providing variety within the lesson so that an activity does not outlast the attention span of the class. Some ways of achieving variety are:

- Preplanning a selection of movement challenges. For example: ball control may be developed in:

    Individual situations — on the spot; travelling; at changing speeds; stressing different parts of the body; using the floor, the wall, the air.

    In partner situations

    By adding complications such as targets, zones, offence-defence, scoring situations.

- Preplanning the choice of equipment. For example: jumping might be started by practising landing in a hoop; it might then be practised with a partner assisting; finally it might be done in connection with gymnastic apparatus such as vaulting box, mats and climber.

- Preplanning the flux and flow of the lesson to provide an appropriate beginning, and to bring the work through the development of the concept into a climax or culmination.

The diagrams below show possible profiles of the flux and flow of four kinds of lessons.

A Games Lesson

Introductory activities	Development of skill	Application of skill	Conclusion	Shower
Warm up	or concept	or concept in a game	Verbal assessment	Dress
Free practice with balls		or game-like situation	of what was accomplished	Return to class

A Dance Lesson

Introductory activities	Development of a movement vocabulary	The Dance — developed, assessed,	Dance demonstration	Shower
Free response to selected music	and of a dance idea or concept	and revised in several stages	Assessment	Dress
Warm up of body			Verbal summary	Return to class

A Gymnastics Lesson

Free practice • floor work	Development of skill or concept	Rotation to apparatus stations	Cleanup Assessment	Shower Dress Return to class

A Swimming Lesson

Preliminary activities	Development of challenges	Self testing	Check out	Shower Dress Return to class

THREE

THE NATURE OF
PHYSICAL EDUCATION

It is difficult to give a clear definition of physical education. This may result from the fact that the emphases within the subject field tend to change with the needs of society and with the aims of general education. "Education through the physical will be judged, therefore, even as education for life will be judged — by the contribution it makes to fine living . . . It should therefore be declared that physical education seeks to further the purposes of modern education when it stands for the finest kind of living."[1]

For the purposes of this book, physical education is defined as ". . . the school program of the study of the art and science of human movement needed in today's world designed for (human) development through movement, and (human) performance restricted to the expressive form and/or restricted through the use of representations of environmental reality."[2]

This definition seems to incorporate the idea that the growth and development of the individual in accordance with his needs and talents is of prime importance and that this may be accomplished to some extent through the study of and participation in different forms of movement. It includes expressive forms of movement. It indicates through the phrase "use of representations of environmental reality" that the school swimming pool may be regarded as a substitute for the ocean or lake; the vaulting box and climbing frame as a substitute for a fence or a tree; teams as a substitute for a unit of society. It seems to indicate that an understanding of one's own movement as an art and a science will bring some degree of self-realization and some ability to adapt to the requirements of everyday

[1] Jesse Feiring Williams, "Education Through the Physical," *Journal of Higher Education*, vol. 1, no. 5, The Ohio State University Press, Columbus, 1930, p. 281.
[2] Camille Brown and Rosalind Cassidy, *Theory in Physical Education*, Lea and Febiger, Philadelphia, 1963, p. 36.

life. Since it restricts physical education to a school program of study, it infers a planned developmental experience.

At the present time, the main kinds of planned developmental experience in most school curricula can be divided into the areas of: 1) games, 2) gymnastics, 3) dance, 4) track and field, 5) aquatics, and for some 6) calisthenics.

Some school systems have extensive skating programs and others include a course in outdoor education. For the purpose of this text, track and field, if mentioned at all, will be included in the games area, and skating and aquatics will receive virtually no attention. While acknowledging the increasing importance of outdoor education, a consideration of this area will not be included within the scope of this book.

Since the emphasis of this text is upon movement education — the art and science of human movement — it is necessary to examine the various areas of physical education in an attempt to determine their movement implications.

DISTINCTIVE FEATURES IN THE NATURE OF GAMES, GYMNASTICS AND DANCE

All too often teachers and pupils alike are unaware of the basic challenges of games, gymnastics and dance. Perhaps they understand the nature of games better than they do the nature of gymnastics or dance. Even so, these matters can bear examination because a clear awareness of purpose can make a great deal of difference to the way movements are done. Often it is the particular stress of a movement which makes it significant.

If these three areas of physical education are examined for their particular stress with regard to competition some interesting and significant comparisons result.

Question yourself. In which area is competition the *raison d'être* for the activity? Surely the answer is *games*. All team games have a method of scoring and the purpose is to achieve a winning score. Likewise, dual and individual games are competitive and the winner is determined by the score. Even games of chance are a form of competition against the vagaries of luck.

It is interesting to note that an examination of different forms of games can produce examples which range from highly competitive to minimally competitive: team games being examples of the first category; singing games being examples of the latter. This is an important fact for the teacher to keep in mind, for if he teaches according to the needs of the pupils he will be conscious of the stage of their development. When their skills are unsure, they will need a slightly competitive situation. As their skills increase, they will need the thrill and challenge of a more highly competitive activity.

Much of one's philosophy of sportsmanship is determined by one's understanding of competition. Pupils should be helped to become aware of the relationship which exists between themselves and other players. The very young and very unskilled will work in a cooperative way with others of like ability. For example, the young pitcher will try to send the ball in such a way that the young batter can hit it. This really changes a competitive situation into a cooperative one. The pupils should be aware that they are cooperating with each other. This stage should be allowed to exist as long as their level of skill demands it. However, when they are skilful enough to compete, then they should understand that *within the rules*, they should strive to plan a strategy which will aid their cause. They should enter into play with pupils of equivalent ability and they should expect to exert themselves to the limit of their skill and mental power.

Because the natural development moves from cooperative play to competitive play, pupils should have many opportunities to make up their own games. They will find that scoring is a necessity, rules are needed to give purpose to the play and to provide safety. They may also come to realize that a referee facilitates the play. This type of education should help them to understand and respect the meaning of sportsmanship.

If it can be agreed that the area of *games* is distinctly competitive, let us consider the situation pertaining to *gymnastics*. Is there any form of competition present in a handstand or a dive over three people or a handspring off a box? Question yourself as to why one wants to do these events. What is the attraction? Surely, it is the challenge, "Can I do it?" So one says, "Can I manage that?" It is a form of self-testing in the matter of body management. What are the difficulties? Almost always the performer has to deal with the force of gravity. It is a form of competition — one's strength, speed or body alignment against the force of gravity. This is a very subtle form of competition and children will have a clearer concept of what they are trying to achieve if they are helped to become aware of it. The awareness should, in turn, help them to show more virtuosity in the challenges they invent for themselves. If teachers understand the challenges, they will be able to help pupils enjoy a wider experience and achieve higher standards.

It may be noted in passing that an externally competitive situation is structured in the case of a gymnastic meet. The scoring on the basis of subjective judgement permits one entrant's performance to be ranked qualitatively with that of all other entrants. Thus a champion or winner is declared. Similar circumstances exist in diving and figure-skating championships.

Consider next the situation related to *dance*. What is the joy of dance? Basically it is to move for movement's sake or to communicate ideas or feelings to others. Neither of these elements is competitive. In folk dances, the form which dominates is a social relationship to other dancers. In ballroom dance, it is a matter of melding one's movement into a harmony

---

with one's partner and with the music. Thus, dance would appear to offer an experience in cooperation rather than in competition.

The following diagram shows these three areas of physical education on a continuum between the poles extending from competitiveness to cooperativeness.

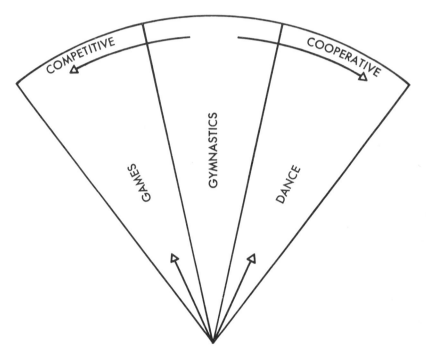

The basic experience provided by the three different areas of physical education.

COMPETITIVE   **COOPERATIVE**

Games   Gymnastics   Dance

Team Games		
Dual Games		
Individual Games and Contests		
Games of Chance		
Meets: Gymnastic, Swim, Skating, Track		
Ballroom Dance Contest		
Self-Testing: Stunts, Tumbling, Apparatus		
Singing Games		
Acrobatic Dance		
Gymnastics (Movement Education Type)		
Modern Dance (Concert Type)		
Modern Educational Dance:		
Ballroom		
Folk		
Square		

If the same three areas are examined on the basis of the degree to which the activity is a social one or an individual one, another continuum can be constructed. For the purposes of this analysis "social" may be defined as having a significant element of interaction between individuals. "Individual" may be defined as containing no element of interaction with others.

Games, then, are seen to range from highly social to individual in nature. Team games present two opposing experiences. One is the opposition of one team against the other resulting in the competition mentioned earlier. The other is the cooperative interaction of the teammates to achieve their goal of a winning score. Dual games such as doubles in tennis or "Two on Two" in a soccer dribble game offer the same experience in a simpler situation. Singles in table tennis, fencing, or "One on One" in basketball shooting offer a competitive experience which is limited to "action and reaction". Certain games like golf or "jacks" or solitaire can be entirely individual with the action being related to the equipment and/or the environmental conditions. Thus it can be seen that games offer the full range of experience between interaction of individuals within groups; action and reaction between groups or between individuals, and, finally, solitary play. It is interesting to speculate on the curve of popularity of these forms of social experience. The two-year-old child, unsure of himself, is likely to favour individual, but parallel play. The primary child, if allowed to choose his own circumstance, shows a progression of choice from individual play to partner play, and then to small group play. The junior child will continue to enjoy the same three variations of situations but will also thoroughly enjoy larger groups, "gangs" and intergroup play. The thirteen-year-old and his older cousins accept the greater challenge of organized team play. This remains attractive for a considerable number of years but gradually dual and parallel activities such as badminton and golf re-assert themselves.

If the teacher appreciates these tendencies as evidences of readiness for the experience offered by the organization of the games situation, a valuable contribution to the social growth of children should accrue.

Examined from the same point of view, dance tends to offer more of a social experience than an individual one, although both are possible. Social dance is nomenclature found in the literature. It indicates the emphasis immediately. Social dance is usually a name applied to ballroom dance or its derivatives, such as couple dances with a folk-dance flavour or the "Play Party Games" types of dances. The purpose is to enjoy the society of one's friends, neighbours and associates in a dance setting. Folk dances and square dances are similar in nature but rooted in ethnic origins. In all these forms of social dance there is a basic theme of boy meeting girl. In some societies, the dances may be frankly courtship situations which follow a strict social protocol. In others, there is a greater freedom for the individuals to use the situation according to their own fancy. But the degree of freedom or ritual is prescribed by the custom of the community. The school situation should take into account the outlook in the community. Folk-dance lessons and parties which are limited to girls and women are unrealistic. Couple dances for very young children are equally senseless. Usually, the dances which place a stress on enjoying the society of one's friends in a dance setting are the dances most suited to the physical education program.

The art forms of dance, commonly called Modern Dance, Creative Dance or Creative Rhythms in school curricula offer differing types of social experience. The dance may be a group dance with interaction between members of the group, or it may be an intergroup dance with two or more groups reacting to one another. Partner dances may contain the same range of interaction or action and reaction in a simpler set of circumstances. A great number of dance experiences can be individual in nature. It is possible that thirty individual and unique solos can be danced simultaneously by a class of thirty children.

If children are allowed to select their own set of circumstances, they will follow approximately the same pattern as that outlined in the discussion about games. That is, very young children will "dance" alone. As they get older, the emphasis is on pairs and then on small groups. At an even later age they will use all these forms and add the larger groups. On the whole, the tendency is for the favourite organization to remain the group, thus indicating that the basic stress in dance is a social rather than an individual one.

Finally, an examination of the stress in gymnastics will draw attention to the individual nature of the activity. Essentially, body management and self-testing are very much an individual challenge. Pupils like to work in the presence of others but it is their own arch or roll that they are executing. Older children will enjoy placing their work in juxtaposition to a partner's work, thus achieving a design of movement. This can be enlarged to include groups of four to six members who may cooperate on a sequence. Nevertheless the dominant stress is upon the individual rather than the social experience.

Placed on a continuum the three areas offer contrasting experiences in the social element, as shown in the figure on the opposite page.

Functional or *objective* movement and *subjective* or *expressive* movement offer the participant two opposing experiences. Objective movement may be defined as the type which is geared to accomplish a practical task. Simple examples are to kick a ball; to vault over a fence; to pull a sled; to run to the bus stop. It is easily seen that the kick is to project the ball from one place to another; the vault is to get oneself over the fence; the pull is to move the sled; the run is to arrive in time. The body is the tool for doing the job.

Expressive movement conveys a thought or feeling. The body is the instrument of communication. Simple examples of expressive movements

Social-Ballroom Folk Dance	*Team Games	Group Gymnastics Sequences	Partner Gymnastics	Partner Dances	*Dual Games	Skating	Single Games	Solo Dances	Solitary Games	Gymnastics

*Cooperative interaction for the purpose of meeting the opposition.

are: the angry stamp of a foot; a startled jump of fright; a slow, cautious tiptoeing. The interpretation of expressive actions is not as simple a matter as that of understanding or assessing objective movement. However, most people are surprised to discover how often they "read" such movement accurately.

Where do these two types of movements occur?

Movements which constitute games' skills are developed to effect the control of the ball and/or equipment in an efficient manner. The batter wants to hit the ball; the fielder wants to recover the ball and to direct it to the appropriate base as quickly as possible. The movement used will be objective, though it may have overtones of expressive movement. This might occur as the expression of the fielder's haste in sending the ball to the base as quickly as possible. But in the main, the action is performed to accomplish a job.

Dance as an art form is expressive in nature. The body is used as an instrument for communicating thoughts, feelings, moods or situations. The movements of the body are selected and arranged to convey the desired impressions. Thus a leap, a turn, or a run may be modulated to convey such meanings as joyousness, fright or a sense of playfulness. The quality of the movement — its speed, tension, flow and spatial characteristics — is selected to communicate the meaning of the dance. Of course, dance as an art form is expressive movement which ". . . is highly selected, spatially designed, and organized through (its) rhythmic structure . . ."[3]

[3] Marjorie Turner, *Modern Dance for High School and College*, Prentice-Hall, Englewood Cliffs, New Jersey, 1964, p. 4.

Folk dance is expressive also, although perhaps, not as emphatically so. Hence there are folk dances which are joyous, others which are dignified, some which are comic. Some are imitative of harvesting routines, or of wine making or fishing chores.

Gymnastics, concerned with body management, is mainly objective in nature. One tries to balance on the beam, climb the rope, vault the box, roll across the mat. The onlooker feels very uncomfortable if he finds himself watching a performer "emote" on a piece of apparatus. He is embarrassed to see a performer soulfully cling to a rope. Subconsciously, he recognizes that he is not observing a dance, nor is he witnessing a self-testing situation in body management. Thus he realizes that something is out of place and he becomes uneasy. Movement which should be objective has become inappropriately expressive.

Thus these three areas of physical education would appear on a continuum spanning degrees of objectivity to subjectivity in movement as follows:

FUNCTIONAL MOVEMENTS   **EXPRESSIVE MOVEMENTS**

Games   Rhythmic Gymnastics   Dance
Gymnastics   Ball or Hoop Routines
                         Acrobatic Dance

In summary, the three areas offer to the pupil different sets of experiences. Thus it would seem advisable that the pupil be given opportunities to participate in activities from all three areas.

COMPETITIVE   **COOPERATIVE**
  • Games   Gymnastics   • Dance

SOCIAL   **INDIVIDUAL**
  • Games   • Gymnastics
  • Dance

FUNCTIONAL   **EXPRESSIVE**
  • Games   • Dance
  • Gymnastics

The reader is invited to examine the areas of track and field and calisthenics for himself and to identify the nature of the experience afforded by them.

It is suggested here that aquatics and skating are similar in nature to gymnastics in that they are forms of body management, essentially individualistic, objective in purpose and self-testing against the force of gravity. Their distinctive feature is that they happen in a modified environment. For skating the ice surface offers little or no purchase. For swimming, a ballistic field is provided by the water, which also adds the factor of interference with normal breathing, as well as the complication of having to move in a three-dimensional spatial environment. It should be added, however, that figure skating and synchronized swimming in some situations have moved, or are moving, into an expressive form of activity.

FOUR

SOME CONCEPTS
OF MOVEMENT

Thus far, an attempt has been made to describe the nature of the child, the teaching-learning process and the nature of physical education. Physical education is undergoing change due to the better understanding of the child and the teaching-learning process. It is also changing as a result of the influence of Laban's theories of movement. Up to this point no description of those theories has been attempted. It has merely been stated that his theories are based on a detailed study of the movements of men and women in all situations characteristic of human endeavour.

Laban has stated that "Today research becomes more and more a matter of teamwork."[2] He recognizes the contribution of the physicist, mathematician, engineer, physician, anthropologist and other specialists who have investigated motion. He recognizes that "rationalistic explanations of the movements of the human body insist on the fact that it is subject to the laws of inanimate motion"[3] but states that "The use of movement for a definite purpose, either as a means for external work or for the mirroring of certain states and attitudes of mind, derives from a power of a hitherto unexplained source."[4] He defines living movement as "movement in which purposeful control of the mechanical happening is at work" and gives the name *Effort* "to the inner function originating such movement."[5]

---

[1] These concepts are derived from those expounded by Laban in his writings, particularly the ones listed in the footnotes.

[2] Rudolf Laban, F. C. Lawrence, *Effort*, Macdonald and Evans, London, 1947, p. xii.

[3] Rudolf Laban, *The Mastery of Movement*, Macdonald and Evans, London, 1960 (Second edition revised by L. Ullman), p. 22.

[4] *Ibid.*, p. 23.

[5] *Ibid.*, p. 23.

The situation facing the teacher of physical education in terms of the nature of the materials to be taught is to recognize that there are laws governing the mechanical nature of movement and, in addition, principles which deal with the voluntary control of human movement. The former have been examined in great detail and applied to the training of athletes or of students by such writers as John W. Bunn[6] and Marion R. Broer,[7] and a host of physical education graduate students in their thesis studies. Coaches of professional teams and those connected with international competitions such as the Olympics pursue the investigation and test out the application.

The principles governing the voluntary control of human movement and the inner function originating such movement are the areas which have been studied by Laban and his associates. These principles have been applied to physical education and dance by teachers in the field and will be the concern of this book.

A WAY OF REGARDING MOVEMENT

When movement comes into being certain facts are observable. Suppose you extend your hand in a greeting to a friend. Observe that the hand and arm, as parts of your *body*, are used as the instrument of your greeting gesture. The gesture may be made in response to the appearance of your friend and, therefore, in *relation* to an occurrence in your environment. The movement is directed towards him, perhaps forward; thus making a track in *space*. Furthermore, the particular quality of your movement is affected by your feeling for your friend. If you are pleased to see him, you may hasten, wholeheartedly, to offer a gesture of greeting and the *effort* content of your movement, as a consequence, is swift, firm and to the point.

The example given demonstrates the fact that when voluntary movement is examined, four components must be considered: *body, space, relationship, effort*. The chart on the next page is an attempt to show this concept in diagramatic form.

Thus, our starting point for examining movement is that it is an entirety, an "all or nothing thing." (It either happens or it does not happen.) When it occurs, four components will be present, namely, the *Body* representing the instrument of the action, the *Space* into which the movement is projected, the *Effort Quality* with which it is executed and the *Relationship* which it makes with the objects or persons in the environ-

---

[6] John W. Bunn, *Scientific Principles of Coaching*, Prentice-Hall, Inc., Englewood Cliffs, 1955, p. 201.

[7] Marion R. Broer, *Efficiency of Human Movement*, W. B. Saunders Company, Philadelphia, 1961.

ment. The examination of a specific series of movements will demonstrate that, while all these components are present in some degree, some may exert a greater stress on a movement than others. This will occur because the mover usually has a particular intention which motivates the movement. For example, in a dance sequence, the effort quality of the movement may be of particular concern, while in serving a tennis ball particular consideration is given to the relationship of the ball to the net and to the opponent.

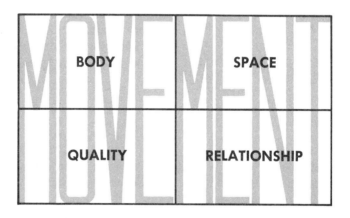

MOVEMENT EDUCATION

The study of the principles which govern the purposeful control of living movement and the acquisition of skill in exerting that control, together with the self-understanding which attends such learning, is the purpose of movement education. Such study delves into specific details which comprise each of the component parts, gradually creating an awareness of their functioning in one's own movement and in the movement of others.

The chart opposite presents an overview of the important subdivisions of each of the components of movement. Movement education must take into account the effect of each of these aspects upon movement, both from the point of view of developing the power to analyze movement and the power to execute it precisely and at will.

DESCRIPTIVE ANALYSIS OF THE IMPORTANT
ASPECTS OF THE COMPONENTS OF MOVEMENT

Movement is a language in its own right and it speaks for itself. Any attempt to give an understanding of it through words is bound to have a limited result. Consequently the descriptions which follow should be converted into movements and felt and observed by the student.

OVERVIEW — COMPONENTS OF MOVEMENT AND THEIR IMPORTANT SUBDIVISIONS

Body Awareness	Space Awareness
1. Basic functions: bend or curl, stretch, twist	**1. Recognition of and adaptation to space: General and personal** A. Recognition B. Adaptation to general space
2. Body parts A. Recognition (i) Of the part used 　　　　　　　(ii) Of the part stressed B. Body parts can bend, curl or stretch, twist C. Body parts can lead an action D. Body parts can meet and part E. Body parts can be used symmetrically or asymmetrically	**2. Orientation to personal space** A. The three-dimensional cross B. Diagonals C. Planes
3. Weightbearing A. Support — parts taking the weight B. Transference of weight C. Balance	**3. Levels:** low, medium, high
	4. Pathways in space: floor patterns: air patterns
4. Body actions A. Identification (i) Locomotion 　　　　　　　　(ii) Elevations 　　　　　　　　(iii) Turns B. Gestures C. Holding or carrying actions which establish stillness	**5. Extensions in space:** large, small, near, far
5. Body shapes: pin, wall, ball, screw	
6. Symmetrical and asymmetrical uses of the body	

Effort	Relationships
1. Effort qualities of movement A. Weight: firm (strong), fine touch (light), heavy B. Time: sudden (fast), sustained (slow) C. Space: direct (straight), flexible (wavy) D. Flow: bound ("stoppable"), free (ongoing)	**1. With objects:** A. The manipulative relationship B. The non-manipulative relationship 　(i) An obstacle 　(ii) An extension 　(iii) A target
2. Emphasizing one element	**2. With people:** A. Alone B. Alone in a mass C. Partners: cooperative, competitive D. Groups E. Intergroup relationships
3. Emphasizing two elements simultaneously	
4. Basic effort actions	

1. *Basic functions*

A. BEND OR CURL. *Bow your head.* Notice that in doing this the top of the head has moved towards the feet or knees, and the spine has tended to become slightly rounded. This illustrates the curling or enfolding function of the body. Curling involves the movement of the parts of the body towards the centre of the body with the tendency to round into a ball shape. It may be done in a limited way as for a bow or it may be done to the extreme of the anatomical range as when the body is curled into a ball.

Bend your head forward. Notice that in this case the action is limited to the joint(s) of the neck.

Bend your elbow. Notice that the action is limited to the elbow joint.

Thus, bend and curl are related in that parts of the body *approach* one another. However, "bend" gives a stress to the action in the joint(s) while "curl" gives a feeling of enfolding the body or a fairly extensive segment of it.

B. STRETCH. *Sit tall. Lift the top of the head towards the ceiling. Feel the elongation of the spine.* This illustrates the *stretching* or unfolding function of the body which comes about when the parts on either side of a joint or joints move away from each other. This may be done as a moving towards the point of complete separation of two parts; as, for example when one straightens the knee. Or, it may be done so as to carry on the elongation until the greatest possible separation of the parts is achieved in the whole body or a major section of it. This elongation occurs when one "stands tall" or "sits tall."

C. TWIST. *Stand squarely facing a wall, with feet apart. Adjust the hips and shoulders so that they are parallel to the wall you are facing. Turn the head and shoulders to face the left hand wall.* Notice that as the shoulders become parallel to the new wall, the hips partially rotate, the knees do so to a lesser extent and the feet remain in the starting position. Feel the rotating action running through the various parts of the body. By definition a twist is the rotation of one part of the body against another part which remains fixed or which moves in a counter-direction. If the rotation goes to the extreme limit of its range, there is a locking of one part against another. The part which remains fixed may support the body weight, as was the case in the above example; or it may be held in position by muscular counter-tension, as is the case in a twist while jumping.

All body movements are composed of fluctuations or transitions between these three basic functions. In most cases, the movement does not reach the limit of its range before a transition into the succeeding function takes place.

Two kinds of stretch and one twisted curl.

2. *Body parts*

A. RECOGNITION. (i) *Of the part used.* It would seem ridiculous to suggest that a person would not know what part of the body is being used for a given action. Yet how many people know where on the heel they put weight as they walk? Probably only those who have seen the effect on the heel of the shoe recognize this. Similarly, one could ask, which side of your mouth is used to chew the tough meat. Most people would have to experiment to find out. Thus, when a new skill is learned, or an established one modified, it is necessary to become aware of the parts of the body which are significant in the action.

(ii) *Of the part stressed.* Some people can be identified by the sound of their footsteps. This could be because one foot is stressed more than the other as they walk. In walking it is not necessary to stress the use of one foot more than the other, but in taking a corner in skating it will be necessary to stress the stroking of the left foot when travelling counterclockwise. In a square dance swing, it will help to stress the foot closest to your partner. In a badminton net shot, it is necessary to use a light wrist action and not a full arm action. In short, specific skills will often require the ability to discriminate between the different parts of the body and to stress the action of one particular part.

The body is twisting.

B. BODY PARTS CAN BEND, CURL OR STRETCH, TWIST. *Hold the open palm of the hand before you. Gradually close the fist.* Notice that, in doing this, the fingers fold in to touch the palm and the thumb folds over the fingers. This is the curling action limited, in this case, to the hand. Other parts of the body can curl or bend. That is, two parts on either side of a joint can move closer together giving the feeling of enfolding. Similarly, those parts can open, elongate or separate. This means that the parts of the body can stretch. Similarly, many parts, but not all joints, have the capacity of rotating to some extent. When this is possible, those parts have the ability to twist. Thus, one can put a spin on a bowling ball by executing a slight twist in the wrist and fingers. It may be said that the parts, as well as the whole body, have the capacity to bend or curl, stretch and twist. This means that one must become aware of when these functions are being used or should be used. For example, the pathway of a bowling ball may be affected by a slight twist of the wrist. Or, in a headstand, one may have to check to be sure that the general body stretch is complemented by stretched ankles and toes.

C. BODY PARTS CAN LEAD AN ACTION. *Lean well forward and then sit back in a relaxed position. Repeat the forward lean in three different ways:*
(1) as if trying to hear something
(2) as if trying to smell something
(3) as if trying to see something.
If these actions are done effectively, it will be easy to see that the ear, the nose, the eyes lead their respective actions. A performer could do these actions in a jumbled order, but it would still be possible to discern which action he was doing from observing the part which led the action. In ordinary life, in games, dance or gymnastics, it is often imperative that a specific part of the body lead the action. For example, if you wish to get through a crowd without bumping anyone, lead into a narrow space with one shoulder. In the long jump, the heels lead into the landing in the pit. In dance, a knee may lead into a body turn. In gymnastics, the hands will lead the catspring. The conclusion is that specific parts may at times perform the important role of leading the body action.

D. BODY PARTS CAN MEET AND PART. This form of action was discussed when the functions of bend (curl) and stretch were described. However, parts may move toward or away from each other in such a way that the meeting or parting is more significant than the enfolding and opening which was the characteristic of the curl/stretch actions. Hence, heel clicks, hand claps, astride jumps, leg kicks to touch the hands or head tend to put the emphasis on the point of contact. Frequently, the meetings and partings are accomplished by a form of swing and the point of contact is at the ends of the extremities of the body. At other times, the stress may be on surfaces of the body meeting and touching. For example, the legs with knees straight may part in splits or scissor kicks and the meeting will be in terms of the inside surfaces. This may develop into an awareness of the fact that the body parts may operate as instruments or tools such as scissors, pincers, hammers and so on.

E. BODY PARTS CAN BE USED SYMMETRICALLY OR ASYMMETRICALLY. The right and left arms can be moved simultaneously and in such a way that they match each other in action, pathway and effort. For example, two hands may be offered to a partner; two arms can be used to flag down a car. Similarly, the right and left legs can be used in exactly the same way in certain jumps or when lifted while the individual is seated. Other parts of the body such as the shoulders, elbows and knees can also be used in symmetrical movement. In other instances, the paired parts of the body can be used independently. For example, the right hand can be used to write while the left hand controls the paper. Similarly, the right foot may tap idly on the floor while the left foot supports the body weight. The symmetrical or asymmetrical use of the parts of the body is particularly important because either use tends to lead the whole body into a similar type of movement, thus causing the body to attain stability or mobility as explained on page 48.

3. *Weightbearing*

A. SUPPORT — PARTS TAKING THE WEIGHT. Different parts of the body may support the body weight: we may be on two feet; on the seat, one foot and two elbows; on the back and so on. In this case, we are examining our contact with the floor or its substitute. It is also possible to hang from the base of support, as from a cross bar. In this case, such parts as the hands, knees, or ankles hold the body weight. The cultivation of body awareness should include a real awareness of the parts and combinations of parts which support the weight.

B. TRANSFERENCE OF WEIGHT. The support can be shifted from one part of the body to another. The transference of weight is one of the most important movement phenomena in the body. In most situations it produces *locomotion* and becomes the means of moving the body through space. *Walk four steps forward.* Notice how the weight is transferred. Roughly, it moves from one foot to the other alternately. But in a slow barefoot walk, notice how it rolls forward from the heel to toe of the supporting foot and is received on the ball of the foot and rolls back towards the heel. A careful study of the transference of weight will show that a roll of some degree very often precedes the actual change of weight from one part to another. If a direct transference is made, it is almost always made through some degree of spring. In this case, the body weight is projected into the air and comes down on the new base of support. Even under these circumstances, the spring is usually preceded by a roll to give the necessary momentum.

C. BALANCE. *Walk forward four steps.* Ordinarily you experience no difficulty in balancing your weight. In fact, you are rarely aware that balance is involved until you experience the problems of walking on an iced surface. The secret is that you have become skilled in keeping the body weight over your feet which are functioning as your base. In the

The body action is a *spring*. The weight is momentarily removed from the supporting base.

human body, the centre of the body mass is located approximately in the hips.[8] When the centre of gravity remains over the base, the body is *on balance*. In many positions, it is easy to retain the *on balance* situation. These cases are incidences of *stability*. In walking, running, and skipping the transference of weight is executed in such a way that the centre of gravity is kept over the base. Stability results. Standing, sitting, kneeling are also stable situations. Handstands, headstands, arabesques are far less stable because, in these cases, it is much more difficult to hold the centre of gravity over the base. There are movement situations where the centre of gravity is moved beyond the base. This brings about the condition of *over-balance* or *mobile balance* and the movement becomes one of flying (as in a jump through space) or falling (as in overshooting the landing after a jump). Overbalance or mobile balance is the result of under-control. Recovery of stability can be achieved by establishing a new base under the centre of gravity. Thus, an overbalance in a headstand may be controlled by making a bridge with weight supported by feet and hands and head. Alternatively, the weight may be transferred through a roll and established over the feet in a standing position.

[8] Marion R. Broer, *Efficiency of Human Movement*, W. B. Saunders Company, Philadelphia, 1961, p. 21.

The development of an awareness of all the aspects which are involved in balance, namely, the centre of gravity, the base, stable balance, mobile balance, and the transference of weight, is a very important part of the skilful use of the body as a tool for movement.

4. *Body actions*

While the body movement is a fluctuation between the curl, stretch and twist function and must take into account the pull of gravity upon the body mass, the movement itself takes the form of certain types of *actions*.

A. IDENTIFICATION. *(i) Locomotion.* These actions move the body from place to place through space. It is done in different ways according to the manner in which the weight is transferred from one part to another. The transference may be from one adjacent part to another and the result will be a *roll*. For example, one may lie on the back on a given location on the floor. By transferring the weight onto the right side, to the front, to the left side and then onto the back, a single roll to the right has been executed and the body has been moved one body width to the right. Notice that in the forward roll, the weight starts on the feet and is transferred to the hands which have been placed near enough to the feet to become adjacent to them. Similarly the back of the head must be *placed* adjacent to the hands to make the roll smooth.

In *step-like* actions the weight is transferred to non-adjacent parts of the body. Thus in crawling the weight moves from right hand, to left knee, to left hand, to right knee.

In *jumps* which cause travelling, there is a moment of elevation and of flight when the body rises clear of the floor and the weight drops back again onto the same or a different body part but in a new location in space.

In a *slide*, the body weight is retained on certain body parts as it moves through the space. The power required for that movement will come prior to the slide from the momentum of step-like or jump actions. If it comes concurrently, the action becomes a drag and the step-like or jump movements of, for example the hands, will supply the force to pull the legs along in a sliding action.

In summary, locomotion is achieved through the transference of body weight to various parts of the body. This may be done in different ways, namely by rolling, jumping or step-like actions.

(ii) Elevations.[9] These actions are springs or jumps which propel the body upward, momentarily removing the weight from the supporting parts. The flight is followed by a falling of the body weight which is usually

[9] Rudolf Laban, *The Mastery of Movement,* Macdonald and Evans, London, 1960, p. 50-52.

caught by the receiving part and absorbed into a landing of some sort. Elevations may be on the spot, as in hops which move up and down in a vertical plane. They may also be used as a form of locomotion. This occurs in the long jump. To feel the characteristic ballistic nature of this action, it is necessary to feel the lift in what Laban calls the "centre of levity"[10] in the region of the breastbone. It is necessary to lift the chest and to feel airborne or to feel a moment of suspension. This overtone is most likely to occur in dance jumps. It may also be experienced in jumps off the trampoline and the springboard.

The term "elevation" has been extended to include the lifting of a body part, such as the arm or the head. The tension which is required to overcome the pull of gravity is similar to the impetus required for the execution of a jump. However, it is used with less intensity and probably with less suddenness and, therefore, flight does not result.

(iii) Turns. Stand in a forward stride position with the right foot in front. Keeping the feet in their original spot, turn left about face. Your left foot will now be in front of you and you will be facing in the opposite direction. This is a half turn. It brings about a change of face.

Stand with feet together, facing a chair. Cross the right foot over the left and twist around on the ball of the feet so as to turn a complete circle and finish facing the chair. This is a full turn and it brings about a loss of face and a re-establishment of it.

Turns can be on the spot or travelling. They can be full or partial. They can be led by different parts of the body and can proceed in different directions. Different parts of the body may be used as a base. Thus a turn may be a sitting, standing or even a flying turn, to mention three possibilities. A twist function of the body is involved. A common characteristic of the turn or spin is a loss of orientation in space. When a number of turns are executed in swift succession, a temporary dizziness builds up and there is likely to be a loss of orientation and perhaps balance. This creates a feeling of excitement and gaiety. One becomes caught up in the flow of the movement. Single or partial turns will give a change of face, often with surprising suddenness.

B. GESTURES are movements of parts of the body which are not, at the time, supporting the body weight. Examples are arm or leg swings, a trunk tilt, and a knee raise or toe tap. The gestures of the arms and legs are often organized as scooping, surrounding or scattering type gestures. The gestures of the head and spine usually echo or accompany these movements of the limbs. An important use of a gesture is to provide a counterbalance which keeps the centre of gravity over the base as, for example, when the head is raised or lowered to adjust the balance in a handstand.

[10] *Ibid.*, p. 58.

C. HOLDING OR CARRYING ACTIONS WHICH ESTABLISH STILLNESS. *Shake the hand vigorously and very fast. Suddenly stop! Hold the hand still.* Notice how much positive action is required to establish and hold stillness. *Similarly hold the arm extended diagonally forward and downward so that it holds or carries its own weight for a full minute.* Once again you will feel the positive grip that is exerted to hold the state of stillness. The awareness of the state of stillness as a positive effort to arrest movement and to resist the pull of gravity must come through experiences in which the exploration of the phenomenon is the purpose of the movement study. Stillness is usually required as the state for the beginning and ending of sequences of movement. Dramatic impact can be created by contrasting phrases of stillness with phrases of movement.

5. *Body shapes*

These can be seen as silhouettes in space, but they also need to be felt in the body for they require an awareness of the position of one part relative to another part of the body. For example, some beginning gymnasts cannot feel the elongation of the spine which makes for a good handstand. The coach may help by reminding them that they should strive for a *pin-shape* in the body. This is also an efficient shape for the basketball lay-up shot, for it enables the player to penetrate narrow spaces between opponents. Similarly, the *wall-shape* is useful for the rebound player who hopes to block out the opponents. This shape is wide and spreading, usually in the door plane. It is seen in the cartwheel and in most guarding positions.

The *ball-shape* is the result of curling the body up and is found in a very complete ball in the forward or backward rolls or the cannonball dives in swimming. The handspring and walkover are examples of the ball-shape inverted to form a circle or a wheel. In dramatic movement or dance, it may be used in bows or to indicate withdrawal and protection of the centre of the body. In everyday movement it can be used for protection from attack or from falls. It is essentially a mobile shape, offering a surface for the transference of body weight.

The *screw-shape* arises out of a body twist. As demonstrated by the discus thrower, it can be used for a source of power which is produced as the body rotates out of the counter-twist. Thus, it is used for throwing, wrestling, turning.

Movements which generate clearly defined body shapes can be used in dance composition for their design quality. They can be used in drama for the meaning they express. In sports or working actions they can be used for their functional advantages.

6. *Symmetrical and asymmetrical uses of the body*

Stand with feet astride and arms stretched wide apart and diagonally upward. Look directly ahead. Feel the "X"-shape of the body. Notice how similar the right and left sides of the body are. This position brings the body into a symmetrical posture. *Now return to an "attention" position using symmetrical movement.* It is easy to move the arms symmetrically and there is a considerable choice of ways of doing it. For example, they can both spread sideways and downward, or close forward and downward, or the elbows may bend to bring the hands in to the shoulders before they extend downward. However, since the feet bear the weight, it is more difficult to move them simultaneously. A jump to bring them together seems to be the most evident way of solving the problem. This little experiment demonstrates the nature of the symmetrical use of the body. The right and left sides must be matched in simultaneous movement. Further experiments will lead to the conclusion that this use of the body gives great stability, and therefore it restricts mobility and locomotion.

Using phrases of four steps each, walk, run, skip and side gallop trying to be aware of when each of the two sides of the body is active. You will notice that in the walk, run, and skip, the two sides of the body are used alternately but the arms and legs are used in opposition. You will notice in the gallop that one side is consistently emphasized. These are examples of the asymmetrical uses of the body, but the gallop is more completely asymmetrical than any of the other actions. The asymmetrical use of the body gives greater mobility but less steadiness.

From a standing position, kneel down. Did you use a symmetrical or an asymmetrical method? *Try the opposite method.* Which gives the greater mobility? It should be possible to build up a sensitive awareness of these two uses of the body by analyzing a wide range of your own movements.

In summary, the body is the tool of human movement. Skilful control and a good understanding of its movement possibilities should be the rewards of becoming aware of the organization of its movement life.

SPACE AWARENESS

It was pointed out in the beginning of this chapter that movement takes place in space. The student of movement will need to become aware of the different aspects of space which may be involved in any movement or series of movements. These aspects are outlined on the chart on p. 39 and will be elaborated here.

1. Recognition of and adaptation to space: General and personal

A. RECOGNITION. Observe the following response to the command: "Hands up!"

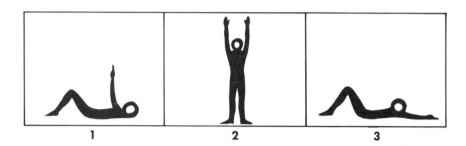

All think they are correct and yet there is a difference in the result. Number 1 is reaching to the ceiling; Number 3 is reaching above the head. Number 2 may be thinking in either of these terms. The explanation of the different results lies in the difference in orientation. Number 1 is taking his orientation from the pull of gravity and is using the ceiling as "up" and the floor as "down." His response is in relation to a direction in the space in which he finds himself. Number 3 is taking his orientation from his body, regarding the normal position of the head as "up" and the feet as "down." Thus regardless of all else, he orientates himself in relation to the head-feet axis of his body.

How would these two respond to the cue to "raise your head" while doing a handstand?

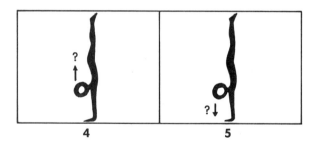

These situations demonstrate that there can be more than one point of view with respect to one's orientation. If *space in general* is taken as the basis of orientation, then "up" and "down" are represented by the vertical to the earth. "Right-left" and "forward-backward" are taken from the sides and the front of the body. If a room is the area to which one is to become oriented, the upward and downward movements are made towards the ceiling and floor respectively. These directions concur with the vertical to the earth. However, in a room, the "front of the room" is usually specified and it determines the orientation of the forward movements. Backward, right and left sides are then automatically determined. This, for example, is done in American square dances, although it is a convention to regard the caller as being at the front of the room. These situations are two variations of an orientation to *general space*.

There is also the possibility that the individual may take his orientation from his body. In this case, "up" is described as headward, "down" is feetward, "forward" is in the direction of the breastbone (wherever it may be turned) and "back", "right" and "left" follow accordingly. Therefore, when one is asked to reach forward, one will move in the direction toward which the chest is directed. The orientation thus described may be regarded as *personal* since it is taken from the body.

In certain situations, the orientation to space, room or body will not differ and, therefore, a distinction of the basis of orientation is not vitally important and the consideration of it will not arise. (See figure 2, page 50.) Occasionally confusion arises, and it might be useful to check the basis of orientation. (See figures 1, 3, 4 and 5, page 50.)

B. ADAPTATION TO GENERAL SPACE. A vast empty space may intimidate or stimulate. These reactions may become evident when a class of very young children is taken to the gymnasium for the first time. They may crowd together as if for comfort; or they may tear off on the run, enjoying the freedom afforded. Even adults react in these ways when meeting in an unfamiliar room. Furthermore, a confined space may irritate, depress, or frighten, particularly if it must be shared by a crowd of people. Hence we realize that we are faced with the need to adapt to space.

Already it has been implied that we can react by *moving freely around*, filling up all the space, visiting all parts of the room; i.e. we can penetrate the space by moving through it by means of locomotion. This may be done with an emotional response: we may be intimidated by it and shrink into ourselves, or lured into it, progressing freely through it even to the extent of using elevation in the form of jumps or an upright carriage. In dramatic situations we may even use it as if it were a partner, and ward it off, using the arms to push against it or bar it from encroaching upon us.

2. *Orientation to personal space*

Personal space may be described as that sphere which immediately surrounds the body and which can be reached without moving away from the original starting spot. The orientation is taken from the normal standing position of the body. The directions established are: up-down, right-

---

left, front-back. This orientation forms a triple axis cross and is known as the:

A. THE THREE-DIMENSIONAL CROSS. It has three dimensions which describe the construction of the body.

(i) The length of the body lies upon the vertical dimension and has two directional possibilities, namely, *up* and *down*. The line may be visualized as passing through the centre of the body just in front of the spine. A good way to experience this orientation is to reach with one hand as high as possible directly over the head and to follow the vertical line down to the floor between the feet and move up again in the same line. It will be noticed immediately that the whole body is brought into play and rises or sinks as a means of assisting in the movement. The experiment should be carried on until the performer is aware of how the body may behave and feel as it sinks and rises in the vertical dimension with or without the hand being used as the point of emphasis.

(ii) The width of the body lies across one of the horizontal dimensions and has the two directional possibilities of to the *right* and to the *left*. This dimension passes through the middle of the body approximately above hip level and can be experienced by reaching out to each side at that level with each hand and swaying from side to side without changing the position of the feet. The maximum width or reach can thus be determined. It may be noticed that, in this situation, the front of the body is open. If the right or left hand alone were to mark the reach on each side of the body, the movement would cause the body front to open and close alternately. This situation is even more complete when both hands simultaneously mark the outward reaches on their own and then on the opposite sides of the body. Thus the body situations of *opening* and *closing* are linked with the use of the horizontal dimension and the directions of *right* and *left*.

(iii) The depth of the body lies along the sagittal dimension which passes through the centre of the body above hip height from front to back. It has the two directional possibilities of *forward* and *backward*. This dimension may be located by starting the hands touching the body, one in front and the other behind, and extending them as far out from the body as possible above hip level and drawing them back into the body. Later, explorations should include reaching with one hand as far forward and then as far back as possible. This can be extended in range by allowing the right foot to accompany the right hand, so long as the *front* of the body remains facing forward. This exploration will reveal that the movements which are engendered by restricting oneself to this dimension are the *advancing* and *retreating* forms of movement.

It is important to notice that the *direction* of the movement is merely one consideration. The changes which take place within the central area of the body in terms of rising/sinking; opening/closing; advancing/retreating are probably more important because they force adjustments in the line of gravity. See diagram on page 172.

While the dimensional cross represents a basic personal orientation to space, the human body is capable of participating in a myriad of movements which do not lie along these dimensions. Presumably, given the dimensional orientation, the other possibilities could be plotted. For systematized plotting of the use of space in human movement and the spatial harmonies which arise from the transitions between these spatial pathways, references should be made to Laban's books *Modern Educational Dance*[11] and *Choreutics*.[12]

As indicated on the chart on p. 39 only limited guidance is given in this text. Therefore, attention is drawn to the fact that the dimensional scale gives the basic orientation from which other manifestations of spatial orientation such as the *diagonals* may be determined.

B. THE FOUR DIAGONALS. There are four diagonals which are most easily found by imagining oneself standing in the centre of a cube. By reaching to the forward upper right corner of the imaginary cube and following a pathway which goes directly to the backward lower left corner of the cube, passing through the centre of gravity of the body, it is possible to locate one diagonal. In a similar manner the other three may be found. Movements into the extreme high or low reaches of the diagonal, done while retaining the forward focus of the body, tend to pull the centre of gravity beyond the base which will cause one to create a new base or to move into flying or falling movements. Thus diagonal movements are characterized by mobility.

C. PLANES. *Stand in a doorway with the feet and hands at their respective corners.* Notice how flat the body feels. It is as if it were the door which divides the space in front from the space at the back of the body. The policeman directing traffic at an intersection uses just such a posture to block off the traffic from in front and behind him. The basketball guard uses a modified form of the same position. It is called the *door* or *vertical plane* and it grows out of a combination of the length of the body with the width of the body. Movements up and down or sideways are most compatible with this position.

Do a forward roll and feel how the weight moves around a circular spine. In this case, the body is in the sagittal or *wheel plane*. It grows out of a combination of the vertical and the sagittal dimensions. It is used in such actions as bowing, walking on a narrow beam, sitting down or standing up when done with the body focussed straight forward. Many gym-

[11] Rudolf Laban, *Modern Educational Dance*, Macdonald and Evans, London, 1948.
[12] Rudolf Laban, *Choreutics*, Macdonald and Evans, London, 1966.

---

nastic movements such as handstands, headstands, springs, bridges and rolls are done in the wheel plane. It is the plane which is compatible with loco-motion forward or backward and the sprinter works hard to keep his movements within it.

Do two or three "Coffee Grinder" stunts. As one leg circles under the body, it is seen to be held as parallel to the floor as possible. This means that an attempt is being made to keep it in the *table plane.* This plane is made up of a combination of the horizontal and sagittal dimensions. The movements may sweep from side to side or forward and backward as required, but they cannot be allowed to rise up and sink down. Most of the movements in the table plane lead into turns or partial turns bringing the body into opening or closing attitudes. Thus sweeping or sliding, batting, the backhand return in tennis or badminton are likely to be in the hori-zontal plane unless deliberately moved out of it.

As suggested earlier, the movements in the table plane can be parallel and close to the floor, but as the name implies they can be raised to the table level and indeed, higher if associated with the ceiling. This makes us aware that movement can take place at different levels.

3. *Levels*

Three major levels are considered: *low, medium* and *high.* The low level is located roughly on or near the floor; the high level is considered to be upward toward the ceiling and the medium level is between these extremes. The distinction becomes clearer when translated into movement. The medium level is considered to be the normal operating range of move-ment felt by reaching out and around the body. The low level is experi-enced by bending well down towards the floor and it is most clearly comprehended by changing the base of support to kneeling, sitting or lying on the floor. The high level can be appreciated by reaching upward with arms and head, by rising on the toes, by jumping upward. Sequences of movement which take the body from high through medium and into a low level are very demanding on the energy and balance of the body, but they offer a very enlivening and varied experience.

Sometimes, children experimenting with levels feel that they are work-ing in the high level when they have climbed upon the vaulting box. This is true from the point of view of general space, but they can also be challenged to discover that they are in a new situation. Within this situa-tion, they should discover at what level their movements are in their personal spatial field.

Another experience can be given by examining the fact that certain parts of the body normally operate at a particular level. Then experiments can be aimed at discovering what happens when these parts are taken into other levels. This may bring about such ideas as inverting the body in space.

4. *Pathways in space*

Locomotor activities leave tracks in the snow and draw invisible patterns on the floor. The figure-eight weave of the forwards on the basket-ball team is one example. The grand right and left in American square dance is another. Lines of traffic, whether on the highway, or among the visitors at Expo are guided into floor patterns designed for efficiency.

The *floor patterns* of the weave and grand chain are made up of curving lines. Other patterns are made up of straight lines. These may be organized with sharp changes of directions which build into zigzag patterns. Experimental work with these patterns will reveal the different charac-teristics of these forms. For example, curving patterns are helpful for passing through a crowd without bumping. Zigzag patterns are erratic and surprising and therefore, often used to enliven a dance or to entertain in a gymnastic routine or to shake off a guard in a game.

In a more precise way, step patterns may be built up into dances. The "step, close, step" becomes both the floor and rhythmic pattern of the two-step. Circles, spirals, figure eights, straight lines can be used for the design of the dance or as an accompaniment to the chosen movements. Precise step patterns can be important in such situations as the take-off for the high jump or the basketball lay-up shot.

Air patterns can be vital in certain activities. For example, the design of most dances is found in the patterns made by the movements of the arms, head and trunk as well as by the legs. These patterns help to estab-lish the symbolic meaning of the dance. The flight of balls makes air patterns which must be strictly controlled to score a goal or hit a target. Working actions such as chopping wood or rowing a boat have clearly defined air patterns. The existence of these patterns needs to be recognized in order that the mover may achieve excellence of control and beauty of movement as well as meaningful form.

5. *Extensions in space*

Extensions are concerned on one hand with the size of the movement shape; and on the other with distance from the point of reference. *Hold the hand, palm forward, fingers pointing upward, just in front of the chest, (i.e. "near" in distance). Describe a twelve-inch circle, clockwise in the door plane. Repeat making the circle twice as large. Repeat making the biggest circle possible while remaining in the door plane.*

The circles were probably *small, medium* and *large* in size. The large one should have been so large that the trunk, head and arm were drawn into the action. In ordinary circumstances, most movements are done in a small or medium size and distance from the body. For this reason, changes in extension should be cultivated. In badminton, tennis, volleyball and other games, players can make phenomenal returns if they will really extend themselves in an effort to reach the bird or ball. Patterns which contrast the different sizes of the same movement can be used to good effect in dance compositions. Variation in the size of movements can relieve fatigue in the course of a routine job. One can become aware of movements in the centre of the body. These are essentially small in extension. Such movements extend outward towards the limbs and thence into space. The reverse may take place. Thus it is possible to experience the capacity for growing and shrinking which is continually present in the heart and lung movements.

All the aspects of space which have been discussed in this chapter should be subjected to individual experimentation. The student's personal movement should be supplemented by the careful observation of the movement of other people pursuing their normal activities. The observer should try to identify movements which stress any one of the aspects of space which have been analyzed. For example, one observation task could be to identify movements in any of the three planes. In this way the theory can become personal experience.

EFFORT

1. *Effort qualities of movement*

Stamp the foot hard! Smooth the fingers gently across the brow. Suddenly snap the fingers! Point an accusing finger directly forward. Try these movement ideas separately first. Then link them all together with an appropriate phrasing, feeling the dramatic statement emerge. All of these movement statements could be regarded as having an emotional overtone. As the dramatic feeling emerges, the expressive qualities in the movements will become more noticeable both to the mover and the observer.

Run on the spot for twelve counts. Double the speed of the run for twelve counts.

Walk in a circle for six steps. Repeat, but put a strong accent such as a stamp on the first and fourth step.

Approach your partner on a straight line. Then walk around him to arrive behind him. Allow him to remain stationary for the entire experiment.

In each of the last three movement tasks there was a change in the quantity of certain elements within the action demanded. These changes were required in order to achieve slightly different objectives. The requirements brought about a change of degree of speed, force and curvature respectively; and the degree of change could have been measured in each case. If the response to the instructions was carefully watched, as the change to the new tasks takes place, a change in the inner attitude of the mover would also be noted. For example, increasing the speed of the run will involve a different attitude of mind than decreasing the speed of the run. This change in inner attitude will be reflected in the movement exhibited in response to the task.

The two sets of examples are used in an attempt to illustrate the fact that we can give either a qualitative or a quantitative stress to the execution of our movements. If the intention aims at expression and communication as it does in dancing and acting, then the qualitative elements will be highlighted, while in an operational situation, where a particular practical objective has to be achieved, the quantitative elements are more likely to be stressed.

However, both aspects are always present. This is because the attitude of the mover always exerts an influence upon the resultant movement. Thus some degree of personal expression or communication always exists in an individual's movement. This accounts for the quality of the movement. Also, all movement requires a suitable degree of force, speed and curvature to function properly. This accounts for the quantitative aspect of the movement. Nevertheless, when the intention of the mover is expression or communication, the qualitative elements will be stressed. When the intention is to perform a particular task, the quantitative elements will be stressed.

If several persons are observed while they perform the same tasks, individual differences will be evident in the movement and in the attitude of the different persons to the tasks.

In everyday life, it can be recognized that through the way we move or carry ourselves we are constantly expressive of self, although we are rarely aware of this. This is illustrated when people doing the same tasks exhibit differences in their movement patterns. Thus, our movements when manipulating objects show not only the efforts required in order to be operationally effective but also certain overtones of effort qualities which are expressive of the personal attitude of the mover. Laban called these "shadow-movements."[13]

For the purpose of the study and identification of shadow-movements, observe several people engaged in conversation. Study the hand movements which accompany their verbal expression. Compare several individuals. Try to identify the way the movements are expressive of the individuality of the person concerned.

If the actions described in the experiments at the beginning of this section are examined, three factors which, among others, are observable in the effort quality of a movement can be identified. Words such as "stamp," "hard," "gentle" are related to the muscle tension which characterizes the movement. Words such as "suddenly" and "double speed" give a hint that a time factor is involved in the movement. "Directly," "straight" and "around" give an indication of the presence of a spatial factor which is of significance in movement. These three ingredients are factors requiring consideration in a study of human effort and they must be examined in detail. A fourth one, *flow*, was not used in the experiments but would have

---

[13] Rudolf Laban, *The Mastery of Movement*, Macdonald and Evans, London, 1960, pp. 12, 110.

---

been present in the movements. It will be included in the following discussions.

We have noted that Laban included four factors in his consideration of human effort: namely, *weight, time, space* and *flow*. He explained that the varying qualities of our movements can be discerned by recognizing the particular combinations and intensities of our effort in dealing with the motion factors of *weight, time, space* and *flow*.

A. WEIGHT: The effort exerted in relation to weight can produce either a *firm* or a *fine touch* movement.

This statement may be clarified by the following description.[14]

> In all our movements, whether they are intended to be expressive or used to achieve a practical objective, we have to handle *weight*; either that of our own body or that of an object. The weight of our body or of an object requires us to apply appropriate muscular exertion which ranges between strong and weak tensions. When concerned with bodily expression, we have to produce an appropriate effort quality which springs from a feeling or inner state and our muscles will react with an increase or a decrease in tension which will correspond to the fluctuations of that inner state or feeling. The effort will show qualities tending toward a firm, robust expression or toward a gentle, delicate one, depending upon the nature of the inner feeling.

Thus we may walk with firm, determined steps at certain times even though we may habitually use a rather light quiet pace. The tension evident in our steps springs from our purpose or inner attitude at the time. In summary, in handling the weight of our bodies or of an object, we use the appropriate degree of tensions within the ranges of from *strong* to *weak*. When concerned with body expression the effort qualities shown may range between *firm* and gentle or *fine touch* movements as may be appropriate to our inner feeling.

B. TIME: The effort exerted in relation to time can produce either a *sudden* or a *sustained* action.

Sudden movements are *quick* and of *short* duration. They explode into being. Examples of such movements might include an explosive jump, repetitive staccato jabs of the hand, or a sudden turn of the head. Explosive starts and unexpected stops are likely to be sudden in quality. The attitude of the mover is one of urgency and sometimes even of hastiness.

Sustained movements are *slow* in speed and have the sensation of going on for a long time. Sustained movements could include a slow continuous sinking or raising of the arm, or the sinking or raising of the whole body with the feeling that the on-going action is enjoyable and that there is no urge to finish it.

---

[14] Ullman, Lisa; excerpt from a letter addressed to the author dated February 7, 1968. By permission of Miss Lisa Ullman.

C. SPACE: The effort exerted in relation to space can produce either a *direct* or a *flexible* movement.

Direct movements go from one place to another in a *straight* line and the sensation of a *threadlike, linear* use of space may be felt.

There is a *direct*, linear quality to this child's walk.

Flexible movements go in *wavy* pathways with the sensation of *filling* space and expanding in a plastic[15] sense.

Direct movements may be exemplified in jabbing, pointing, tapping and pressing. There is a tendency to constrict any spheric expansion into space. Flexible movements include light wiggles or strong twists, flutterings or stirrings. The attitude in this case is an enjoyment in the use of space. There is a tendency to make full use of the ubiquity[16] of space.

D. FLOW: There is a fourth factor which may exert an influence upon the quality of a movement. It is the mover's attitude toward the *flow* of the movement.

---

[15] plastic: used here technically to mean "capable of taking form" in a three-dimensional sense.

[16] ubiquity: used here to mean "the everywhereness of space".

The movement may be restrained and carefully controlled, in which case the flow becomes *bound*. Conversely, it may be easy flowing, in which case it is called *free* flow.

Bound flow movements have the characteristics of being *easily stopped*, and of giving a feeling for *pausing*.

Free flow has a spark-like energy which *drives* the movement *onward*. The feeling is a *fluid* streaming of the movement in which one is caught.

Carry a very full cup of tea and place it on a table without spilling it. The preparation for stopping the downward movement the instant that the table top is reached will cause the selection of *bound* flow so that the movement is indeed capable of being stopped.

Shake a duster. It is an advantage to keep the cloth in motion. Therefore, there will be no necessity to keep a precise control of the movement. This job will likely call for *free* flow movements of flicking.

E. SUMMARY. The effort quality of human movements can be discerned by noting the various combinations and intensities of the effort used in dealing with the motion factors of *weight, time, space* and *flow*. If the main purpose of the movement is to perform some operational task, then the combinations of motion factors selected and the intensities used will be quantitatively suited to the requirements of the task. On the other hand, if the chief purpose of the movement is that of communication and expression — as it is in drama and dance — the qualitative aspects of the motion factors will be stressed and will be in harmony with the inner feeling of the mover. In either case — operational or expressive — both the quantitative and the qualitative elements will be present and thus the movement will be basically characteristic of the individual mover.

The chart on the opposite page shows a summary of the elements which can be combined in different ways and in different intensities.

These qualities need to be observed and felt. A simple experiment is recommended: *Hold both hands in front where you can see them. Keep one still. Move the other upward, trying to use one or more of the elements at will. For example, raise it firmly and suddenly, directly, jerkily. Observe and feel the quality. Repeat the movement using the qualities of fine touch and sustainment, flexibility and easy flow.* Try to feel how the first is an energetic, active movement and the second is an easygoing, dreamy movement. Try other combinations such as firm, sustained, flexible and bound flow.

2. *Emphasizing one element*

The previous experiment (above) encouraged the use of *one* or *more* elements at will; and in the descriptions suggested the use of four at once, namely: firmly, suddenly, directly, jerkily.

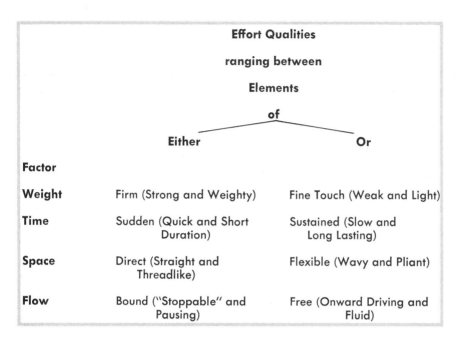

Effort Qualities

ranging between

Elements

of

Factor	Either	Or
Weight	Firm (Strong and Weighty)	Fine Touch (Weak and Light)
Time	Sudden (Quick and Short Duration)	Sustained (Slow and Long Lasting)
Space	Direct (Straight and Threadlike)	Flexible (Wavy and Pliant)
Flow	Bound ("Stoppable" and Pausing)	Free (Onward Driving and Fluid)

A beginner has to sensitize himself to the presence of the various elements in his movements. If he wishes to have command of the effort qualities in his movements, he will probably have to practise assiduously in order to control the selection, intensity and the blending of one element into another.

In the course of gaining this control of the effort elements, it is often helpful to concentrate on one element in particular. Hence, in walking, one might vary the speed, taking fast steps sometimes; slow steps at others. Or, one might become conscious of making a sudden turn or a sustained lifting of an arm. Similarly, one may concentrate on the motion factor of *weight* or of *space* or *flow*.

This idea of placing a particular stress on one element or factor can be carried over into lessons in the various aspects of physical education and will be dealt with at greater depth in later chapters.

3. *Emphasizing two elements simultaneously*

It was pointed out above that in a *sudden* turn the *time* factor may receive the main emphasis, although the other factors of *weight, space* and *flow* will also play a part in giving the movement its particular effort quality.

It should now be added that some movements will be characterized by the stress given to two elements simultaneously. Thus, movements may have a *time-weight* stress. For example, it takes a firm-sudden movement to achieve a handspring off a vaulting box. Light-staccato repetitive jumps may become the preparation for a high jump. A firm sustained stretch may be used to lower the body from a cross-beam. A fine touch-sustained exploratory movement may be used to find the lower rung of a ladder as one descends from a height. The possible combinations of time and weight are shown in the following diagram.

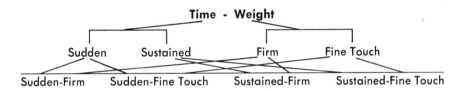

Movements could use a *time-space stress*. For example, aiming at the basketball goal may be done with quick decision from under the basket, or after a slow preparation as in a free-throw. On the other hand, when escaping from a restraint, a sudden flexible movement might be very surprising and elusive. An exploratory movement as, for example, trying to move through a hoop could quite reasonably be done with a sustained and flexible movement. The possible combinations are:

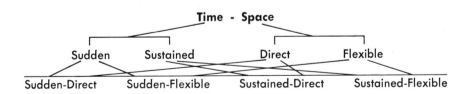

Another set of combinations might be derived from the *weight-space* elements. Straight strong actions such as hard swift kicks in soccer are one example. A springy jump might be done with a stress on the lightness and directness of the movement. Brushing actions, such as brushing a hat or sleeve might be done with a stress of lightness with flexibility if the idea were to flick the bits off. But, the pressure might be increased to firm and the spatial factor of the strokes might alternate between flexibility and directness if some of the fluff were sticking to the garment. The possibilities are:

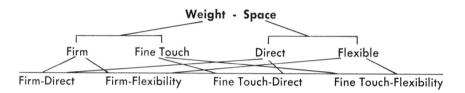

The *flow* factor may be stressed together with one of the other factors. Hence if *flow* and *weight* are stressed the observer may note such actions as: a firm controlled form of lifting which stops at the required height; a fine touch but ongoing twirling or turning; blackboard printing done with a fine pressure but with slight pauses between individual strokes as contrasted with writing done with firm pressure and an onward flow. The possibilities are:

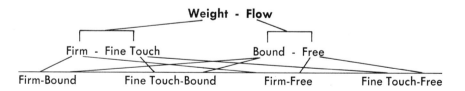

If *flow* is stressed in conjunction with *space* the movement may have the quality of being direct but restrained, as might occur if one reached out to put a pencil carefully into a container. If this were done with the attitude that precision was not necessary and that the pencil could bounce after being released the spatial element could remain direct but the flow element would change from *bound* to *free*. If one were to throw a skipping rope onto the floor so that it lay in an undulating pattern, the movement would probably have a flexible free-flow quality. If, however, you chose to place the rope in a figure of eight, it is more probable that your movement would be *flexible* but with *bound* flow which would bring precision to the positioning of the rope. The possibilities of movements with a *space-flow* stress are:

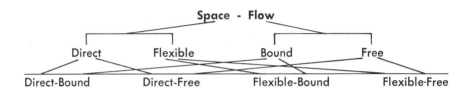

Flow may be combined with a stress on the *time* factor. Slow and cautious movements such as might be used to test the support for steps or which might characterize someone holding back on a backward roll might be examples of a *sustained-bound* stress in movement. On the other hand, a child might make up his mind to do a cartwheel and burst into the take-off with suddenness and freedom and thus show a stressing of the *sudden-free* aspects of effort elements. The performer might bring the cartwheel to an abrupt stop. This would emphasize the *sudden-bound* elements of movement quality. A stress of *sustained-free* flow movements might be present in a lazy form of walking.

The possibilities of movements with a *time-flow* stress are shown in the diagram on the opposite page.

4. *Basic effort actions*

When the purpose of movement is to achieve an operational task, it can be observed that the degree of force involved is linked with the time durations and the pathway or expansion into space. The selection of the three elements from the *weight, time* and *space* factors are compatible with the task to be done. For example, if one pounded on a door, the degree of

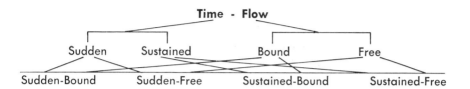

Time - Flow

| Sudden | Sustained | Bound | Free |

Sudden-Bound   Sudden-Free   Sustained-Bound   Sustained-Free

force would be greater than if one tapped on a door. In both cases, the blow upon the door would likely be made with a sudden contact which would be of short duration. The pathway of the hand in movement could be either curving or direct in terms of the expansion of the movement in space.

The combination of the elements can be varied with the result that eight different kinds of actions can quite clearly be distinguished as separate possibilities. Laban has identified these and called them *basic effort actions*.[17] The actions he selected are the eight named and described briefly below.

It should be noted that the names chosen for the Basic Effort Actions are words which are in common use in our daily language. However, the ordinary dictionary meanings of these words do not coincide with the technical way in which they are used here. For example, *thrust* is defined as "Push with sudden impulse or with force".[18] *Press* is defined as "Exert steady force against".[19] The motion factors involved are not the vital concern in the vernacular use of these words. However, as the names are used here the crucial thing to note is the combination of elements which are associated with the particular basic effort action thus named and discussed.

       1. THRUST — *Thrust or dig a shovel into a bank of snow*. The action will consist of *firm* exertion combined with *sudden* time and a *direct* penetration into the snow. All three elements are those which combine to produce an energetic and active movement. This is to say that the firm tension "fights" the resistance offered by the snow; the suddenness "fights" against the tendency to consume

[17] Laban, Rudolf, and F. C. Lawrence, *Effort*, Macdonald and Evans, London, 1947, pp. 14-17.
[18] H. W. Fowler and F. G. Fowler (Eds.) *The Concise Oxford Dictionary*, Fifth Edition, Oxford University Press, London, 1964, p. 1352.
[19] *Ibid.*, p. 964.

time; the directness "fights" against becoming disoriented in space. Other forms of thrusting might be punching, hitting, kicking, stabbing.

2. PRESS — *Press into the floor with the hands as you do a handstand.* The action is related to the thrust in that it requires a firm tension and a direct application of the force into the floor. The time element has changed from sudden to *sustained*. Other forms of pressing may be: lifting, pushing, pulling, squeezing, crushing.

3. SLASH — *Sling a heavy sack onto a table.* The movement has been called a slash. It is related to a thrust in that it requires a firm tension and a sudden application of speed. It is different from thrusting because the movement has a flexible use of space, the pathway being wavy. Other forms of slashing might be: whipping, beating or throwing if kept flexible.

4. DAB — *Blot up spilled water with little dabs.* These movements are related to thrusting in that they are *sudden* and *direct* but the firm tension has been replaced by a *fine touch*. Other forms of dabbing may be: patting, tapping.

5. FLOAT — *Gently yawn and slowly undulate the arms and spine to gain some freedom after sitting still for a long time.* If the movements were *sustained*, *fine touch* and *flexible*, they were a series of floating movements. Notice such movements are the complete opposite in characteristics to *thrust*. The attitude of floating is easygoing. One luxuriates in the length of time available, enjoying the progress of the movement rather than the fact that anything is being accomplished. Similarly the resistance from the antagonistic muscles is minimal; thus the muscular tension required is light. The movement expands out into space, meandering about in it, and one appreciates the freedom offered. Other forms of floating might be: slow, delicate undulating walking; delicate stirring, light polishing, stroking.

6. FLICK — *Whisk a speck of fluff off your sleeve with the back of the fingers.* The action is related to floating in that it is *fine touch* and *flexible* but the sustainment has been replaced by *suddenness*. Other forms of this action might be: fluttering, flipping, quivering.

7. GLIDE — *Smooth your brow.* The action is fine touch and *sustained*, but unlike flicking its spatial factor is *direct*. Other forms of gliding may be: light smearing, spreading, light scraping.

8. WRING   — *Tie a tight knot. Wring out a cloth.* The action is related to floating in that it is *flexible* and *sustained* but the fine touch is replaced by *firmness*. Other forms of this action are: screwing, twisting, strong stretching, writhing.

Conclusion

The effort quality of the movement, therefore, is of great significance. It makes for the basic distinction between mechanical and living movement. The awareness and control of the effort quality of individual movement should be one of the major concerns of modern movement education. Further reference is made to the basic effort actions in later chapters when the analyses of gymnastics, games and dance, respectively, are considered.

RELATIONSHIPS

Oberteuffer has stated that all movement has purpose.[20] If this is so, it must be related to its purpose whether that purpose be an operational or an expressive one. Since the individual is sensitive to his environment, he is capable of modifying his movements to some extent in order that they may adapt to or change that environment. These considerations are basic to the aspect of movement study entitled "Relationships."

Movement may be related to objects in the environment and/or it may be related to people. These possibilities will be examined in detail.

1. *With objects*

There are two basic forms of relationships with objects: manipulative and non-manipulative. In the first case, the performer is concerned with controlling the movement of the object. In the second case he is concerned with adapting his movements to a stationary object.

A. THE MANIPULATIVE RELATIONSHIP. In the manipulative situation he may exercise his control over an object through isolated or intermittent contact with it, or through continuous contact. If, for example, he is controlling a ball, he may throw, catch, bounce, roll, kick or otherwise direct its movement. In most of these situations, the contact with the ball is either intermittent or isolated to one or two instances. If, however, he maintains contact with a ball or a rope or another such object, he may hold, carry or swing it. This situation tends to occur when the object is a racquet, bat, stick or tool. In these cases, the objects become extensions of the body and serve as a means to help the individual to increase his reach or his power

---

[20] Delbert Oberteuffer, *Physical Education*, Revised Edition, Harper Brothers, New York, 1956, p. 18.

to apply force. In either case, his concern is to exercise control over the objects.

This manipulative relationship is clearly evident in games and the actions used to control the equipment are traditionally called games skills. They have been sufficiently defined as to have specific names such as the overhand serve, the hook pass, the soccer dribble, and so on. The particular means of controlling the specific games equipment in each of these action skills has been very well defined by coaching authorities and researchers. However, a skilled performance is subject to many variables and thus, one author[21] points out that the control of moving objects is an open learning situation. This signifies that an absolute level of control cannot be achieved. This is because the performer must be prepared to deal with ever new, ever changing conditions which arise out of such environmental factors as wind resistance, conditions of surface areas, resilience built into the equipment or the oddities of weight and balance found in the construction of the object. The strategy of the opponent also contributes to the varying conditions to which the player must adapt.

Within the general category of the manipulative relationship to an object where contact is not maintained, two alternatives tend to emerge. The individual may be dealing with the control of an incoming object or, conversely, directing the movement of an outgoing object. In the first situation, he must align himself with the object and prepare to absorb the impact. In the second situation, he must prepare himself to apply the necessary force to project the object and if he wishes to control its flight, he must select his target and control the release of the object. These two situations are characteristic of many games.

The manipulative relationship between the mover and an object brings with it secondary relationships. Thus, in the process of manipulating the object the performer may be under, behind, in front of, in line with, beside, close to or distant from the object. These relationships, which in one sense are positional or spatial considerations, are dependent upon the two factors — the mover and the object — and, for this reason, are to be considered possible relationships between the two.

The importance of the manipulative relationship to objects as it applies to games has been stressed in the description given above. However, occasionally the manipulative relationships to objects arise in dance and gymnastics. For example, some folk dances feature such objects as tambourines, castanets, staves, swords, ribbons, rattles and other items which have a significant meaning in the customs of the people. Dances may be created which feature the use of percussion instruments as objects which are incorporated into the movement of the dance, being swung, twirled, hit or otherwise used as an integral part of the movement and/or sound

[21] Knapp, Barbara, *Skill in Sport*, Routledge and Kegan Paul, London, 1963, p. 151-152.

patterns. Some forms of gymnastics, particularly those originating in Europe and designed for use as a recreative activity for girls and women, combine the manipulation of such objects as ropes, hoops, balls and wands with balance or acrobatic activities. In most cases in gymnastics, the necessity of exercising control over the object becomes the distinctive feature and the focus of attention is centred outward upon the object rather than inward upon the movement of the body. This may also be true when objects are used in the dance. On the other hand, in dance, the objects such as tambourines and castanets may be integrated with the expression of the dance and provide the accent or enhance the mood.

B. THE NON-MANIPULATIVE RELATIONSHIP. This relationship with objects includes a variety of possibilities. In each case the performer assumes a positive relationship to the object by adapting his behaviour to it, or by using the object to his advantage. Thus the object may be regarded as fulfilling a role in the movement situation.

(i) An Obstacle. If the object is regarded as an obstacle, the individual may adapt to it, or submit to it. The adaptation may take the form of dodging around it; going over, under, or through it. For example, the gymnast usually goes *over* a box horse. He may go *through* window ladders; but moves *around* or *between* markers. On the other hand, he may submit to the obstacle by being stopped by it. Essentially, this is what happens when a person is confronted by a fence or barrier.

In gymnastics, the apparatus is often used as a form of obstacle. In games, nets are obviously used as obstacles. In dances, props may be used to represent an obstacle.

(ii) An Extension. Some objects are used to increase the powers of the body. They may offer support or protection for the body or augment the range of its movement. For example, climbing ropes or ladders can offer support, can increase the performer's height and/or can bridge a gap. A tumbling mat can provide protection, as can a volleyball net or a service line in tennis. In dance and drama, platforms or stairs can provide an elevation which may be used to enhance a performer's physical height and create an impression of dominance.

(iii) A Target. An object may become a target, goal or focal point towards which the performer relates his movement. The target or goal is obviously of prime importance in many games. In gymnastics, a mat might be regarded as a target and the performer may organize his movements to land or arrive on it. Spaces between pieces of apparatus — such as the spaces defined by window ladders — may be regarded as goals through which the performer may wish to move his body with or without contact

with the apparatus. In dance, a large drum might become the central focus of a group dance. In the Scottish sword dances, the crossed sword and scabbard placed on the floor define the spaces where the feet must be placed. They, therefore, define the target.

When involved in a non-manipulative relationship with an object, the individual must concern himself with his choice of starting and finishing positions as they relate to the object. For example, he may start or finish beside, behind or in front of the object. The amount of weight and the manner in which the weight is applied to the object must be related to the size, strength and stability of the object. In gymnastics, especially, safety depends upon selecting activities which are suitably related to the object or apparatus used. Successful adaptation of the movement to the object is a significant test of the performer's awareness of his relationship to a non-manipulative object.

2. *With people*

Movement may be and often is done in relationship to people. There are several possibilities which may develop.

When observing and analyzing the way in which a movement situation is modified by the relationships present, the point of view taken is: What people are involved and how has their involvement influenced the movement? Some of the answers are given below in the form of varying possibilities.

A. ALONE. The *absence* of another mover, provides a situation in which the performer is entirely free and entirely responsible for his own movement. This situation has its own ramifications. One who walks alone sets his own pace and pathway. By observing him, one can judge something of his mental attitude. Has he a pressing purpose? Is he aimless? A single worker can expect no aid from an assistant. Can he lift the object or must he drag it? A single player may use inanimate objects as substitutes for another person. Hence he may throw to a wall and use the rebound. A gymnast, practising alone, has the apparatus all to himself, but he may have to take rest periods, instead of taking turns; he has no basis for comparison other than the feel of his own successive performances; no incentive other than his own drive. The dancer is free to move how and where he will but he has no one with whom to communicate; namely a co-dancer.

The experience gained through working alone is a positive factor in the development of an individual. It may help to develop characteristics of independence and self-reliance. It may also add to an appreciation of the interaction which may develop in mass, partner and group work.

The *solo* situation, as it is to be used here, describes those times when a performer is moving alone in the presence of others who are watching.

Immediately an interrelationship is set up. The fact that there are observers causes the performer to: strive for his best performance; become unsure of himself; modify his movement in some way either to communicate more clearly or mask the significance of it if he does not wish to communicate. Examples of the solo situation include: presentations by an artist as a solo dancer, singer, instrumentalist or monologist; to some extent certain moments in the work of a pitcher or goalkeeper or penalty shooter when all the action depends on their next move; certain single events in sports such as diving, jumping, throwing contests; and in gymnastics.

B. ALONE IN A MASS. This situation is quite common in physical education classes which use "scatter formation" as a routine way of working. Each pupil finds his own working area and is free to pursue his own tasks so long as they do not interfere with his neighbour. Each must develop a sense of responsibility to assure the safety of all. The principle of "non-interference" is the crucial relationship.

This can be extended to mobile situations where each member can run or move along his own pathway so long as he does not interfere with others. First experiences with this situation may find the individual believing himself to be in a *solo* situation, exposed to the critical gaze of all the other members. Further experience leads him to understand that he and the others are all so concerned with their own movement as to be more or less unaware of what others are doing. This means that care must be taken to develop sufficient awareness to maintain the "non-interference" relationship.

The "alone in a mass" relationship occurs in unstructured situations such as boarding public transportation, viewing art exhibitions, skiing or ice-skating and so on. It is quite different from the mob or gang situation where everyone is united in a common purpose.

"Transient relationships" in a mass is the opposite to the "non-interference" relationship. It is the vital awareness of others for a fleeting moment as one passes by. It is the flash of recognition of the common humanity of the individual members who comprise the mass. In gymnastics, it helps to give the basis of concern for the safety of all. In games, it can be the fleeting indication of appreciation or encouragement to a fellow player. In dance, it may be the acknowledgement of others, a "greeting and passing on."

C. PARTNERS. Two people may participate in movement situations in an interrelated way, rather than as two unrelated ("alone") individuals. The interrelationship may be one of *cooperation* or one of *competition* or opposition. Cooperative relationships can take several different forms:

(i) *Taking Turns.* This might be regarded as a transitional stage between working *alone* and working with a partner. It is a form of sharing

---

— equipment, space or time — leaving each individual free to determine his own movements. Thus, partners may take turns shooting for a basket, using a vaulting box, dancing with a percussion instrument. The relationship between the partners can be increased by relating the finishing position of one with the starting position of the other. Alternatively the timing of the finishing of one and the starting of the other could be related. The actual movements could be related by means of contrasts. For example, one could move slowly, the other very quickly; one could use a low level, the other a high level. When the actual movements bear a relationship to each other the relationship of the two performers may advance into a situation of:

(ii) Question and Answer or Dialogue. In this case the movements are contrasted or they demonstrate a marked variation from one to the other thus appearing to be an argument in movement or an ongoing communication. In games or gymnastics, the sequence may take on the spirit of "Anything you can do, I can do better." In dance, an argument might be made quite evident if strong, sudden movements are used, although other effort qualities may also be very suitable. It will be necessary for the partners to show clear contrasts in movement qualities and/or spatial patterns. If the movements of the pair become too closely related, they may become symbolic of agreement. It should be clearly understood that the "argument" is always within the movement which is symbolic of the real situation.

(iii) Matching is an ultimate form of agreement. The two partners tend to move simultaneously thus obviously matching or *mirroring* the movement of the leader. The roles of leader and follower are present but the roles may fluctuate between the partners very freely. The matching may arise from verbal planning as in gymnastics or early experiences in dance. A more advanced relationship results from a non-verbal communication which may be achieved by means of "reading and matching" the movement of the partner, perhaps in a face to face situation. This frequently develops in dance.

(iv) Follow the Leader seems to be an outgrowth of matching. The leadership is likely to be invested in one partner for a fairly long period of time. It will remain a cooperative relationship only so long as the leader chooses actions which he expects his follower will be able to do.

(v) Meeting and Parting. The situation of meeting a partner sets up circumstances which must be resolved in some way. The resolution may be achieved by *greeting* or *engaging* each other in cooperative action. In dance the bows and curtseys are common forms of greeting. In real life or in acting, handshaking or conversation may result. In gymnastics, two

partners may engage each other in couple stunts which involve the giving or sharing of body weight. For example, the sequence might include: rolling to meet, sitting and standing with hands joined while countering the partner's pull. Alternatively, routines may be invented in which the meeting is emphasized by actions without contact such as high vertical jumps face to face or the placing of handstands close to and immediately in front of the partner.

The meeting might be resolved by *encircling* one another, *withdrawing* from each other, *passing* by without engaging each other in any form of interaction, or by joining the partner in some sort of *merger*. The merger might develop as a form of "Follow the Leader" or as a form of "Matching." These are dramatic actions which are likely to occur in dance drama.

Competition or *Opposition* between partners may develop in several different frameworks. For example:

(i) Question and Answer situations can take the form of opposition. In dance drama, this may develop when the movement symbolizes attempts to gain dominance. To a certain extent, singles in tennis or badminton may be regarded in this light. A long high clear ball may be answered by a smash aimed at an inconvenient location on the opponent's court. In gymnastics, it would be possible, though unusual, to set one stunt or routine against another in a "Do better than this" form of challenge.

(ii) Follow the Leader becomes competitive when the leader chooses things which deliberately challenge the skill of the followers.

(iii) One against One is a clear-cut case of competition with a score being kept and a winner being pronounced. It is the relationship of singles play, races, or contests. It can be portrayed in dance or mime-like movements and dramatic sequences. It can occur in everyday happenings such as may develop at bargain counters or on buses when there is competition for the last seat available.

(iv) Action and Reaction is very similar to Question and Answer except that there is a closer cause and effect relationship between the actions of the two individuals. An example of action and reaction is the interplay of movements between a forward and guard on a basketball team. The forward fakes movements hoping to cause the guard to react and be caught at a disadvantage. In miming operational actions, the reaction of one partner to the other has to be logical in terms of time, weight and space in order to be believable. For example, a strong kick towards a partner's shins requires a sudden withdrawal of the shins. A strong pull must cause the reaction of a strong resistance in line with the direction of the pull.

D. GROUPS. When more than two people are working together to achieve a common purpose the result is a *group* organization with an interrelationship between the constituent members. The size of the membership makes a significant difference to the interrelationships of the members and to the functioning of the group.

(i) Threes. The formations possible are: line of three, file of three, triangle, circle. The contributions of the three members may be kept equal or two may join forces to oppose the third member. Alternatively one member may lead or influence the other two. In games, the line or file of three and the circle of three usually give each member equal status. One against two is a fairly common situation. In gymnastics, the three often match each other or two may lift or support one. In dance, any of the situations mentioned may be used.

(ii) Fours. The formations possible are: the line, file, circle, square and the double partner situation or the leader and followers. This number allows for a symmetrical formation and this permits even competition. This occurs in the tennis or badminton doubles game.

(iii) Fives. This grouping, being an odd number, allows for asymmetrical groupings which are particularly interesting for dance composition. The uneven number makes it possible to have games based upon four in a circle against one in the middle. In gymnastics it allows for pyramidal or triangular formations with a leader in front. In court games, it allows for two-one-two formations which can rotate through defined locations.

Groups of larger numbers may be regarded as extensions of groups of four (i.e. even groups) or of groups of five (i.e. uneven groups).

E. INTERGROUP RELATIONSHIPS. While the dynamics of relationships between members of a group can operate on a basis of equality, this is rather rare. Usually one person in the group either assumes or is given the leadership role. The larger the group is the more likely it is to have a leader. In movement situations, the leader can function without verbalization. Experiences in the leadership role as well as the followership role is of particular value, especially if no verbalization is allowed. In this circumstance, all the participants are obliged to become highly sensitive to the movement of others, interpreting its meaning and responding to it with movement "answers" of their own. It is very valuable to experiment with situations where no leader is appointed at the outset. Then the dynamics of group relationships can be studied with the purpose of discovering if and when a leader is found and how the role materializes.

Two (or more) groups may interact. They may or may not have leaders. The interaction may be facilitated if leaders do exist. The forms of interaction can include all those described for the interaction of partners.

The two basic forms of interaction are the same as for partners, namely, cooperative and competitive.

The experiences defined above are social experiences which have received little attention to date. They are worthy of considerable experimentation and study, especially if they are developed in their non-verbal form.

The dynamics of the group, the interrelationship between members of the group, and the interrelationship between different groups are developed to a high degree in the dance program. These ideas are discussed on pages 170 to 172. The interrelationships between members of a team, the leadership role and the intergroup relationships are particularly important in team games. These aspects of relationship are discussed on pages 101 to 103.

FIVE

GAMES:
A MOVEMENT ANALYSIS

The material to be presented in this chapter will be concerned with the application of Laban's analysis of movement to the area of games. The analysis of movement was described in length in Chapter Four.

Games stress the competitive element. All the movements of the players are selected to achieve a positive score. This is the offensive aspect of the playing strategy. It is supplemented by the defensive play which is geared to preventing the opponent from scoring.

Within this context, the player must develop his own individual skills. A great deal of research has been and continues to be directed towards determining precise factors which affect control, accuracy and proficiency in the required skills. Studies have been directed towards applying the laws of physics and body mechanics to the manipulation of balls and other equipment. Coaches and athletes have studied and documented training schedules and methods and have photographed and described specific skills. However, opinion generally concedes that there is no definitive "good form" for any specific skill. Each individual will have to seek out his own best-movement patterns. However the basic laws of mechanics will apply in all situations. For example, the greater the force applied to the ball, the faster it will travel. This is a basic law of the physics of motion. Furthermore, certain skill patterns will have a generally recognizable basic form. For instance, if the ball is thrown underhand, the usually acceptable form will include a step forward on the left foot as the right hand delivers the ball. However, the exact size of the step, the rhythm of the whole movement pattern, the precise use of the body parts will belong to the personal style of the player. Hence, the child or the beginning player is attempting to understand the forces which influence his movement and to become acquainted with the requirements of the game and the idiosyncracies of his own body movement.

The teacher or coach will assist the player in his search for his own personal style by guiding and evaluating the movement on the basis of the

The softball pitch is characterized by a forward step on the foot opposed to the pitching arm.

requirement of the rules, the different forms of strategy, the basic techniques of the skills and by helping the player analyze his own movement patterns.

The theory of movement, described in the preceding chapter should provide one means of analyzing the game and the movement of the players. The chart given on page 78 gives an overview of the thinking which arises when the four components of movement are used as a basis for examining the role and the performance of the games player. An elucidation of these basic questions follows.

BODY AWARENESS SKILLS REQUIRED IN GAMES

In a game, a player is concerned, among other things, with the control of the ball or the other equipment. This is true for volleyball, softball, soccer,

Body Awareness	Space Awareness
1. Body Management Skills. What is the significance of: a. Shifting weight? b. Balance? c. Body actions? d. Body parts stressed? e. Basic functions (curl, bend stretch, twist)? f. Body shapes? 2. Control of Equipment. What is the significance of: a. Basic functions (curl, bend, stretch, twist)? b. Body actions? c. Body parts stressed? d. Weightbearing? e. Body shapes?	1. What directional skills are needed? 2. Of what importance is the change of levels? 3. What is the significance of the pathways of the player, and of the ball? 4. What is the significance of patterns? 5. What value is a change of extension?
Effort Qualities of the Movement	**Relationships**
1. How can the control of the effort quality of the movement (time, weight, space, flow) contribute to a skilled performance?	1. What is the relationship of the player to the playing area, and to the equipment? 2. What is the relationship of the player to the rules, and to the officials? 3. What is the relationship of the player to his teammates, and to his opponents?

basketball and the simple ball games which receive the main emphasis in the elementary and junior high school curricula.

The player is also required to manage his body efficiently during the times when he is not personally handling the ball. At these times he still has a very important function in the game. He will revert to his guarding responsibilities or will attempt to position himself for receiving the ball from a teammate. These roles put a premium on good body management skills. In tag and chasing games, track and some field events, the body management skills are of prime importance.

These two needs of a player — skill in controlling the equipment (i.e. specific games skill) and skill in body management (i.e. personal strategy) — will be examined in terms of the pertinent aspects of Body Awareness given on the chart on page 39, Chapter Four.

BODY AWARENESS AND BODY MANAGEMENT SKILLS IN GAMES (PERSONAL STRATEGY)

Shifting the body weight

The unskilled games player is often characterized by his lack of mobility. He stands firmly rooted to the ground as if he expects the ball to come to him. As a result, if it does come to him, he is unable to move fast enough to execute an effective play. Furthermore, his inactivity reduces his opportunities to enter into the main stream of the play.

It is of prime importance that his "mental set" should be directed towards keeping on the move in order to create opportunities to receive the ball. This is a *relationship* concept. But, given this mental set, he can implement it by becoming aware of the feel of the weight upon the balls of the feet. He must feel the shift of weight from one foot to the other. He must discover the foot patterns which result (sliding, lunging, stepping, running). The player needs to become proficient at keeping the feet moving while he controls the ball by bouncing or volleying it. He should also be able to arrest the foot action while he deals with the ball. He should discover the most advantageous location of the weight for purposes of shifting his position quickly and for sudden bursts of running which may follow a period of waiting with expectancy. He should discover that the use of a slightly bent knee, coupled with weight on the balls of the feet, assists in achieving the mobility required for dodging and for a quick getaway.

Balance

The mobility discussed above is closely related to the balance provided by keeping the weight over the balls of the feet and by using a bent knee. This condition might be regarded as a form of mobile balance. A more extreme form of mobile balance will occur while the body is in the air during a jump. In this case, the different parts of the body must counterbalance each other in order to give the jumper the control he needs.

Experimentation with situations which involve balance may be directed towards finding the effect of: size of the base; position of the centre of gravity; transference of weight. These factors need to be clearly understood and translated into skilled performance.

Some such situations of balance might include:

(1) being able to stop suddenly without falling over (size of base; height of centre of gravity above base; shape of base in relation to the drive of power)

(2) being able to change directions readily (placement of weight over the base)

(3) being able to control an overbalance (fall) and recover quickly (transferring weight through successive parts of the body, shaping the body to facilitate the weight transfer; e.g. rounded for rolling, parts available to make a new base)

(4) balancing while in the air (location of parts of the body which serve as counterbalances).

Examples of situations in games which could provide opportunities for understanding the controlling features of balance are given below.

(1) the lunge to reach a low ball in volleyball will require a wide base with body weight (hips) low or a controlled overbalance

(2) a vigorous batting swing in softball requires an increase in the size of the base and a hit requires a quick change of balance in order to move immediately into a run to first base

(3) a pass from a fast soccer dribble requires a control of weight over the base especially if it is a pass which travels to the right while the passer moves to the left

(4) changes of direction in dribbling a basketball may need a wide base (long stride) and weight low (bent knees)

(5) remaining behind the restraining line in throwing events in track and field will require a control of balance (need to keep upper body weight over the base or to counterbalance it if it goes beyond).

Body actions

The body actions which have relevance to body management skills in games include turns, elevations and landings and locomotion.

1. TURNS, when competently performed, contribute tremendously to a player's efficiency. For example, the pivot is an important skill in basketball. It often frees the player with the ball from tightly guarded situations and opens the game up. A good turn in base-running in softball may allow a runner to reach second base in safety. Less clearly defined turns are required in the general progress of soccer, basketball, softball and even volleyball.

Many players find turns difficult to execute. Experiments to discover and understand the principles involved should make subsequent practice more valuable. The following principles are important:

> Balance is involved. Experiment with ways of stopping a turn or spin. Assess the effect of the size and shape of the base upon the ease or difficulty in stopping the spin. Note the effect of the relationship of the body weight over the base in terms of balance. For

example, discover how, in a pivot, if a wide stride and bent knees are used, the weight is lowered and the control increased.

Body parts are involved. Experiment with different parts of the body leading into the turn. Some of the more usual parts are: one shoulder, one leg, one knee.

A body twist is involved. Experiment with ways of starting a turn. One part can cross over another, thus leading into the turn. There may be a counter-twist out of which the turn springs. In other turns, the rotation develops out of a shift of weight.

Occasions in games play which may offer opportunities for use and analysis of turns may include:

- turns to follow the passes of the volleyball within your own court
- reversing direction in base running in softball
- soccer dribble with weaving pathways
- the pivot in basketball
- roll forms of high jump
- in general games play, instances of dodging.

2. ELEVATIONS AND LANDINGS. The more accomplished a player is, the more likely he is to be able to use jumps to his advantage in games. Hence pupils should be given opportunities of becoming aware of how to achieve elevation when they need it. This may involve exploration of the take-off, the body in flight and the control of body weight in landing. Refer to page 116 under the section on gymnastics for details.

Instances during games play when elevations may be used effectively include:

- going up to meet the ball in a high volley return
- jumping to 'pick off' a high hit in softball
- going up to meet the ball when body trapping in soccer
- jumping for control of the rebound after a shot in basketball
- high jump in track and field.

3. LOCOMOTION. Reference should be made to page 114 under the section on gymnastics for a detailed analysis of forms of locomotion and to the section on feet and ankles on page 82 of this chapter. However, it should be mentioned that all games demand great mobility from the players and great stress is placed on footwork. Versatility can be improved by increasing the variety of footwork which pupils can do well.

Some suggestions follow:

- volleyball — slide step sideways, short runs, single steps, lunges, jumps, step-hop
- softball — speed running, slide steps sideways, jumps, sliding, single steps, lunges
- soccer — running (different speeds), step-kick, jump
- basketball — running, walking, slide step sideways, jump, lunge, step-hop, cross-over steps
- track and field — running, jumping, hop-step-and-jump.

Body parts stressed

The head, the knees and the feet have a particular contribution to make to body management in games.

1. The *head* is significant enough in size and weight to affect the body balance. Its function in relation to seeing is also of importance. Both these roles should receive the attention of both coach or player. For example, these situations should be explored:

- use of head in faking a guard out of position, particularly in basketball
- role in body alignment in sprint starts and sprint running
- use in maintaining balance and creating velocity in spins and turns in any game.

2. The *knees*, in their ability to bend, provide a means of absorbing the shock of bringing the body weight down from a height. They also supply part of the spring by which the body weight is propelled into jumps which lead into various directions. Most pupils need a great deal of continuing help before they become really aware of the feel, power and timing of the related bend/stretch function of the hips, knees and ankles in the control of the body weight.

Some examples of the significant use of the knees may help the teacher to search out further instances:

- in volleyball, bending both knees quickly to get under a low ball
- in softball, using a knee bend to drop down to recover a grounder
- in basketball, using a knee bend to check progress and avoid taking steps
- in long jump, using a deep knee bend when landing.

Furthermore it should be noted that the knees, in conjunction with the feet, ankles and a rotary hip movement, have actions which should be carefully and *cautiously* explored. For example, what difference does it make to the knee bend if:

- the toes are turned slightly outward?
- the toes are pointed straight ahead?
- the heel is kept off the floor and the weight remains on the toes and the ball of the feet?
- the heel is kept in contact with the floor?

3. The *feet and ankles* are extremely important to good body management. Good footwork does not often happen naturally. Pupils should be guided in the exploration of how the feet and ankles work. They should become aware of:

- the part(s) of the foot which receive weight
- weight transference from one part to another to produce power or spring, lightness and resilience.

Some games situations which could give opportunities for increasing awareness of footwork are:

- weight on the balls of the feet allows the player to be ready to move quickly on volleyball court, etc.
- base-running in softball is improved by tagging the inside corner of the base with the *right* foot
- in soccer, being able to change the size of the running stride
- in basketball, changing from a run to a sudden stop or a sideways slide
- the alignment of the drive of power out of the foot in track running
- for primary children, ways of using the feet while playing with different kinds of inflated balls.

Basic functions: curl, bend, stretch, twist

The curl, bend, stretch, twist functions are used in the general body management skills of the games player. For example, in outreaching an opponent, a player will emphasize the stretch function of the body. In faking and dodging, the twist will be emphasized. In falling, the curl of the body will offer protection. Usually, beginners do not regard such activities as being of importance. They tend to regard the contact with the ball as the only important moment in the game. However, the study of a film of a modern soccer or volleyball game should reveal the importance of the times when the player works without the ball. Such a study will make clear the pronounced use of the curl or bend, stretch and twist function of the whole body.

Body shapes

Reference should be made to Chapter Four, p. 48 for a descriptive analysis of the ball, pin, wall and screw shapes of the body.

The games player often concentrates so completely on the movement of the ball that he overlooks his own body as a component in the game. The shape of the body may be adapted to serve the requirement of the game, each of the four shapes offering a different contribution.

1. WALL-SHAPE. In guarding roles, the body can become a wall or physical blockage. The basketball guard uses the wall shape very consistently. In fact, at the beginning of the game, all the team members may assume such a shape until it is determined which team has the offensive. The wall shape (adapted) is also useful for both in-fielders and out-fielders in softball, creating the impression that there is not a clear spot on the field where a hit may be placed. Similarly, the receiving side on the volleyball court may appear to cover the entire territory. For track and field, however, it is rarely seen since there is no defence role as such, and the whole intention is to become as streamlined as possible.

2. PIN-SHAPE. In offensive roles, where there may be a need to penetrate through a limited amount of space without contact, the elongated shape of the body is useful. For example, a basketball player may use it as he breaks through a group in order to isolate himself to receive a pass on the move.

In situations where streamlining of the body is an advantage, the pin shape will tend to be used. For example, the runner strives to eliminate all sideways projections of the arms or legs and becomes as far as possible one-dimensional: forward/backward.

3. BALL-SHAPE. The ball shape is often used if personal contact is expected. It creates a modified cannonball type of impact when used by the attacker. It provides some protection for the receiver. When the body is shaped like a ball, the vital organs are somewhat protected and the force of the blow can be lessened by rolling with the punch. The shoulder or hip girdle can be used for pushing. Some football, ice hockey and wrestling situations, where personal contact is permitted, make use of the ball shape of the body. In some styles of long jump this body shape is used.

4. SCREW-SHAPE. This body shape tends to be limited to the incidental shaping of the body which occurs when a player twists and dodges during a game. Other uses of this body shape tend to be associated with particular games skills rather than with personal strategy.

BODY AWARENESS AND THE CONTROL OF THE EQUIPMENT. (Specific Games Skill.)

As soon as the player is in possession of the ball, his responsibility is to control it so that he or his teammates can score a goal. The control of the ball can take at least four forms: receiving it, seizing it, retaining possession of it, getting rid of it. The operation of receiving it may involve stopping it, containing it, or holding it. Seizing it is an active and aggressive form of play which occurs, for example, when the player jumps to intercept the ball. Retaining it might involve holding it securely; keeping it moving but under control, as is done in dribbling; or, keeping it in spite of the efforts of the opponents to take possession. Getting rid of it may take the form of passing it to a teammate or aiming it at the target or goal. Furthermore, sports equipment such as bats, racquets and hockey sticks are used as extensions of the body in projecting a ball toward a goal or teammate. The lacrosse stick, hockey stick and softball glove are used as extensions of the body in receiving, seizing or retaining possession of the ball. Practice will be needed to adjust to the implement-eye coordination which differs from the hand-eye coordination. The following *relationship* concepts are discussed here in order to give meaning to the use of the body in these situations.

Seizing the ball!

Basic functions: curl, bend, stretch, twist

The body moves by bringing about transitions between these three basic functions. Therefore, the curl is often a preparation for a stretch. A stretch may merge into a curl. A twist may provide momentum and power for a stretch or it may dissolve into a curl. Consequently, as the movement flows from the preparation into the action and thence into the dissolution or recovery from the action, the analysis can be directed towards understanding how these three functions can best operate in support of one another. For example, the body, and especially the arms and fingers, are slightly stretched toward an incoming ball but as the catching takes place the fingers, arms and body curl slightly, "giving" a little to cushion the force of the impact. As the catch is completed the fingers curl around the ball more completely to hold it securely.

As the above illustration indicates, curl is stressed in situations where the body is used to receive and retain an incoming object. Conversely, the stretch or twist functions are stressed when the ball is projected away from the body. The twist is also used to change the direction of the ball, as might happen in a basketball jump ball strategy. In each situation, the preparatory phase of the action may call into play a contrasting body function. This pattern can be summarized as follows:

Games Situation	Preparation	Action	Recovery
Receiving	1. **Stretch** to prepare to meet and get into alignment with the incoming ball.	2. **Curl** to produce a give which will lessen the impact and bring the ball under control. 3. Increased **curl** to grasp it.	4. Relax the grasp.
Retaining		1. **Curl** of the whole body to cover the ball making it difficult for an opponent to reach it.	
Seizing	1. **Curl** to prepare by supplying a source of power for the spring.	2. **Stretch** to meet the incoming ball at a point as close as possible to it, followed very quickly by a **curl** to grasp and obtain possession of it.	3. Slightly relax the grasp.
Getting rid	A. 1. **Curl** to prepare by supplying a source of power for the spring.	2. **Stretch** to project the ball away from the body.	3. Slightly **curl** the body.
	B. 1. **Counter-twist** to prepare the source of power.	2. **Twist** to fling it away from the body.	3. Return slightly to the forward orientation.

The analysis given above indicates that there is a rhythm built into skills which consists of a coordination of the preparation, action and dissolution or recovery. The exact rhythm is likely to be personal to each performer, and influenced by the particular demands of the situation. Hence, the coach must take into consideration how much analysis is helpful and what teaching methods are most useful. Knapp[1] indicates that for activities "in which the performer acts on his own, — the evidence, though not conclusive, is predominantly in favour of whole method for beginners."

Since most beginners tend to place their entire attention upon making contact with the ball, the stress should probably be on "giving" i.e. curling to receive the ball, "bending" to get under it for power, "crouching" to protect the ball. This should emphasize the basic function of curl, stretch or twist in the total body.

Some examples of these functions being required in games are now listed.

1. CURL — crouching to get under a low ball in volleyball. Crouch will give power for subsequent stretch used when ball is volleyed
— "giving" when body trapping the soccer ball. The resulting concave shape of the body will cause the ball to fall close to the feet
— "giving" when receiving a strong pass in basketball
— "giving" when catching a softball

2. STRETCH — in volleyball, fingers and forearm are stretched so that the ball is not retained even for a moment
— in soccer heading, the body is in stretch and driving into the ball to project it away
— in basketball, the jump ball requires the extended reach which comes through the stretched body as the jump takes it upward
— in softball, the pitch is delivered as the body moves into a stretch

3. TWIST — in volleyball, some forms of spiking use a twist as a means of directing the ball to an unguarded location
— in the soccer pass, a twist is often required to send the ball in the desired direction
— in basketball, a cross-over lay-up shot requires a twist
— in softball, batting requires a twist.

Body actions

The control of the equipment such as balls, pucks, bats, racquets and sticks is one area of major concern to the player, coach and teacher. Of

[1] Barbara Knapp, *Skill in Sport*, Routledge and Kegan Paul, London, 1963, p. 62.

In basketball, the jump ball requires the extended reach.

the body actions listed on the chart on p. 39 gestures are of greatest importance in handling the equipment, although locomotion and elevations are also significant.

1. GESTURES. Games skills such as batting, catching, kicking and throwing are readily recognized by sight and by name to even primary grade children. However, the efficient performance of these skills has to be developed over a period of time through maturation and through analysis, learning and practice. Eventually these skills and other more specialized ones have to be modified to suit the game with which they are associated. Many coaching books present a detailed analysis of the various games and their associated skills.

All this information continues to be used in the teaching of games, usually as criteria for guiding the exploration process. However, from a movement education point of view, the skills which are executed by parts of the body which are not supporting the body weight are recognized as *gestures*. The study of gestures used for the control of equipment will include a consideration of:

(a) the relationship between the gesture and the weightbearing action of the body. The example of rocking the weight forward from the back to the front foot as the arm swings forward in an underhand pitch is an illustration of this relationship. The volleyball serve, softball batting, the overhand throw all require a change of weight from back to front foot as an accompaniment to the arm action. Catching will require that the transfer of weight moves from front to back *in coordination* with the arm action.

(b) the purpose of the gesture, which may be one of the following:

- to *project* the ball; that is, an *outgoing* action which will include all hitting, volleying, throwing and kicking
- to *secure* the ball; that is, an *incoming*, containing action which includes all catching and trapping.

The significance of understanding these purposes is evident, for example, in volleyball, when the player must overcome the impulse to catch the ball and think clearly in terms of projecting it. Similarly, in trapping the soccer ball, he must make a real effort to allow the body to receive the impact, to absorb the blow and redirect the ball so that he retains control of it.

(c) the relation of the gesture to the curl, stretch and twist functions in the main body movement (see p. 85). If the projecting of the ball is done with a stretch or a twist in the gesture a similar function is found in the main body movement in most cases. It is also usual that, in the gesture, a curl provides a preparation for a stretch and vice versa, and a counter-twist may be the preparation for a twist.

2. LOCOMOTION. Occasionally a ball is controlled by *means* of loco-motion. For example, if a basketball is intercepted with one hand, it may not be possible to catch it. The player may direct it into a bounce and keep it moving in a dribble. Similarly, in trapping a soccer ball with the legs or feet, it may be easier to control it in locomotion rather than to stop it. This is a form of "containing" the ball. Ordinarily, dribbling is used for the purpose of moving the ball through the space and not for the specific purpose of controlling it; however in some cases the locomotion may serve to keep an opponent from seizing it.

3. ELEVATIONS. There are a few occasions when the movement of the ball takes place while the body is travelling upward in a jump. In these cases, the jump may be considered to be a means of controlling the ball rather than a body management skill as described on page 81.

Some instances of this are:

(a) the lay-up shot in basketball
(b) soccer heading.

Body parts stressed in controlling equipment

It is easy to imagine that a performer knows exactly what part(s) of the body plays a significant role in performing a games-skill action. Yet, upon examination, it is clear that this is not necessarily the case. Young children and beginners should be helped to discover the effect of a particular use of a given part of the body for achieving control of the ball or equipment. The more advanced player should become competent in using specifically selected actions in the body parts to achieve surprise, variation,

The body carries the ball as close to the basket as possible before releasing it.

virtuosity and strategy in play. The Harlem Globe Trotters set an excellent example of the exploitation of unusual ball control.

Exploration might include the use of such body parts as the following:

1. THE HANDS which may be stressed to give effective control in such
    circumstances as:
    — in volleyball (high volley): use of strong, sudden thrusts of fingers rather than a flabbier action supported by a follow through in the wrists
    — in softball (underhand pitch): use of various types of finger grips (tripod, etc.)
    — in soccer (the throw-in): use of a wrist snap to support the finger-tip grip
    — in basketball (dribble): use of finger tips which are spread wide
    — in track (relays): use of the thumb and palm of the hand to receive a relay baton

— in general ball games (free play): use of the side, top, palm of the hand in free play with a playground ball.

2. THE HEAD, INCLUDING THE EYES, may be stressed in the control of the ball. In many game situations it is necessary to keep the eyes on the ball. For example, this is true in any batting situation. At other times it is necessary to have the eyes on the target. Basketball shots require this. In some cases, such as dribbling in soccer or basketball, it is more important to be watching the players and teammates and the head should be up.

Situations for exploration might include:

(a) use of eyes in the volleyball serve

(b) alignment and positioning of head for batting, catching a fly, picking up a grounder, throwing to base in softball

(c) parts of head used for controlling placement of ball in soccer heading

(d) various original and unusual uses of different parts of the head in exploratory play with lightweight inflated balls.

3. THE FEET are particularly stressed in soccer. The study of the use of different parts of the feet to propel, check, or control the soccer ball should form a basis for the development of soccer skills.

Ball control in soccer may include the outside or the inside of the foot.

Footwork is very important in basketball. The rule on "steps" defines limitations to the movement of the feet when a player is in possession of the ball. Pupils should be given opportunities of receiving the ball while the feet are off the floor in a stride, hop or jump. They should develop foot patterns for the pivot, and for the lay-up shot as well as controlling the balance of weight over the feet during foul shots.

The foot action during the pitch in softball must be related to the pitcher's plate and to the pitching arm. The batter's footwork must promote a transfer of weight from the back to the front foot as the bat meets the ball.

4. OTHER BODY PARTS STRESSED. Although the hands, head and feet are of particular importance in the control of balls, the significance of other parts of the body in special games situations may become apparent if the player has learned to look at movement from this point of view.

Weightbearing and the control of equipment

Weightbearing and weight transference have a major role to play in the control of the equipment. They affect the power and accuracy with which a ball is thrown or kicked. The swing of a bat or racquet is also affected by the way the weight is supported or transferred. It is very evident that if the ground is slippery, a player cannot get the usual power or accuracy into his movement because his body weight is not securely based. Likewise, it is clear that by transferring the body weight from the back to the front foot, the weight of the body is added to the force of the arm action and a stronger throw or hit results. Furthermore, the line of direction taken by the body influences the pathway made by the throwing arm and thus the accuracy of the throw is affected. These principles hold true for throws, kicks, hits, and volleys with any of the standard items of games equipment.

Body shape and the control of equipment

In the pursuit of excellence in the control of the games equipment such as the ball in basketball or volleyball, or the bat in softball or the stick in hockey, the changing shape of the body may be used to exert a significant influence upon the degree of skill achieved. Often it means that the player participates with a full body movement rather than with an isolated gesture of the arms or legs. The four basic body shapes are usually associated with specific purposes in the game. Some examples are used to illustrate such occasions.

1. WALL-SHAPE. This shape tends to be used as a defensive measure. Thus, basketball players jumping for a rebound, often spread their bodies into a wall-shape on the upward jump in order to block off other players.

The body trap in soccer will tend to be wall-shaped although the body will withdraw into a concave shape as a means of lessening the impact.

2. PIN-SHAPE. This shape helps the player to penetrate a restricted space without making contact with the opponents. It may be seen in soccer heading, in the basketball toss-up jump and in the jump which is used for a lay-up shot in basketball. The spiker in volleyball usually assumes a pin-shape in an attempt to jump high while avoiding contact with the net. The fielder who catches a high ball in softball will tend to use the pin-shape as he reaches for the ball.

3. BALL-SHAPE. This body shape tends to be used for the purpose of protecting a ball with the body. Hence, some forms of defensive dribble in basketball make use of an adapted form of this shape. It may be seen in football as the runner tries to carry the ball through the opposition. The underhand serve in volleyball and badminton makes use of a slight ball-shape in the body as a means of generating force for the serve. The sprinter's start is another adapted form of the ball shape, used as a means of generating a forceful forward drive.

4. SCREW-SHAPE. This shape is used very widely as a means of generating great force in ejecting the ball or object. The discus thrower depends on the counter-twist to help to develop enough force to throw the discus a great distance. The counter-twist brings about the screw-shape of the body. This use of the body is found in modified forms in the overhand throw for distance, in batting skills, in the backhand strokes in tennis and badminton, in the tennis serve and the overhand serve in volleyball. In fact, most skills concerned with achieving a distance throw or hit are likely to make use of some form of the screw body shape.

SPACE AWARENESS REQUIRED IN GAMES

A player must develop a good "space sense" to become really efficient. The accuracy in placing the ball is important, but selecting the location for placement can be equally so. Awareness of the play which is centred around the ball is important, but awareness of the zones into which the play may go will allow a player to anticipate the next move. A heightened awareness of space should make a performer more valuable to his team.

Studies in the use of space may be concerned with the player (his body) in space, the equipment (ball, etc.) and zones (court line, goals, nets) in space. Alternatively, the player and the equipment may be considered together.

The reader is referred to Chapter Four, p. 49ff. for a detailed analysis of space.

Changing directions

The player may deliberately use unpredictable changes of directions as he travels alone or with the ball. This strategy should make it difficult for the opponent to anticipate the play. It will also keep the game mobile and make a team member more effective.

The ability to pass one way and break in the opposite direction is very useful in basketball. The ability to comprehend the whole playing area and realize which zones have been over-stressed can enable a player to distribute the play. This can introduce the element of surprise and can challenge the opponent's adaptability.

Controlling the direction of the ball

From a spatial point of view, this may mean selecting a good pathway or target area. For example, most passes between teammates who are advancing down the court should be diagonally forward into the space slightly ahead of the receiver. Balls should be volleyed into the back corners or the sides of the volleyball courts. Softballs should be hit into areas in the field which have been left unprotected by the opponents. Soccer balls should be directed into the corners of the goals. These ideas can be appreciated by most players, but it takes a great deal of experience to be able to use them. The difficulty is that an open space is a much more abstract target than a post or bull's eye. In the first situation, the player has to create his own point of focus before he releases the ball. In the other cases, he may select a target by relating to the goal post, the rim of the basket or a moving player.

Handling the direction of bodily movement

This is an application of the use of the Three Dimensional Cross which was described on page 52. It is sometimes necessary to control, very strictly, the direction into which the body or its parts move. For example, in the spike in volleyball, the direction required is up/down. Forward action will bring the player in contact with the net or cause him to step over the centre line. Similarly in a jump ball in basketball, the up/down dimension is required for the body in the jump. In running, the movement of the arms and legs should be restricted to the wheel plane. All lateral action is wasteful. The direction of the follow-through in any throwing, kicking or hitting action has to be controlled in order to achieve the required pathway for the ball. Faking plays usually depend upon the forward starting to move into one direction and suddenly changing to another one. This requires a great deal of control in the use of directional changes.

CHANGES OF LEVELS

Players tend to choose the easy way of doing things unless it is brought to their attention that this makes defence easy for the opponent. Medium level is usually the easiest and is used most often. Players who will use changes of levels, or the extremes of high and low levels as surprise tactics will improve their standard of play. Defence players should be ready to deal with either high or low play from a clever opponent. With experience, they may even be able to predict from the preparatory movements which level to expect.

PATHWAYS

The success of such games as basketball, soccer and hockey is greatly affected by the pathways chosen by the players. Dribbling should be done in as varied a pathway as possible. The player, who is running free while awaiting a pass, should create for himself an open receiving position. However, such events as swimming and track sprints and base running in softball require the shortest possible pathway since success depends on economy of time.

Where the ball goes after it is released by the player is another aspect of pathway. On the ground, it will cut a straight line, usually diagonally forward and across the playing area. Occasionally, it may be directed straight forward or sideways. When thrown, it usually describes a slight arc. When hit, volleyed, kicked or shot as in basketball, it may have a pronounced arc. The particular pathway of flight will depend upon what is required in terms of the height and/or the length of the arc, the desirability of lateral curve, the required angle of flight upon arrival at the target. These considerations may be determined by the threat of interception or by whether or not the angle of flight can be used as a form of strategy.

PATTERNS

Pathways can be organized into patterns. The patterns of play used by a team are usually a form of games strategy and require the development of cooperation between teammates. The cooperation is a *relationship* concept, but the positioning in the playing area is a *spatial* concept. The usual patterns which are found in games such as basketball and hockey are: the figure-of-eight weave; the zone or channel pattern. Zone or area play is also used in softball, volleyball, tennis and badminton. The pattern by which the ball is worked down the playing area gives a logic to the game. The concept is difficult for beginners to comprehend and the execution of planned patterns is a challenge to the most advanced teams.

As was mentioned in discussing the use of levels, the performer tends to take the easy way of doing things and can fall into lazy, unenterprising habits. Hence, there is a need to make players aware of the use of changes in the dimension of actions which can create variety and surprise. The height of the jump used for interception can determine its success or failure. The extension of the follow-through in a volleyball serve may affect its accuracy.

Not only may the size of the body action be varied, but the distance of a throw, hit or pass may also be made unpredictable. The player may ask himself:

- Is the serve sometimes short; sometimes long?
- Is the goal shot sometimes from close range; at other times from further out?
- Is the length of the pass varied?
- Is the softball catcher's return sometimes to the pitcher; sometimes to the other basemen?

Players must become aware of the contrasts of small/large and near/far and use them to advantage during the game.

THE EFFORT QUALITY OF THE MOVEMENT

Since games are concerned with the matter of scoring goals and employ operational movement, the effort quality factors will be selected to achieve success in the competition. It is important, however, that players can use the appropriate effort quality of movement at will.

Reference can be made to Chapter Four, pages 56-67 for the descriptive analyses of the effort qualities of movement. The present discussion will draw attention to how the theory may be applied to games action.

Early in their play experience, pupils can be assisted towards increasing awareness of the range of effort quality available to them. For example, they can bounce a ball faster or more slowly, or use a change in timing to outwit the opponent. Similarly, they can run faster or more slowly, or use a change of pace to their own advantage. It will be a truer application of the effort quality of movement, if the judgement of speed is taken from the point of view of *how the performer moves* rather than from that of how the ball or equipment moves. For example, a sudden hit or tap is required in a volley because the rule does not permit the ball to be carried on the fingers. Therefore, the hitting action must be short and sharp, sudden as well as strong. The player who can break with a sudden dart for the basket has a fair chance of success because his movement will have an unexpected quality which will surprise the defence. The guard is likely to need a sudden action as a countermeasure. The examples given should help the teacher to seek out instances when a stress on one of the time elements (fast/

sudden; slow/sustained) is being used effectively. Pupils can then explore other opportunities for using these effort qualities effectively.

Similarly, the *weight* factor can be significant in the movement of a player. A softball hit may call for a *strong* quality, thus, the player will take a firm grip and apply the bat to the ball with forcefulness. Alternatively, a bunt may be more appropriate and loose grip will be used initially, and a finer force applied to the hit. Sometimes, a fine touch must be used as, for example, in a net shot in badminton. Graduating the amount of power in the serve will help to control the placement of it or the speed and force with which it arrives. Awareness of this form of control is important to finesse in a game.

Sometimes the *space* factor in the quality of the player's movement is important. For example, some people who have a natural tendency toward a *flexible* use of space may have trouble producing the *directness* needed to achieve a satisfactory follow-through on a basketball foul shot or to use an effective jab in field hockey, or to keep the leg action in the sprint in an economical wheel plane dimension. Alternatively, players who have a strong tendency toward *direct* quality of movement may find difficulty in getting sufficient flexibility into such actions as treading water, high jumping or hurdling. They may not be able to deliver a ball with a spin or use a side-arm throw. Patience will be required in such situations. Work on effort qualities of movement in dance and gymnastics lessons should bear fruit in the games lessons and vice versa. For example, in gymnastics, twists which are used to transfer the body weight from one body part to another may establish the feel of a twisting movement in the body. Later, when a twisting action is required in a dodging movement in games, appropriate reference can be made to the earlier experience and a carry-over of the learning may occur. It is usual that some form of compensatory movement can be found if the player cannot readily use the appropriate effort quality. This is one of the reasons why it is now being conceded that there is no "one perfect form" but that, within bounds, players must find their own playing style.

The *flow* factor is often very important in games action. It is likely that the overhand throw will be characterized by a free-flow action. The follow-through on a two-hand underhand foul shot in basketball may also be a free-flow movement in the direction of the target if that effort quality is in accordance with the player's movement pattern. Catching, particularly as the hands "give" to reduce the impact of the ball, is likely to have a bound-flow quality which assists in checking the progress of the ball. This will be true of the actions which are concerned with stopping the ball or the body. In the long jump, in order to hit the take-off board without overstepping it, the last stride, at least, is likely to have a bound-flow quality. After that, the rest of the jump may be characterized by free flow or, perhaps, during the flight, the body posture will be held momentarily by bound flow, before the free-flow landing occurs. Actions such as trapping in soccer or cradling in lacrosse which are aimed at containing the ball may have a free-flow quality which keeps it in motion while redirecting it. The need to check the movement, or the need to allow the movement to carry on to its normal conclusion determines the type of flow quality required.

When the basic games skills such as hitting, kicking and throwing are analyzed in terms of their effort elements, it will be discovered that many of them are variations of the basic effort actions. The examples given below will indicate the important use which is made of the basic effort actions in the playing of games.

Hitting (i.e. a *thrust*: firm, sudden, direct action) is used in batting, serving, kicking, volleying, sprinting actions, take-offs for jumps.

Dabbing (fine touch, sudden, direct action) is found in badminton net shots, some light volleys, many versions of the lay-up shot, some faking actions, some forms of soccer dribble.

Pressing (firm, sustained, direct action) is required for pole vault, the hand and foot action in the "Get-Set" position in the sprint start, foot action in a basketball pivot, some forms of body checks in soccer, some stick work in the bully in field hockey.

Slashing (firm, sudden, flexible action) is needed for the whip-like action of the overhand throw, the overhand serves in volleyball and tennis, the body roll in high jump, the spike in volleyball, many of the guarding plays in basketball and the slap shot in ice-hockey.

Floating (fine touch, sustained, flexible action) is used in treading water, after the release of the ball in some basketball shots such as the overhand set shot, the one and two hand free shots.

Wringing (firm, sustained, flexible) is used in the wind-up for an overhand pitch, some aspects of wrestling, tying a ball in basketball.

Flicking (fine touch, sudden, flexible action) may be found in some badminton wrist shots, some hand actions used in guarding in basketball, some actions used by the hands in tipping a jump ball, some methods of deflecting a rebound in basketball, the flick shot in hockey.

Gliding (fine touch, sustained, direct action) can be found in the face float in swimming, the glide sections of the breast and side strokes, some forms of skating action, some swings used for underhand serves or throws or bowling, some forms of flight in jumping.

The above suggestions may help teachers and pupils to develop observation skills and to sharpen their kinesthetic awareness. A precise control of the quality of movement is obviously a great advantage to a player and well worth working for.

RELATIONSHIPS

It is obvious that a player moves in relationship to the boundaries and court lines, to the equipment, to his partner or teammates as well as to his opponents, and in a very particular sense to the rules of the game.

An analysis of relationships in movement was given on pages 67 ff. An application of those principles will now be made to games.

The players are required to respect the boundaries of the playing area and the special lines which are used to regulate the game. These may make special demands on a player's skill. For example, the soccer player (throw-in), volleyball server, softball batters and pitchers all have lines which restrict their movements to some extent and which add to the difficulty of balance. They also give rise to particular plays and planned strategies being developed by teams which play together often enough to consolidate their team play.

The kind of playing surface — grass, wood, tile — and the exact condition of it, exert differing influences on both ball and player and, therefore, affect the circumstances of play. For example, softball or track on a wet field can be dangerous. Other physical conditions, such as the lighting, the tension in the volleyball net, the amount of resilience in a basketball backboard may at one time or another affect the players and cause them to make adjustments in relation to their physical environment.

RELATIONSHIP TO THE EQUIPMENT

Most games are focussed around a ball or similar object. Some games, such as soccer, require that the ball be controlled by the body or its parts. Others, such as hockey, require that the ball or puck be controlled by means of a tool such as a stick or a racquet. The relationship of the player to the equipment is one of manipulation.

Manipulative relationship

This relationship to equipment has several stages which depend on the player's experience and the stage of the development of his skill.

1. PRE-CONTROL STAGE. At this level of skill the learner tends to handle the equipment quite experimentally to "get the feel of it." This stage, in a very much shortened form, is likely to characterize the early part of the warm-up period of even the professional player. The answers he seems to be seeking appear to be directly related to the equipment in terms of:

How much bounce is there in this ball? How much rebound is given by this surface? How high is this net? How much space is allowed? How much traction can be relied upon?

In the case of the beginner, he may also be relating the manipulation to his own capacities in terms of:

What can I do with this ball? (bounce, toss, catch, roll, hit it?) What part of my body can help me control it? (hands, one hand, foot, general body action?)

2. CONTROL STAGE. As the player enters the control stage, he relates himself to the equipment on the basis of using it at will. He can start and stop it. He has a selection of things which he can do with it without loss of control. For example, he may be able to manipulate the soccer ball well enough that he can coordinate the dribble and goal kick. He may lapse into experimental manipulation but it will now take the form of trying out more complicated ways of manipulating the ball. For example, he may increase the speed, the height, the force or the distance involved.

3. UTILIZATION STAGE. As soon as he has some degree of control, he will use it to hit a target, keep the ball from another player, race with it or otherwise provide himself with a further challenge. At this point, he is likely to be participating in simple versions of the major games. For example, he may play "Five Man Field Hockey" or "Mass Volleyball." His manipulation takes on a competitive spirit, although at the same time he may be developing a spirit of cooperation as he plays in conjunction with a teammate.

4. PROFICIENCY STAGE. The final stage of manipulation is reached when the player has control over the ball in most situations. He will then be testing and enjoying his mastery of it in the playing of the game.

The movement situation is so dynamic that different skills will be developing at varying rates of speed. The player may have mastered several ways of controlling the ball while other ways of handling it will be at one of the earlier stages. For example, the soccer player's footwork might be excellent, but his heading skills might be very poorly developed.

Hence, it would be inaccurate to say that a player had reached the mastery stage in a game. However, he is usually aware of his competence in certain skills or in specific situations.

Non-manipulative relationships

The player has to relate his own body and his ball to such objects as a net, goal or target. Goals and targets become the focal point of his efforts and influence all his actions. Nets and other obstructions cause him to adjust his movements to find acceptable ways of relating his or the ball's movement to them. The volleyball player uses the up/down dimension in an effort to avoid touching the net. The softball pitcher regulates his pitching action to retain contact with the pitcher's plate until the ball is released. These are adjustments made in order to retain an acceptable relationship with the non-manipulative equipment of the game.

RELATIONSHIP TO THE RULES

It has always been realized that the play is regulated by the rules of the game. It has not always been understood that the player actively relates to the rule by modifying his movements to conform to it or take advantage of it. Hence, when the volleyball rules disallowed any form of cushioning as the ball makes contact with the fingers, the 'dig' became the usual underhand pass. In this way, the ball contacts some part of the closed fist, usually on the thumb side and no cushioning or cradling is possible. Similarly, in girl's basketball, the dribbler had to learn to protect the ball when the rule made it legal for an opponent to steal it (without personal contact). Because the rules directly affect the movement patterns which make for efficiency, the player should work, i.e. explore, select and practise, with the rules clearly in mind.

RELATIONSHIPS TO OTHERS

There are several relationships with people which may develop in games situations. These include the cooperative, competitive and non-engaged situations. Each of these give rise to some variety within the category. To some extent the level of skill of the player determines the relationship which develops. These circumstances are discussed next.

Non-engaged situations

The characteristic relationship here is that of being "alone-in-a-group." This usually occurs with very young children or with beginners who wish to practise their basic skills. Each player has his own equipment, his own share of the playing space and such non-manipulative equipment as nets, goals, targets and backstops. The individual responsibility with respect to other players is to avoid interference. Each player works in such a way that he limits his choice of activities to those in which he has sufficient control of himself and his equipment and not to encroach upon his neighbours. His interest is centred on controlling the vagrancies of the ball. He recognizes that he is at a stage of development when the problems of relating the ball to another player are too complex for his level of skill.

Cooperative situation

As soon as a player can exercise a reasonable degree of control over his ball, he tends to extend his frame of reference to include another player who probably has a similar level of skill. They will pass the ball between themselves, pitch so that the other may hit or catch, serve so the other may return and generally assist each other to control the ball. Speed, force and placement are all selected to assist the partner. In this way, a cooperative relationship is maintained.

Different forms of cooperative relationships may develop. Players may *share* the ball by passing it between them. They may *take turns,* one pitching while the other bats or one bouncing while the other one rests. They may play *Follow the Leader* which remains cooperative only so long as the leader chooses things which the follower can do.

The number of players who cooperate with one another can be enlarged from two to ten or more. In some situations roles are assumed by different players who take on special functions on behalf of the group. Hence, in softball, the pitcher, catcher, basemen, short-stop and fielders each play special roles which contribute to the purposes of the team. When this degree of specialization is required, the individual players are usually chosen because their skills are sufficiently advanced to meet the demands of the role.

As soon as the relationships have reached the stage where roles are assumed, teamwork is required. This means that a common goal must be accepted by all members. It is likely that some form of leadership will develop. Under the best circumstances, individuals will sacrifice personal aspirations for the good of the team, doing their best within the assigned role and supporting other members to the full. The teamwork stage requires not only a reasonable level of skill in controlling the ball, but also sufficient maturity in social and emotional development to put the good of the team before their own individual purposes.

Competitive situations

Competitive relationships tend to arise out of cooperative situations when skills become sufficiently advanced to make such a change possible. The mere repetition of a skill already mastered is boring and the player tends to seek out a test of the skill with the attendant stimulus of a chance of failure or a possibility of triumph. The first competitive situation for the young child is almost invariably against one other player. On other occasions, two or three players may be cooperating when, quite spontaneously, there arise small tests or comparisons of skill to which each responds. Finally, there is the more usual situation where skilled players voluntarily undertake to play a game.

The actual group composition can range from singles play, as in badminton and tennis, to doubles play and to team play.

Reference should be made to Chapter Four, pages 67 to 75 for the analysis of relationships as they are found in movement. A more precise application to games will be added here.

Competitive situations can be simple or complex in terms of the demands made upon the individual. "It" games pit *one* player against the group. This is a relatively simple form because the focus is upon the action of one individual. However, some degree of confusion arises among the individuals within the group. They have to guard themselves against collisions. The "It" player has difficulties arising out of the size and shape of the playing area. He is faced with rather obvious embarrassment if he does not succeed in tagging someone within a reasonable time limit. The usual point of the game is for "It" to exchange roles with the first player tagged. This purpose can be modified so that the number tagged within a given time limit becomes significant. Then the relative success of the different "Its" may be compared.

Other organizations for competition can include, for example, one *vs* one; one *vs* two; two *vs* two; twelve *vs* one; twelve *vs* four situations. That is, the competition can be between equal numbers or many can oppose a few or a few can resist many. The shapes of the groups (circles, lines, zones), the boundaries and whether or not the attack is made upon players or upon objects, have a bearing upon the experience offered by the game. For example, *Dodgeball,* which is an attack upon the person of the opponent, may require different safety rules than *Club Guard,* which is an attack upon the skittles.

The most complex form of competition is probably the form exemplified by team games such as soccer, basketball, et cetera. In these games the greatest demands of cooperative play, as described on page 101, are required within the team; while the individual player is faced with opposition on a player to player or a zone basis. The complexities which arise in these games require excellence in body management and skill in controlling the equipment. They demand a maturity of emotional and social development; a knowledge of rules and a comprehension of strategy. They require a high degree of skill in the cooperative and competitive relationships.

SUMMARY

Games may be analyzed in terms of the four components of movement. Good management of the body and the skill to control the equipment are basic requirements for success as a player. The elements which determine the quality of the movement must be under the control of the performer. He must also be skilled in his use and understanding of space. The ability to relate his actions to the requirement of the rules is a necessity. He must be aware of the nets, goals, boundaries and general playing environment. Finally, one of his most important roles is that of participating as a team member, contributing to the team strategy and assisting his teammates while facing the opponents.

The implementation of these requirements is outlined in Chapter Eight.

SIX

GYMNASTICS:
A MOVEMENT ANALYSIS

In Chapter Four, four components of movement and their subdivisions were presented in a chart form, which was followed by brief explanations with examples. The four components of movement were treated on a theoretical level. The present chapter will be devoted to applying those concepts to gymnastics. A later chapter will make the application to dance.

Gymnastics has been described (p. 29) as being activities which arise when the performer strives to test his ability to control his body movements in relation to the force of gravity in deliberately selected circumstances of difficulty. He draws on his powers of strength, speed, agility and his ability to maintain satisfactory interrelationships between the different parts of the body. He may work on fixed apparatus or on the floor, with or without mats.

The question to be considered here is: "How can an understanding of movement concepts increase the powers of bodily control?" The answer to this question will be arrived at by examining each of the four components of movement in relation to their effect on bodily control.

BODY AWARENESS

In gymnastics, the performer must become aware of how the body is moving in terms of weightbearing, the transference of weight, the actions of the parts and the relation of the parts to each other. The descriptions which follow are presented, to some extent, in order of importance; but not necessarily in the order in which they would occur in a teaching program.

WEIGHTBEARING

Support

The weight of the body must be supported. Certain parts of the body or a combination of parts can do the job. The pupil, over a suitable period of time, should discover the parts which, alone or in combination, can function in this way. The most obvious parts are likely to be: two feet, one foot, the seat and two feet, the seat alone, the front of the body while in the prone position, the hands and knees plus lower legs and, perhaps, toes. At a more advanced stage of experience more unusual parts, and smaller ones, may be found capable of supporting weight. For example, the right hip, the hand and side hip, the shoulder and back of the head (also, perhaps, the upper arms, one knee, the tummy only, two hands only).

The first step toward awareness is the recognition of those parts which "touch the floor." With more experience, true awareness will be achieved. In this sense, "awareness" means knowing, by mental recognition and by kinesthetic feeling, exactly which parts support the weight.

The base of support may be established on the floor, or a substitute, such as a bench or the top of the vaulting box. However, the body weight can also be suspended from a support on a beam or bar. In this case, the

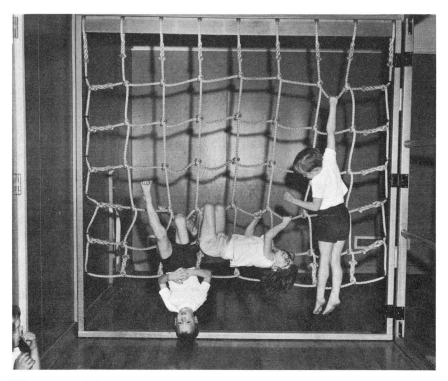

Different ways of hanging with body weight suspended from above. "What parts can hold your weight?"

parts which bear the weight can be both hands, one hand, the back of the knee(s) and so on.

So far, the base of support and the parts which may become the support have been described. This should not be taken to imply that gymnastics is a static activity with the weight held in a series of different statues. The idea that different parts of the body can support the body weight may also be realized by identifying those parts which take the weight in locomotor activities such as cartwheels, backward rolls, running, rolling, crawling and other such actions.

As soon as the body weight is moved from one weightbearing part to another, *weight transference* becomes a matter for consideration. The support of the body weight and the transference of body weight are very closely related.

Weight transference

Weight can be transferred from one part to another. If each new weightbearing part is placed in the original location of the base, the movement takes place "on the spot" and is non-locomotor in nature. For example, running or jumping may be done "on the spot." If each part which receives the weight is placed in a new location, so that the body travels about in space, the resulting movement will be locomotor in nature. Walking forward on the hands, hopping in a circle, rolling backward are all examples of different types of locomotor movements.

If these locomotor movements are examined to determine how the body weight is being transferred, three different methods can be identified.

1. THE STEP-LIKE TRANSFER. In movements like walking or crawling on all fours, the main transfer of weight is from one non-adjacent part to another. For example, in the walk, the transfer of weight is moved from right to left foot alternately. (Notice that within this transference, there is another one, namely, from heel to toe of each foot in turn.) The crawl is likely to be from left hand to right knee (and leg) to right hand to left knee (and leg) alternating in order. In step-like actions, contact with the floor is maintained; that is at any given part of the sequence, at least one weight-bearing part is in contact with the floor. The alternation of weight is from one non-adjacent (or distinctly separated) part of the body to another.

2. THE SPRING-LIKE TRANSFER. In movements like the run, hop or jump, the weight is transferred from one non-adjacent part to another or from one part and back on to it again — in both cases with a moment of flight as the transfer takes place. In the run, the weight moves from the ball (and toes) of one foot to the ball of the other alternately, with sufficient spring to clear the feet off the floor. If the flight action is emphasized by being made higher or longer the run becomes a bound. In the hop the spring

carries the weight off one foot and back onto the same foot. In the jump, the spring carries the weight off one foot and onto both feet; or off both feet and onto both feet; or off both feet and onto one foot.

Other forms of weight transfer which are initiated by a spring include: the cat spring (from two feet onto two hands, onto two feet); neck spring (from neck — shoulders — hands onto feet); handspring (from two hands to two feet); hand jumps on the horizontal ladder (from two hands onto two hands). Original forms of springs may be added to these examples.

3. THE ROLL-LIKE TRANSFER. In this type of movement the weight is transferred along the surfaces of the body so that successive segments receive the weight in turn. Thus in a log roll, the movement may start with the weight being transferred from the back to the left side, across the front, onto the right side and thence onto the back. In an ordinary walking step, the weight moves from the heel, forward through the ball of the foot and partially onto the toes before it is pushed off the foot altogether. As these illustrations indicate, a roll is considered to be a transference of weight through adjacent parts of the body. In many cases, these parts are anatomically adjacent to each other, as are the back and the left side of the body. However, on other occasions, specific parts of the body are placed adjacent to other weightbearing parts in order to provide a continuous surface on which to roll. For example, in the forward roll, the weight starts on the feet and is transferred to the hands which are placed adjacent to the feet, and then to the neck and shoulders which should be placed adjacent to the hands. From there, the weight moves along the spine where the vertebrae and hip girdle are located adjacent to one another by virtue of anatomical structure. The weight then moves to the feet which are placed adjacent to the hip girdle. The secret of a smooth roll is in the performer being able to judge the point of placement required for these parts in relation to the speed and force of the roll. Similarly, the cartwheel can be executed as a series of step-like actions, or, by judging the placement in relation to speed and force, can be made to roll around the circumference in a smooth wheel-like way.

Balance

The body may be supported upon the weightbearing parts which are in contact with a base in such a way that a position or posture of stability is achieved. For example, the performer may be standing with two feet astride, or half kneeling with weight on the right knee (and lower leg) and left foot, or crouching with the weight on "all fours." In the examples given, each in order is a more stable position than the one which precedes it. In other circumstances, he may be holding a handstand balance, or be poised on the balls of the feet prior to springing into a forward roll. In these cases, the balance would be relatively unstable.

The required degree of stability is determined by the performer in accordance with his purpose. He controls the degree of stability chiefly by altering the relationship of the centre of gravity to the base. The centre of gravity in the body is located approximately in the centre of the pelvic area at the level of the hips. The base may be created by one or a combination of weightbearing parts.

If a stable balance is required, the hips should be kept over the centre of the base. They should be kept low; that is, close to the base. The base should be relatively large. When these criteria are applied to the handstand and to the headstand, it is clear that a well-executed headstand should be more stable than a well-executed handstand.

The shape of the base is also a factor in the stability. For example, the head and the hands in the headstand provide greater stability when arranged in the shape of a triangle rather than in a straight line.

If the centre of gravity begins to be drawn beyond the base, the head, arms, legs or other parts of the body may be used as counterbalances to shift it back over the base. Thus, if the performer assumes an angel stand on a balance beam, the forward lean of the trunk is counterbalanced by the raising of one leg behind and the centre of gravity remains over the supporting foot. The principle of counterbalance is in constant operation in daily life, because there is an almost continuous movement in the body at all times. This brings about a constant shift in the position of the centre of gravity which is countered by a movement elsewhere in the body. However, in gymnastics this condition is deliberately exaggerated and exploited to provide a challenge to the performer's control of balance and to test his skill and virtuosity.

There are occasions when the centre of gravity is moved beyond the base, no counterbalance is made and an overbalance results. Such stunts as the prone fall, the walkover or the dive roll are examples. In these cases, the skilled performer retains control of his movement by preparing for a transference of weight to new weightbearing parts with sufficient force in take-off and sufficient give or resilience to establish his weight on the new base.

There are a number of rotary stunts performed in gymnastics in which the body rotates around an axis which passes through the hips. This is true if the body is unsupported, as is the case in a somersault. In the cartwheel or roll where the weight is being transferred through a succession of body parts the rotation is around an axis which passes horizontally through the centre of the body. In these situations the force of gravity is used to aid the rotation. This is done, in part, by keeping the centre of gravity in advance of the base until stable balance is once more required. Thus the performer experiences stable balance merging into unstable balance which in turn merges into stable balance. A headstand which moves into a forward roll which finishes in an upright standing position illustrates such a sequence. Similarly, a headstand (relatively stable) which overbalances (unstable to mobile) into a bridge (stable) uses the technique of controlling an over-balance by establishing a new base.

BASIC FUNCTIONS: CURL (BEND), STRETCH, TWIST

Body movements are composed of alternations between the bends, stretches and twists of the various body parts. The movement results from the contractions of muscle groups coordinated with the relaxation of their antagonistic muscle groups. Such contractions exercise a pull upon the bones which then move at the joints so that two parts tend to approach one another or separate from one another; or rotate about one another. These movements give rise to the three basic movement tendencies in the body.

In certain instances all parts can contribute to the enfolding and the total body becomes curled. Such is the case in forward or backward rolls or egg rolls sideways. On other occasions all parts of the body tend to contribute to the outward extension of the body. The cartwheel, the vertical jump, the log roll are all examples of actions which stress a full body extension. The round-off, spiral roll, jumps with twists and twist movements while hanging from beams are examples of activities which stress the twist function in the body.

Not only is it possible to experience the feeling of each of these basic movement functions being brought into full range in the body, but it is also possible to feel the body moving from a full range twist into a full stretch

Body movements showing twist, stretch, curl.

and then into a curl. The fluctuation between the three functions can be combined in different orders. For example, the stretch may sometimes dissolve into a curl, at other times into a twist. As these alternations occur, the centre of the body becomes the focal point of the movements: curling movements close around it; stretching movements radiate out from it; twisting movements rotate about it.

In many sequences of action — in gymnastics or in the movement of daily life — the stretch or curl or twist is not used at full range. In such a case, for example, a partial bend of the legs (curl) is used as a preparation for a spring (stretch). Or, from a back lying stretch, the body may partially curl over a shoulder base before extending (stretch) into a twisting roll (curl). Thus, a tendency toward a curl may be changed before it brings the body into a full range curl. The change may be into a tendency toward a stretch which lasts only long enough to result in an "uncurl" and which dissolves before it becomes an evident stretch. For example, a dive into a forward roll may be executed as a partial curl into a pronounced curl, finishing in a stretch which develops into an erect standing position. However, it may also be done as a stretched flight (layout) into a pronounced curl for rolling. This precise appreciation of the use of the body functions is one of the aims of gymnastics.

There is another ramification of the bend/stretch/twist functions of the body which is significant in gymnastic movement; namely, that the bend/ stretch alternation tends to be used in the more stable situations and the twist/countertwist alternations in the more mobile ones. Hence, most of the landings depend upon the bend of the ankles, knees and hip joints which then extend to raise the body into a vertical stance which is a body stretch. Twists and countertwists or twists into curls keep the body moving, the twists often bringing about a change of direction. The stretch of the body can be used to bring the movement to a halt.

PARTS OF THE BODY: AWARENESS OF THEIR ROLE IN MOVEMENT

Some movements place a marked emphasis upon the role played by a particular body part. For example, in the fish-flop the front of the body must be held in a convex curve to provide a rocking surface. In a mule kick, the legs must lash out in a backward high dimension. In some vaults, the legs must move in a special pathway. These examples draw attention to the fact that the action of various parts of the body must be given consideration.

Recognition: use of part

The performer should become sufficiently aware of his movements to recognize that a specific part of the body is being, or should be, used in a given situation. The use might be for a weightbearing or for a non-weighting function. For example, it is necessary to know which part of the head is bearing the weight in a headstand. If the weight is placed too far towards the back an overbalance may result. If it is placed too far forward, an exaggerated back arch will develop. In the handstand, the position of the head may be used as a counterbalance in keeping the centre of gravity over the base.

Recognition: part stressed

Frequently a movement depends upon a special stress being placed on the action of one body part. For example, the legs may be used to create momentum in a swing when mounting or dismounting from a beam. Or the knees should be kept bent during a crouch jump. Or the balls of the feet may be used to achieve spring in a run or the take-off for a jump. The recognition that the emphasis is being placed on the action of a special part of the body is an important stage of body awareness in gymnastic work.

In a slightly different sense, an awareness of the effective use of such body parts as the knees, ankles, hips and feet is especially important to efficient body movement, especially in gymnastics. The following details should become part of the understanding and performance skills of the pupils.

1. KNEES are important to landings. A controlled bending helps to absorb the body weight and prevents a jar to the body as the feet make contact with the floor. The initial bending is followed by a stretching as the feet push against the floor to drive the body weight upward until the momentum is dissipated and the body comes to rest over the feet. In the take-off for a jump, the knees should bend to prepare for the subsequent extension of the legs which drives the body into flight.

The straightening of the knee is important when a forceful leg swing is required because it lengthens the leg and increases the centrifugal force generated by the swing. The leg which leads upward in a handstand makes use of this power to help elevate the hips. It can be useful in the cartwheel, particularly in the one-hand or handless cartwheel.

2. ANKLES. Beginners in gymnastics usually have "dead" feet and ankles. The ankle spring is achieved through an alternation of bend and stretch in the ankle joint coordinated with similar action in the hip, knee and foot joints. The bend absorbs shock. It also positions the foot for the strong push which comes as the ankle joint extends. Spring in the ankles will make the footwork resilient.

3. FEET. The ball of the foot is a source of power for elevations and landings and also for running. The heels do not receive the weight in a landing until the momentum has been absorbed. They are lifted from the floor to allow the foot to push for a spring. The toes help in balance as a countercheck against too great a bend in the ankle and they give the final push against the floor in a jump.

Nimble footwork will take into account the spring and cushioning functions and also the relationships developed between the two feet. Double and single take-offs and landings can be featured. The relative positions of the two feet, for example, one leading or crossing the other, can also be a test of nimbleness.

The feet may also grip a rope, bar or the floor. They may be anchored to climbing equipment. These possibilities are increased when the performer works barefooted.

4. HANDS. The hands are used instinctively to help with the transference of body weight in rolling, rocking and crawling. They can also be a base of support in different balances and hangs. The fingers are used in opposition to the thumb when the hand grips. The fingers and thumb are usually widely spread and slightly bent when used for balances. The direction in which the fingers point and the grouping of the fingers — tripod, fanned — will be selected according to the function they perform.

The function of the hips, shoulders, elbows, wrists may be stressed, each in its own way, in the various action sequences which arise in gymnastics.

Body parts and the functions of bend, stretch, twist

Recognition of interrelationships between the parts of the body is necessary for good control and a high standard of performance. For example, in the cartwheel, the knees, ankles and toes should be stretched in harmony with the general extension of the body. In landing from a jump, the foot, ankle, knee and hip joints should bend in succession as a means of absorbing the impact of the weight of the body against the floor. They then extend, each in succession, to push the body upward as the momentum is reduced. The successive bends and stretches will be repeated on a smaller scale while balance is maintained and until stillness is established. The interrelated action in the different joints is essential for a coordinated movement. In asymmetrical rolls, the twist of the spine may be accompanied by the rotations of the wrists and ankles. Thus, although the major twist occurs in the spine, the accompanying twist in wrists or ankles (which bear the weight) is important because it adds to the range of the movement.

In addition to entering into the general body functions of bend, stretch and twist, it is also possible for the parts to assume a special and contrasting movement. For example, in the caterpillar walk, the knees remain straight while the body is bent at the hip. In the crouch jump, the knees and hips bend while the ankles are stretched.

The performer with a high degree of body awareness, will know when the movement of body parts harmonizes with the general tendency of the movement and when it provides a contrast.

The consideration has so far been directed toward the function of the individual part. Taken in broader terms, pupils will find curls, stretches or twists which involve adjacent joints. For example, surfaces or areas of the body may be curved or arched through curls or stretches of the spine. The "stomach" can be made concave or convex, creating arches and curves, providing stable balances or facilitating rolls or rocks as the weight is transferred along the curved surfaces. The back can be curled or arched. The sides of the body can also be thus considered. Twists may arise from entwining the legs, the arms, or a leg and an arm. Difficulty may arise in managing the transfer of weight as one action leads into another. Curved surfaces tend to facilitate rocks or rolls. Arches tend to supply bases of support and the transfer of weight tends to be by means of steps or springs. Such movements are often seen when partners are composing movements which create spaces through which one of the pair may move. They also tend to arise when the surfaces of the body are being used to transfer the body weight, or, conversely are being kept out of touch with the floor.

Parts leading an action

The part which leads usually draws the centre of gravity beyond the base so that a transference of weight must take place. If, for example, the performer is kneeling, the hips can bend and twist to the right until the weight is taken on the right hip. At that point, the hip lead might cease, the back and then the shoulders might take over the lead as the weight is rolled along those surfaces. Subsequently, the knees or one leg could assume the lead. After a roll along the top of the vaulting box, the feet might lead the descent onto the mat. It is important to realize, that the part which leads must eventually come to the end of its range (usually when it receives the body weight) and another part may then take over. In jumps, the head, one shoulder, and one hand are examples of some parts which may lead the movement. Different sides or surfaces of the body may lead in such actions as running, sliding or jumping.

Parts meeting and separating

The legs are caused to separate in split jumps and to meet in heel-click jumps. The hands may touch the toes in a jump or a pike position. One knee may touch the forehead in a balance. The arms may separate in an upward and downward, a forward and backward, or a side position. The feet may alternately meet and part as in a gallop step. These examples should indicate that there are many ways in which this situation may be developed. The most extensive movement usually occurs when one part of the upper body meets a part of the lower extremities. The movement may involve combinations of bends, stretches or twists, and it may or may not bring about a transfer in weight.

Body parts used symmetrically/asymmetrically

The parts of the body which receive weight or lead an action or are otherwise stressed in a movement may be selected from one or both sides of the body. If a turn, a jump or a swing is led by the right (or left) shoulder, for example, the body will be engaged in an asymmetrical movement. If, however, both legs are raised simultaneously in a headstand, the movement will be a symmetrical one. Double take-offs and landings, jumps with both sides of the body matched, and rolls which move evenly along the spine, will be symmetrical. Runs, slides, turns, twists, and balances on one side of the body, will be asymmetrical. The symmetrical use of body parts is rather more restricting than the asymmetrical use. The latter provides ready mobility and a continuity of action.

BODY ACTIONS

The movements of the body which develop out of fluctuations between the bend, stretch and twist functions can give rise to certain categories of actions. These actions are used in gymnastics to test the performer's bodily control although at times the control aspect may be linked with a more closely defined purpose such as to clear an obstacle or to travel from one place to another. The actions fall into five types.

Locomotor

These actions move the body through space from one location to another; or if the point of arrival is unimportant, along pathways in space. The travelling may be accomplished through steps or step-like actions, springs which propel the body into a new location, and rolls. These were analyzed on pages 106 and 107 of this chapter from the point of view of weight transference. In addition, locomotion can be achieved by slides in which the power is developed prior to the slide and the weight is held on the part concerned as the progress across the surface of support takes place. Locomotion can also take place by dragging as, for example, in the seal walk, or a partner stunt when one is pulled by the other. The drag is always passive and the power is in advance of the part being dragged. In the seal walk, the body is divided in its function — the arms using step-like actions, the legs passive weightbearers.

INCIPIENT LOCOMOTOR ACTIONS. Running and hopping on the spot are step-like or spring-like forms of locomotor actions which are kept on the spot because the part which receives the weight is moved into the location of the part which transmits the weight. By changing the spatial factor, the actions become locomotor.

In gymnastics, locomotor actions may be used to create momentum as a preparation for a subsequent action, as occurs when a run precedes a vault. Alternatively, the momentum achieved in locomotion may prove to be a challenge in controlling the subsequent action. This is the case if a cartwheel precedes a handstand in a floor sequence.

Gestures

These are actions which, by definition, are made by those parts of the body which are not, at the time, supporting the body weight. It will be necessary to discover which parts are free and which are bearing the weight at different points in a sequence. The performer should be aware of how the bend, stretch and twist functions can be used to create gestures. An increase in control can be acquired when it is realized that the gesture may shift the centre of gravity and change the stability of the balance. This may be directed toward increasing stability by providing symmetrical gestures or by creating counterbalances. Conversely, it may be directed toward decreasing stability and leading the body into a transference of weight. Gestures may lead into a change of direction or they may, as in the case of swings, provide momentum for springs or a change in the level of the centre of gravity. Gestures may contribute to changes in body shape with or without changing the base of support. For example, a handstand may change from pin, to wall, to tuck, to twist, before a change of base occurs. Or, on the pommel horse, the hand grip may be established but a leg swing may be used momentarily to cut off the support of one hand.

Gestures provide a major category of activity which may be used in gymnastics to test the ability of the performer to control his movements.

Stillness or pause

At first impression this category may seem to denote an absence of action. However, this is far from true. An active contraction of muscles must occur to hold the weight steady for a significant length of time over the base of support. The action can be examined to determine the "on balance" or stable nature of the stillness or the relatively "off balance" or unstable nature of the pause. This will lead to a disclosure of the features which affect balance (discussed on pages 107 and 108) namely, size and shape of the base, position of the centre of gravity over the base and its height above the base.

Stillness may be used in gymnastics as a halt which occurs in the continuity of a sequence of movements, particularly in the form of a moment of stable balance. It is also usually required as evidence of complete control of the body at the start and the finish of a sequence of movements.

Turns

Turning actions are rotations of the body around selected axes. They have an important spatial ingredient. They may bring about a change of direction. The turn may be in one of the three main planes in space: in the sagittal plane (*wheel plane*) as are forward and backward rolls; in the vertical plane (*door plane*) as are cartwheels; or, in the horizontal plane (*table plane*) as are such stunts as the spinning top. Asymmetrical rolls may be discovered to be moving between these planes, and sequences which combine turns in the different planes will offer the experience of transitions between the planes.

Successive turns tend to create dizziness and a loss of orientation and/or a loss of balance. These difficulties are usually accepted as a challenge to bodily control in the gymnastic sequence. If the turn is less than, or more than, one complete rotation it creates a change of direction which adds variety to the movement and increases the sensitivity to the use of space.

Elevations

In gymnastics, elevations are exemplified by flight in which the body is elevated to such an extent that it moves through space without a base of support. An analysis should include the aspects of take-off and landings as well as the actual flight. The take-off is in the form of a spring which is usually preceded by a run, a swing or preparatory spring which builds up a momentum for the flight. Studies have shown that a crouch and hard stamp off the take-off foot[1], followed by a sudden and strong push-off gives the greatest elevation. According to the type of spring used, the take-off may be from one or both feet. Springs can also be generated off the hands. A preparatory bend in the elbows aids the explosive power. A coordinated swing of the legs and hip girdle often accompanies a spring off the hands. Neck springs, head springs and hand springs use the momentum of the legs and hips to add to the push of the hands.

Landings on the feet are described on page 111 where the action of the knees is discussed. When landing is on two feet, the knees should be well bent to absorb the impact of the body weight upon the base. An alternative is to land with a deep knee bend and allow the momentum to decelerate over a roll. If the landing is onto one foot, it is usual to dissipate the impact by spreading it over a series of running steps. When the landing is onto the hands as in a catspring, the weight is held only momentarily before being passed onto another part of the body — the feet in this case. In dives, the hands take the weight initially and pass it on to the neck and spine as the flight is merged into a roll. Occasionally the hands continue to support the body weight, as in a handstand, or a spring to hang from a rope or crossbar. In such cases, the spring may be somewhat minimized.

A word should be said as a reminder that the parts of the body which receive the impact of a landing should have the power to absorb the impact.

[1] John W. Bunn, *Scientific Principles of Coaching*, Prentice-Hall, Inc., Englewood Cliffs, N.J., 1955, p. 121.

The feet and legs and hip girdle are more powerful than the arms and shoulder girdle and should, therefore, be used for the greatest impacts. Parts of the body such as the knees, spine and head can receive the body weight as a form of transfer, but not as a form of impact.

The interval of flight between take-off and landing can be subject to considerable variation. The flight may stress height or distance. It may include an accompanying gesture such as a heel click or a pike. It may feature a special body shape. These additional stunts are particularly appropriate in gymnastics because they indicate a high degree of bodily control.

The flight may be used to mount the apparatus or to spring off it. It may be used to travel along it or to fly over it. When it is used in these ways, the performer is often working on a vaulting box, horse or buck, although he may be using a partner as a base of support. Alternatively he may be mounting or dismounting a Swedish beam, using a horizontal rope or a wall climber.

BODY SHAPE

The emphasis in gymnastics is on action tasks. These tasks bring into being varied and changing body shapes. Thus the performer will have the opportunity to develop an appreciation for the relationship between the action of the body and its shape. Extensions of the body give rise to elongated shapes (*pin-shape*) as occurs, for example, when the starting or finishing position is an erect stand. Body actions demanding flight may result in extensions such as the pin-shape in the dives. However, during an extended flight, the body is free to assume many different shapes. Extensions during the balances may result in pin-shapes, asymmetrical shapes or partial *wall*-shapes. The emphasis in the cartwheel is on a lateral extension and this results in the characteristic *wall*-shape of the body. Vaults and balances with legs parted will also tend to become wall-shaped. The *ball-shape* is the natural shape for the body in forward, backward, egg and shoulder rolls where the body is curled as completely as possible. Twisting actions will create *screw*-shaped body forms. The shape of the body grows quite naturally out of the basic function being used, but the awareness of, for example, curling to make a ball-shape usually brings about a more precise shaping of the curl movement.

SUMMARY OF BODY AWARENESS

Body action tasks place a particular stress on the self-testing challenge of retaining control of the body in movement under circumstances deliberately chosen for their difficulty. The management of the body weight in positions of greater or lesser stability is a major feature. The movement grows out of fluctuations between the basic functions of bend, stretch and twist. In some actions the movement of the parts is integrated into the major movement tendency of the whole body. In other movements, specific parts provide a contrast to the general movement tendency of the body. The actions of the body can be grouped into five categories: locomotion, gestures, turns, elevations and stillness.

The skills which have traditionally been regarded as the basic gymnastic movements — rock, roll, balance, hang, inversion, jumping down from a height, have now been considered as —

1. ways of transferring weight — rock, roll, jump
2. ways of supporting the body weight — balance, hang
3. inversions — a variation of support. Inversions will be more carefully analyzed under Space Awareness on page 124.

Thus a broad base is provided from which the individual performer may discover his own movements, some of which will be original to him, and some of which will be a rediscovery of traditional gymnastic movements.

EFFORT

In gymnastics, the first concern is predominately related to the body. The body action is the focus of attention. "What do I want to do — a roll, a balance, a vault?" is the question. However, as soon as the performer tries to execute what he has in mind, he is faced with the problem of *how* he will do it. Certain demands must be met. How strong an action is required? What speed is most suitable?

These questions indicate a need to consider the effort content which may be appropriate. The precise combinations of efforts used to execute the task will differ with the individual performer and the specific performance. However, some general considerations of the effort qualities appropriate to gymnastics can be discussed. An outline of analyses is given in Chapter 4.

EFFORT QUALITIES

If the real spirit of gymnastics is present, there is a strength and speed to the movement which gives it its characteristic vitality and vigour. This is true of the movement of the young child in particular. Older children, as they become more aware of their ability to control their movements, will also use lighter, finer tensions and slower actions.

Since the various activities which comprise this work are concerned with moving, holding or supporting the body weight, a good deal of muscular energy is expended and there is a need for an adequate degree of muscular strength particularly in the legs, the arm and shoulder girdle, and in the abdomen. The ability to support the body weight (above the floor or suspended from above) gives a great freedom of movement to the individual. The ability to spring — thrusting the body weight into space — and to land, absorbing the impact safely — adds further freedom.

However, the skill is not guaranteed by the presence of adequate muscular strength. The performer must become aware of the need for a degree of muscular tension whether he is moving or holding a position. This is the operational use of the *weight* factor (described on p. 58). If adequate tension is not retained heaviness will result and the body will become inert and unready for action. Over-tension is a waste of energy, cramps the body and causes it to be unprepared to move readily.

Strong action is required for the take-off for a jump, for the kick-ups used for handstands, for levering the legs upward in headstands or hangs from bars or ropes, for lowering the legs and hips slowly, for heaving a partner into the air, for landing on the hands from a spring in the air, or for landing on the feet from a flight. Gripping, pushing, pulling when working on apparatus or with a partner require strong movement. Swinging actions of the legs which build up momentum for a shift of weight, or the release of a twisting action which is used for the power it generates will demand strong tension.

While it is essential to become aware of the need of a strong tension for the purpose of raising, lowering or ejecting the body weight, the ability to create the required tension and to associate the feel of it with the action is also necessary.

However, true command of the situation requires that there be an awareness of the changing degrees of tension which make for efficient movement. For example, in a take-off, the step which precedes the spring has less tension than the spring itself. Once in flight there should be a decrease in tension and the feeling of elevation and of being airborne should be sought. In kicking the legs up to an inverted balance, there is an increase of tension up to and including the thrust off the floor and, thereafter, a decrease of tension until the point of balance is achieved. Then there may be an increase of tension to check the movement and keep it in the line of gravity. Once the point of balance is found, the tension decreases and an effort is made to feel an elevation upward. This is achieved by using fine tension.

Occasions where the stress is placed on lightness and fine tension do not predominate in gymnastics. Nevertheless, fine tension and lightness do play a vital role. The movement of suspension in a flight, the upward stress in a balance, the moment of arrival and pause on the apparatus will be characterized by lightness. Of course movements such as bouncing, running and landing can be done with a stress on lightness, in which case the intervals of flight will receive the emphases.

Changes in the degree of tension can be exploited to bring accents to a sequence of movements. The parts which quite clearly require strong tension will form a contrast to those which have a moment of suspension or pause. When the movements flow from one into the other with continuity, the moments of fine tension become the preparation for, (or the recovery from), the moments of firm tension. In this way the energy is conserved, efficiency promoted and a vital and interesting movement pattern developed.

While the effort qualities of firm and fine tension with their resultant strong and light actions give vitality to gymnastic movements and implement the control of body weight, the *time* factor also plays an important part. The speed of the movement can affect its efficiency. For example, a long dive into a roll requires a speedy run prior to the take-off. Coming backwards off a vaulting box to meet the floor with the shoulders, head, or forearms will require a slow movement backward and downward in order to prepare a base of support for the body weight — particularly because the parts touching the floor have no mechanical possibility of resilience or give.

Take-offs which depend on a spring will require a sudden push off the floor. The catspring explodes into action. A sudden twist may be required to change the direction of a flight. Sometimes the onward movement must be checked with a sudden tension as, for example, when the kick-up for an inverted balance has been too strong or when a landing has to be held to a confined spot.

Lifting the legs into a balance and arching backward into a bridge can be done slowly. Sometimes shoulder rolls or backward rolls or twists have to be done slowly in order to prepare for a transfer of weight to successive parts of the body or to free certain parts of the body to receive the weight.

There are occasions when the movement can be done quickly or slowly according to the proficiency or the whim of the performer or to the requirements of the challenge. For example, rolls, runs, and cartwheels can be done at various speeds.

As the proficiency of the performer develops the movement will be characterized by fluctuations in the degree of speed used. The variations of speed may take place within a single action or within a sequence of actions. The first situation may be illustrated by the changes required for a successful nip-up. The preparatory backward leg swing is likely to be slow, followed by a fast return swing and sudden whipping down of the legs coordinated with a sudden strong thrust off the hands. Within a sequence, contrasts and moments of accent may be built into a rhythmic pattern. A fast dive into a roll may decelerate into a slow levered headstand which is suddenly lifted into a handstand which moves into two accelerating rolls which burst into a catspring, then decelerates sharply bringing the sequence to a standing hold. For safety, the speed changes must be logically related to the action being performed.

Frequently strength and speed are linked as is the case in a vigorous take-off. However, strength and slowness are characteristic of some levered actions where strength replaces the momentum built up by a vigorous swing. Speed with relative lightness are linked to give the resilient bounce used in repetitive jumps or the hops which precede some flight patterns. Lightness and decelerating speed usually combine to give light arrivals onto apparatus from preparatory flights.

The characteristic zest and exhilaration felt in gymnastics depends in large measure upon incorporating the changes of tension and speed into the performance of even the simplest action. The basic inclination toward the use of speed and strength is present in young children and should be retained and modulated as they become older and more experienced.

Much of the work in gymnastics is done with a *direct* spatial quality to the movement. This is especially true of symmetrical actions. For example, the dive, forward and backward rolls, leapfrog, the levered head or hand balances, and two foot take-offs all tend to be done with a core-like direction in space. The body approaches or leaves the base of support in a direct line. The force generated by the thrust off the floor passes through the centre of gravity and the body moves in a straight line. However, there are other situations which permit or require flexible movement. These occur in asymmetrical movements when one side of the body leads through turns and twists. For example, asymmetrical rolls, and jumps, twisting into or out of balances, hangs from beams or bars when twists and turns are used, twisting through small spaces such as window ladders, hoops or partner's legs or body arches; all these situations give rise to flexible movements.

As in the cases of speed and strength, the movement may stress directness to the exclusion of flexibility or it may show one merging into the other. Hence a twisting backward shoulder roll may merge into a symmetrical and direct forward roll out of which may emerge a levered headstand done with directness followed by twisting into a stance. Within a single action such as an asymmetrical flight, the body may be brought into symmetry and a direct, two-foot landing achieved.

The *flow* factor plays its part in gymnastics. It will aid in safety by giving the control found in *bound* flow as well as making available the vitality and attack which comes with a *free*-flow quality. Activities which have moments of stillness and stable balance are likely to be characterized by a degree of bound flow which promotes stopping. Kicking up to hold a hand balance, jumps to arrive and stop on a chosen spot (top of a box horse, window ladder) finishing positions, check points before a change of direction, can be expected to be done with an increasing degree of bound flow. These movements may be preceded by a free-flow take-off. In this case, the familiar fluctuation between the two types of flow will take place. Flights, rolls and spins are likely to be characterized by free flow and the performer must be prepared to "go with the action," being caught up, at least momentarily, in the flow. Within a sequence, the performer may determine whether the moment of pause will become a significant stop (with marked bound flow) or whether it will be a collecting point (with either a decrease in free flow or a slight degree of bound flow) before moving into the next action. For example, a series of four successive rolls could be examined for the extent of pause (decreasing free flow) between each roll.

Beginners tend to do an action and stop; do another and stop; and so on. At this level there is no sequence or phrase of movement. There is no rhythm or climax, shape or continuity to the work. When the sequences flow with continuity, rhythm and shape, the body actions have been coordinated with appropriate effort factors. The transference or support of weight is done in such a way that the finishing position of one action becomes the starting position for the next one. The efforts fluctuate so that, for example, a strong tension decreases into a weak one or slow speed builds up to an accent of speed, or directness dissolves into flexibility or free flow is replaced by bound flow. The development of a sequence starts with the body actions which develop one from another in a logical way. The refinement comes through developing the appropriate efforts, judging what contrasts are already present and emphasizing them.

EFFORT ACTIONS

It is possible to think of gymnastics from the point of view of the operation being performed. For example, the feet *hit* the take-off board; the hands are *pressed* into the floor; the legs *slash* out to turn the body on a rope. These are appropriate uses of effort actions in performing certain operations. Since the performer is usually concentrating upon lifting, propelling or receiving the body weight, the effort actions which receive the emphasis are:

1. THRUSTS OR HITS (sudden, firm, direct): often used for take-offs and springs off feet or hands. They are also used immediately following the receipt of the first impact of weight in landings on feet or hands.

2. PRESSING (firm, sustained, direct): frequently used for slow lifts and lowerings; pressings onto the floor or apparatus to receive or raise the body weight; hand grips on apparatus; pushing and pulling. Many parts of the body are used in the various situations of pressing. In particular, the hands, feet, head, shoulders, knees, hips and some of the surfaces of the body press against the floor, apparatus or partner, as balances or transfers of weight are being done. In most cases slow, firm pressure will be applied straight through the line of gravity.

3. SLASHING (firm, sudden, flexible): may be used in such situations as the descent from a high inverted position to a landing on the feet. Sometimes it may be emphasized in the lower half of the body while the trunk or arms retain the support, for example, on climbing ropes, horizontal ladders or the beam. The whipping, twisting actions have the strength,

suddenness and flexibility to create the required momentum and power to lift and turn the body. It is the action required, for example, for a handless cartwheel or a round-off.

4. WRINGING (firm, sustained, flexible): may be used occasionally in asymmetrical actions. An example could be a descent from the beam with the legs or hips leading the action. A wringing effort action is particularly appropriate when the weight is taken on the hips, shoulders or other parts which have no resilience or spring to absorb an impact. Weaving the body through the window ladder may require wringing actions.

The lighter, fine-tension actions of dabbing, floating, flicking and gliding do not receive the same emphases in gymnastics as do the firm actions. They are not usually suitable for the main gymnastic action of lifting or lowering the body. They are more likely to be used as preparatory or recovery actions. For example, in a resilient bounce, there is an alteration of thrusts and glides. Preparations for twisting or wringing asymmetrical rolls often take the form of floating actions. Preparatory swings tend to be glides which are transformed into thrusts as the body weight is moved.

However, the actions of recovery and preparation are very important to the conservation of energy, to finesse in movement, and to the satisfaction derived from a sequence of movement. Initially, the main actions will dominate but as the sequence is practised and mastery is attained, the relationship between preparation, action, recovery and/or preparation for the next action, will become a reality. The rhythm, the ebb and flow of successive actions will be given their proper place. The appropriate effort actions help to bring control and, indeed, are essential to proper execution. The accenting of appropriate qualities can bring beauty, interest and thrill to gymnastics.

SPACE AWARENESS

Gymnastics require that the body be controlled in space. Therefore, the performer must develop an awareness of the various concepts of space which relate to his movement.

The theory is presented in Chapter Four. The application of the theory to gymnastic movement is made in the following section.

PATHWAYS IN SPACE

In the beginning stages, locomotor movements will tend to be done with the body moving forward, and most pupils will circulate about the periphery of the gymnasium. This is quite reasonable, because it is an easy way of avoiding collisions. However, it is very restricting. Greater freedom is possible if the pupils move in their own pathways, seeking out open spaces and consciously avoiding others. This will tend to produce weaving pathways. However, as soon as jumps, running take-offs, handsprings, cartwheels or balances are being used, there will be a greater need to dodge one another. Thus sharp changes of direction tend to give rise to zigzag and angular floor patterns.

The selection and placement of apparatus will stimulate varied pathways. Different angles of approach to the apparatus; varied ways of moving from one piece to another; attention directed toward making good use of the floor areas close to the apparatus, will all influence the pathways used.

In floor and matwork, concern for the relation of one movement to another and to the area allotted to the individual will make demands on the pathway used.

DIRECTIONS

The direction of a movement must be comprehended in terms of a personal orientation. That is to say, the performer distinguishes a forward or a backward roll in terms of bending forward into the former, and in terms of tipping backward onto his seat and spine for the latter. (See page 52). He jumps forward, backward, to the right or left according to his orientation to the front, back and sides of his own body. He jumps to reach upward or he crouches down in relation to his vertical axis.

Simple directional changes can be found in the movements of primary children, but it takes a good deal of experience and maturity for a genuine orientation in space to be established. Such complications as a swing to the left with the right arm or leg; a crab walk to the right, left, forward and backward are difficult to comprehend. The body's orientation in the inverted, tipped and twisted movements and positions may have to be clarified for even the experienced performers. This precise awareness of direction is much more than a mechanical labelling. It is a kinesthetic feeling within the body that must be given opportunities to grow. Its growth will require the help of the teacher in terms of the challenges which make demands on the sense of direction; the use of apparatus which elicits directional changes; the number of times the pupils enter into these experiences throughout their schooling.

It is natural to overuse the forward direction. Pupils should be encouraged to try out the backward, upward, sideways or downward directions. They will discover that some directions are more compatible to a given movement than others. For example, a body curl forward has greater range and can be done with greater ease than a body curl backward. The part of the body which is used as a base will affect the directional changes which may develop. The use of the transference of weight may be found to stimulate successive changes of direction. Conversely, it may facilitate retaining the original direction throughout the action. Asymmetrical rolls with different parts leading into them result in successive changes of direction. Symmetrical backward rolls usually maintain a constant directional focus.

Gesture movements or movements which are led by a special body part may be directed outward into particular points of orientation in space. For example, in the window ladder, the performer might be supporting the weight on the pelvis while the arms and legs are extended sideways and backward. The head might be inclined forward and upward as a counter-balance. In a star jump, the body will retain the vertical axis while the legs and arms are extended diagonally outward. Movements like these are called *chordic* movements because two or more parts of the body are moved simultaneously into specific and different directions in much the same way as the fingers strike their own particular note in a chord of music. These tendencies will appear spontaneously when balances or outward extensions are being sought. When they are recognized and understood, the movement will become more meaningful and will be executed with greater clarity.

In some movements, the body (or part of it) passes through a succession of points which lie within one of the three planes. In the case of forward or backward rolls, walkovers, headsprings and handsprings, the movement lies in the sagittal or *wheel* plane. Cartwheels, lateral swings, side rocking, log rolling and similar activities move in the *door* plane. In some activities such as the spinning top, the sweep of movement lies in the horizontal or *table* plane. Horizontal swings of the legs while the body hangs from the apparatus, turns which flatten out parallel to the floor or which are done with the body lying flat will also be in the *table* plane.

Sequences can be composed of movements which lie within one particular plane. Conversely, the sequence can be built on movements which lie in the three different planes. Moving within a plane will lead to the development of special types of movements. Alternating between the planes will help to clarify where in space the movement occurs and challenge the performer's balance and ingenuity in developing the transitions between the planes.

So far the discussion has been upon the direction of the performer's movement. The direction has been understood in terms of "forward" being the same as "the direction into which the breastbone is pointed" (See p. 52).

However, it is also necessary to consider the occasions when the orientation is upon space in general. For example, the performer may choose to do a series of forward rolls, each roll being done in a different direction on the mat. This would result from making a turn into a new direction between the recovery from one roll and the take-off for the next one. Such a concentration would bring about variety in floor pattern and add changes of direction with a repeated rebuilding of the focus; but, insofar as the action in relation to the body is concerned, the directional orientation remains fixed. It is always forward. In other cases, the performer may wish to play with a change in personal orientation and use, for example, forward, backward and side rolls while at the same time moving continuously down the mat from one end to the other.

The varied movements which are used in gymnastics lead towards participation in the three levels of space. Some forms of locomotion such as rolls, crawls and springs onto or off the hands make use of the *low* level. Running, cartwheeling and forms of movement which stress the feet as a vehicle for travelling tend to be done in the medium level; while leaps, jumps and reaches move into the high level. Activities which carry the body through different levels are a challenge to the control of body weight. To run, leap, land, roll and recover is very demanding in terms of bodily strength and balance. As the body moves through the three levels, the ability to select appropriate movement qualities, body shapes and parts of the body to receive weight, is tested. Similarly, to mount onto apparatus and to dismount from it causes the body to move through at least two levels. It should be noted that, once mounted on the apparatus, the body is found to be in a newly created situation. It will then move in levels which are related to the new base. Hence, in jumping onto the vaulting box, the body enters the high level. In rolling along the top of the box it is moving at a low level in the new situation. In holding an inverted balance on the top of the box, the medium level is used. In springing high to leave the box, the high level is used; but in arching down from a stride sitting position a low level descent is used.

Parts of the body have a level of normal operation. The head, and the arms, when they are raised, normally move in the high level. The legs normally move in the low level. Many gymnastic activities bring about an inversion of the body in space. This happens when the arms, head or shoulders bear the weight at a low level and the hips, legs and feet are extended upward into the high level. In other movements, the legs may swing up into medium level, or the whole body may be taken into the low level. The extent to which the performer encompasses a good range of levels in his movement will be largely dependent upon the strength and energy available for moving his body from one level to another. It will also depend upon his confidence in his ability to control his body weight and upon his awareness that the levels do, in fact, exist.

EXTENSIONS IN SPACE

Movements may be made on a small or a large scale, or of a size somewhere between these two extremes. The possibility of varying the size of a movement does not often occur to a beginner. However, it may be discovered that forward rolls can be extended into dives and dives can cover a short distance or an extended one. Jumps may vary in height or distance covered. Swings which build up the momentum for a transfer of weight usually start fairly small in size and develop into a full swing. The ability to use large movements or to extend the distance or height covered is closely linked with increasing ability to control the body. A high degree of strength and a good sense of balance and timing are usually required before the pupil begins to attempt these variations.

While on one hand, extension is related to the size of the movement, on the other hand it is related to the distance from the point of reference. In most cases, the point of reference is the base of support. Hence, hangs and swings from a bar can be done with a long or short arm grip. Back rolls can be done with the body in a tight ball or with a body extension. Inverted balances can be done with knees bent or legs straight; with weight on head and bent arms or on hands and straight arms. Once again strength and a good sense of balance are required before most extended forms are attempted.

In sequence work, a movement may be repeated with a change in size or extension. This will give variety, rhythm, contour and climax to the sequence and gives evidence of mastery of the more difficult forms of the activities.

To summarize, the foregoing aspects of space study seem to have most significance for the work in gymnastics. However, it may be well to remember that the body action which is being used is the starting point. Only after the purpose of the movement is established and the control of the body is generally established can the spatial aspects of the movement become evident. This can lead on to clarification through the growing awareness of use of the various aspects of the spatial component.

RELATIONSHIPS

It is quite clear that gymnastic movements and sequences are made in relation to the apparatus which is being used. It is also possible to have movements develop out of a relationship situation with other performers. Some aspects of the relationship possibilities in gymnastic activities will be discussed next.

RELATIONSHIP OF GYMNASTIC MOVEMENT TO THE FLOOR

The floor can be one of the most valuable assets in gymnastics lessons and care should be taken to see that it is kept clean, free from splinters and reasonably warm. Hardwood floors provide one of the best working surfaces. Cement and tile are hard, allowing no spring or give. They can also be cold and linoleum tile can be slippery.

Mention has been made (p. 111) of the advisability of working barefooted. This point is re-emphasized here with the reminder that the feet are then free to work to full capacity and that to work this way is to improve the strength and versatility of the feet.

Feet and legs are the strongest and most versatile parts of the body upon which to take the body weight. It is likely that attention will be given to foot actions, for example, running, walking, sliding, hopping, with stress on resilience in absorbing the shock of body weight as the foot meets the floor. Hands and arms, although weaker, less versatile, and less efficient than the feet, are other body parts to use in meeting the floor and absorbing the shock of the body weight.

Attention should be given to "meeting the floor" safely very early in the gymnastic experience so that pupils will not be afraid of the floor. Security in this matter gives freedom, reduces tension and resistance to activity. It must be stressed that this is a matter which needs careful attention. It will not take care of itself. Reference should be made to the details given on p. 106 in the discussion on weight transference.

Another point of view is to regard the floor as a working surface and to experiment with activities which are performed "close to the floor," "far from the floor," "off the floor," "coming down to the floor," "going away from the floor" — all relationship themes.

When mats are used, it is profitable to explore the activities which are most appropriate to the two different surfaces. Surely, if the class has a good command of transfer of weight by rolling, and are performing good rolls on the floor, there would be reason to question "Why do a roll on the mat?" Two-part sequences can develop out of contrasting activities which are suited to the floor with those which are suited to the mat. It may be pointed out that in situations where mats are in short supply this sort of discrimination has an added advantage.

RELATIONSHIPS OF GYMNASTIC MOVEMENT TO SMALL EQUIPMENT

Small equipment such as hoops, crossbars supported on wooden blocks, utility boxes (36-inch cubes or 24-inch x 36-inch x 18-inch units), beanbags and individual mats can be used to advantage, especially by pupils aged five to ten. In most cases, the equipment should be left in place and the body manipulated around, over, under, through, in and out, up to and away from it. These words may be regarded as "relationship words" because they describe how the movement is related to the equipment. For example, if a hoop is placed on the floor, there are many ways in which one can go "in and out" of it: by jumping on two feet while always facing the centre of the hoop; by jumping into it, landing on hands first and then feet and coming out hands first. The possibilities are many.

Small equipment can be used for several purposes. It is a stimulus to movement, helping pupils to think of many activities which they can do. It adds interest and fun to a lesson. It gives pupils an awareness of the principle of relationships. It can serve as a preparation for the use of large apparatus. It is relatively cheap and equipment can be supplied in sufficient quantities that the individual may be active for the whole lesson. It helps in making generalizations. For example, it is possible to find ways of going "over" a rope, a hoop, a beanbag, a utility box, an individual mat, and a wooden block. This allows for the question, "What are the characteristics of 'over'?" "Over," means that no contact is made; one has to clear a target; some elevation is required; there will be a form of take-off and a form of landing. Knowledge, i.e. awareness, allied with physical skill is one of the purposes of the lesson.

The small equipment may be combined to help acquaint pupils with sequence building. For example, a rope may be laid out as a line on the floor, and a hoop placed at one end of it. Pupils may find ways to go from one end to the other of the equipment. It is likely and desirable that two different types of actions will be used. For example, a balance walk on the rope might be followed by a hop into the hoop and a jump out of it. So the sequence would become a balance walk followed by a hop and a jump. Floor patterns may be elicited from the layout of two or three pieces of equipment. For example, a right-angled turn may be formed by the way the equipment is placed. Or an increasing or decreasing zone made by placing two ropes in a V formation may elicit an experience of extension in space.

RELATIONSHIP OF GYMNASTIC MOVEMENT TO LARGE APPARATUS

Useful stationary apparatus may include climbing frames composed of vertical window ladders or stall bars. Connecting units may include the horizontal ladder, a beam or two adjustable beams, one above the other, a horizontal bar, a swinging ladder or ropes. Other items may include the vaulting box, pommel horse, bar box, and balance benches, some with clip attachments which permit them to be inclined against the bar box or the window ladders. A curtain of climbing ropes and a generous supply of tumbling mats are also valuable.

Becoming acquainted with the apparatus

There is always a period, long or short depending upon the experience of the pupil, of adjustment to the apparatus. It is tried out for stability, height, working surfaces, intervals between units, amount of spring and so on. The next stage is to find out what use can be made of the apparatus. With primary children, most of the work they do is concerned with these two stages and is in answer to the challenge "What can you do on the apparatus which is safe for you and safe for your neighbour." Junior children will probably need a fairly lengthy experimental period each time the apparatus is regrouped. Intermediates should require a relatively short amount of time at this stage if they have had a good program previously.

Activities concerned with relationships to apparatus

The next stage can be voluntary rather than spontaneous adaptation to the apparatus. In this stage, which is likely to start at the junior level and be elaborated upon at the intermediate level, the pupil may be required to solve a problem of relationship. For example, they can accept such challenges as: "Find ways of *going along* it, different ways of getting *up on* it, different ways of getting *off* it, ways of going *over* it." The relationship challenges are likely to be: along, up, off, across, over, in and out, under, around, through, use it as a support, on and off, up, down. Looked at from the point of view of how pupils will react to the apparatus, these are the ways in which they are likely to use the equipment. Of course, how this is done — with what use of the body, with what spatial ingredients — become further considerations once again pointing up the wholeness of movement.

Sequences related to apparatus

The apparatus may be grouped in different ways so that a series of two or more types of adaptation are elicited. For example, an inclined bench, a bar box placed crosswise and a mat, might elicit "going along, over, down and along." Or it might be handled in terms of "getting up and getting down." For another example, use of the window ladder, beam and mat might allow a sequence which includes up, through, down, along and off. The movements may develop as the performer moves from one piece of apparatus to the next. On the other hand, one piece may be used more than once before the performer moves to the next piece. Occasionally, the teacher may decide that pupils could benefit from the challenge of arranging their own apparatus and then using it suitably. This can be quite a good test of their sense of relating movement to apparatus.

RELATIONSHIPS WITH OTHER PEOPLE

Working alone

The ability to express individuality without interfering with others is a basic learning in personal relationships which must be cultivated early in order to permit the freedom required for this way of working. Pupils can learn to "move in your own pathway" or to "dodge others." The first is a spatial challenge. The second is a relationship challenge. They will bring about fairly similar results, but they will bring them about by different orientations of the mind. In the first, the pupil is concerned with where he goes and he may pause momentarily or speed up briefly to accommodate his progress to that of his neighbour. "Dodging others" has a slight competitive overtone suggesting narrowly avoiding contact but the focus is on the *other* person. "Work by yourself," "Keep out of others' way," "Work so that you touch no one and no one touches you" (often used for very young children), "Do things which are safe for you and safe for others," "Use the equipment in ways that let everyone work all the time," are all relationship challenges where the orientation is upon judging how the performer's actions will affect others. It is fascinating to see how honest and skilled children as young as the five-year-old can be in honouring this challenge.

This attitude of relating personal action to the action of others should be cultivated from the very first lesson. It should be expected as a standard of work in subsequent lessons and if pupils become forgetful, the teacher will have to make them aware of their irresponsibility.

Partners

There will come a stage, occasionally at age seven, and more usually at age eight, when pupils spontaneously seek out a partner with whom to work. Thereafter, pupils enjoy occasions when they can work with one or more people with an interdependence or a unity of purpose involved.

One way of getting on/off a box.

As in games, the relationship might be one of: sharing the equipment, taking turns, matching the partner, or following the leader. Frequently there are gymnastic situations in which partners relate on the basis of adapting to each other. For example, they may plan a sequence that depends on timing to prevent collisions; or on body shape (one stride leaping over the other's forward roll).

When pupils grow large enough and strong enough to partially or wholly take each other's weight a new field of partner relationships opens. Three main ways of working with a partner are:

1. WORKING WITHOUT CONTACT. In this case, the relationships may be around, under, over, through, passing, up to and away from, matching, and following the leader. An example of a usable theme is: twisting through body shapes. Usually partners alternate between transferring weight to parts which create a space through which the partner may twist on the way to halting in a new position which can be similarly used. Continuity of action in these circumstances can be an added challenge.

2. WORKING WITH CONTACT BUT WITHOUT SHARING BODY WEIGHT. The problem is usually given to the class to solve. They should choose the parts which will make the contact, and select their starting positions. They may limit the work to the original contact and find out what movement is possible. They should mould it into a sequence which has rhythm, contrasts, climax and conclusion. A great deal of sensitivity is required for success. In another form, the challenge might require that they build the movements on continually changing contacts using many different parts of the body before the sequence is finished. Varying the form of contact is another way to approach the idea. So it might be a grip, an interlocking, a hook on, a touch. This type of work sharpens the sensitivity and will probably provide ideas which can be used on the apparatus.

3. CONTACT WHICH INVOLVES WEIGHTBEARING. One partner might take the entire weight of the other, or, a partner might take some of the other's weight. In the latter case, partner #2 would be in contact with the floor, the wall or a piece of apparatus. A useful experience is to share your weight with a partner in order to do an action. For example, partners can run to meet each other and help each other turn by locking elbows and using centrifugal force to speed the turn, or they may assist the turn by bouncing off one another with a hands-to-shoulders contact. Other solutions may be sought and other situations, in which a partner's weight can assist an action, can be discovered. It is interesting for partners of dissimilar size to try such things as a Chinese Sit-up or a "two-hand-sit" by sharing each others weight in the right proportions.

These sorts of experiences are fun but they also heighten sensitivity, expose cause and effect, require cooperation and concentration. They widen the individual's range of movement qualities because he is required to adapt to his partner's movement qualities from time to time. The work should probably be taken as far as the level of producing a sequence which has been practised to a high standard of performance and which may be presented to the whole class for analysis and appreciation.

The partner work suggested so far has the advantage of requiring no equipment and, therefore, can be used in schools which have limited supplies. Most of it can also be adapted to include the use of small equipment or of large apparatus.

Groups

Pupils can quite profitably work in groups of threes or fours. Occasionally, it may be suitable to work in fives or sixes, but care should be taken that the size of the group does not cause some to be wasting time waiting for a turn.

True group work means that all members of the group are needed to contribute to the movement being undertaken. For example, a sequence may be developed wherein two members lift, swing, lower or carry the third member. Four, five or six may work at an apparatus station relating their work to each other on the basis of timing, pathways, matching movements and other common goals.

It should be noted, however, that a small number of pupils can work at an equipment station at one time without having a group relationship situation in operation. In such a case, it becomes a matter of working as individuals and being careful not to interfere with others. This situation is common in the primary and junior grades. The teacher and pupils will have an understanding of working rules — talking, personal contact, watching and so on. It is highly recommended, particularly for kindergarten, primary, and junior children that *all* should use the apparatus *all* the time. Therefore, they should know how to make their own pathways, how to keep out of the way of others, and how to choose their own starting positions. The *floor* should be regarded as part of the station and its use will reduce crowding on the apparatus. Of course, teachers must accept responsibility for putting a suitable number of pupils at each station.

This concludes the application of movement principles to gymnastics. While examples of working situations and challenges have been used to illustrate the points being made, a full discussion of teaching methods and lesson themes has been reserved for Chapter Nine.

SEVEN

DANCE

The material to be presented in this chapter will be an attempt to apply Laban's concepts of movement to dance. The criteria of analysis was presented in Chapter Four.

It has already been suggested (Chapter Three) that dance is the expression of ideas or feelings manifested through the medium of bodily movement. It is characterized by a rhythmic content. It may involve one or many people and it may have a high degree of social interchange but it is rarely competitive in nature. For these reasons it offers an experience which is quite different from participation in games or in gymnastics.

Since we are concerned with dance in education, it is necessary to define three kinds of dance experience which may be selected to serve the needs of the pupils at different stages of their development. In this book, the words "dancing," "dance study," "a dance" will be used to identify different experiences. "Dancing" will simply be regarded as responding to the urge to express oneself in dance movement in a spontaneous manner. A "dance study" will designate a simple or miniature composition which embraces many or most of the attributes of a dance. It is used by a student of dance in the process of his dance education. A "dance" will be the term applied to the art form expressed in movement. The art form is an attempt to convey ideas or feelings through carefully selected patterns which are arranged in a form judged to be best to meet the needs of that particular communication. The following quotation is helpful in establishing a definition of dance as an art form: ". . . those festive dances of New Guinea which are prepared for weeks, months, and years in advance until every movement and position is mastered. For it is just this mastery, this conscious and calculated elaboration and formulation which divides art form from play and improvisation."[1]

---

[1] Sachs, Curt, *World History of Dance*, W. W. Norton and Co., Inc., N.Y., Norton Library Edition, 1963, p. 225.

A "folk dance" may be regarded as a dance form, the patterns of which have arisen out of a process of natural group expression rather than out of deliberate selection. Its patterns and spirit have become traditional through the reenacting of the dance in successive generations.

The questions before us now are:
- What is the expression of a particular movement?
- Why does a particular movement convey a particular expression?

BODY AWARENESS

In dance, the body is the instrument of expression. Therefore, a precise awareness and control of bodily movement is very important. The rate at which this awareness and control are developed will vary from one individual to another. It will be modified by the individual's interest in dance and opportunities to dance, as well as by the instruction which he receives.

It is very important for him to discover the flow of movement which moves between the centre of the body (trunk) and the extremities of the body (the arms and legs). A movement may start in the extremities and flow into the centre or it may move in the reverse direction. When such an interchange of movement exists, whether it occurs naturally or by study and practice, an integration of the bodily movement is achieved.

The following analysis starts with an examination of the movement expression in the basic body functions (bend or curl, stretch, twist of the body) and then proceeds with an examination of the role played by the limbs.

BASIC BODY FUNCTIONS (BEND OR CURL, STRETCH, TWIST)

What expression is involved in the curling or stretching or twisting body? The answer may be discovered by exploring these movements and attempting to recognize the accompanying feelings. However, predictions can be listed.

Bending or Curling can be done so that the feeling may be:
- shutting the world out; concentrating on oneself
- protecting oneself
- prostrating oneself: a bow, obeisance, worship
- fatigue, hopelessness, yielding
- shrinking

Stretching can be done so that the feeling may be:
- facing the world, or a situation
- joy, exhilaration, exuberance
- giving oneself
- asserting oneself; pride, dignity, rank
- asserting oneself; attack, aggression
- growing or projecting outward

Pupils are beginning to allow all parts of the body to participate in the movement, thus contributing to the feeling.

Twisting can be done so that the feeling may be:

- shrinking and turning away
- protecting oneself
- rejecting something, someone, an idea
- horror, terror
- hiding
- momentary withdrawal in order to attack unexpectedly.

Bend or curl, stretch, twist

The parts of the body may contribute to the bending or curling, stretching, twisting movements of the trunk. The action could be initiated in one of the parts and flow into the body to become an integrated movement. Or the action could start in the trunk and spread to the limbs, or the movement in the limbs might be used as an accompaniment to the main action. For example, when crouching in an expression of self-protection, the legs may be used to step backward as the arms move up to cover the head. Or, in an expression of increasing fatigue, the legs can be used with increasingly slow and heavy steps and the arms swing limp while the body droops forward from the head and shoulders. In the first situation the parts of the body are drawn into actions as part of the curling of the trunk. In the latter situation, the arms and legs offer an accompaniment to the droop of the trunk. Little children instinctively integrate the parts with the whole, probably because they are genuinely involved in what they are doing. Older children and adults, especially beginners in dance, tend to isolate the movement of the extremities from the movement of the trunk, making disharmonious movements with the limbs, or forgetting to use them at all. This is usually because they are not caught up in what they are doing, but are superficially "going through the motions" without involvement. They have reservations, or are embarrassed, or have preconceived notions about the necessity of dance being "pretty." Much will depend on how the teacher words the challenge. It probably should be stated in terms of feeling or motivation: "Withdraw cautiously. You sense the presence of danger." Or, "The idea is to contrast a withdrawal with a rushing forward. The withdrawal is quiet and unaccented, the rush forward is strong, positive, emphatic."

The point being made here is that the movement of dance stems from the inner feeling of the dancer. Hence, the teacher, in attempting to work in this context, should help the dancer to establish an inner reaction to the theme of the dance. This means that, in dance, the teacher must help the dancer to discover the expressive overtones inherent in the movement situation. This is quite different from the teacher's role in gymnastics or games, where he draws the pupil's attention to the function which the movement is to fulfill. In this latter case, he may point out that as a preparation for a forward thrust, the body is rocked slightly backward before the forward spring occurs. The challenge may be: "Find a way of drawing backward as a preparation for stepping forward as you throw the ball. Feel the body moving in support of the throwing arm." To summarize, in dance the movement is expressive, in games and gymnastics it is functional.

Parts stressed

There are some dances in which the stress is placed very much on a particular part of the body. For example, most folk dancing places a great deal of stress on foot patterns. Running, walking, skipping, sliding, galloping dances are a few of the choices. They are danced to traditional music and the rhythms seem particularly suited to stimulate or accompany the foot patterns. There are also the more complicated step patterns of step-hop, schottische, polka, two-step, waltz, rhumba, tango, mazurka, hambo and so on, which have suitable forms of accompaniment. It is also possible to create dances based on various free forms of foot patterns or locomotion that are done to free rhythms or, alternatively, do in fact conform to metrical rhythms. For example, it is possible to create a "Rain Dance" in which the use of the feet is selected to portray the varying sounds of rain: the single warning drops, the shower, the torrential downpour, the sudden respite between showers. The rhythms are free in the sense that they are not in 4/4 or 6/8 metre but swell and surge and die in accordance with what is being portrayed about RAIN. On the other hand, it is also possible, for example, to portray some characteristics of a train with the feet. Records can be found which offer a musical portrayal of a train, for example, *The Wabash Cannonball*.[2] In this case the dance composition would start with response to the music and it would have a metrical rhythm, though the foot patterns and forms of locomotion might be highly original and thus be classified as "free form."

Foot patterns are only one way of stressing the use of feet in dance. The parts of the feet may be made significant. For example, the heels, the toes, the way the foot is used (toes turned in or out), the stress given to one foot, all these can be used to express certain ideas or moods.

Similarly, the knees, the legs, the hips, the abdomen, the back, the sternum, the shoulders, the head, elbows, hands, even fingers can assume significance in a dance. Hawaiian dances are very much dances of the hands. Rhumba rhythms encourage the use of the hips. Many primitive dances place particular stress on a selected part of the body. In creative dance, young children happily respond to challenges, particularly rhythmic stimuli, which encourage a use of a particular part of the body. Older children, and teachers of limited experience, sometimes need the reminder that these responses are not as unique as they may seem! It is most helpful to experiment with the use of various parts of the body "dancing." It frees the mind from narrow assumptions, it helps the performer to know himself and to feel himself, thus it contributes to an awareness of the body image. It helps to improve muscular control and rhythmic response.

Awareness of the relationships of part to part

If the meeting and parting of different parts of the body are discovered to be a significant part of a dance, or, if in a dance study, a search is made

---

[2] Folkraft F1006B *Wabash Cannonball*.

for the ways in which meeting and parting might be done, certain possibilities of expression may be discovered. These movements may give the impression of a jaunty overflow of exuberance or well-being. For example, heel clicks, jumps with heel clicks, hand claps, finger snaps, jumps with heels kicking the seat, struts with knees meeting elbows or fists all can suggest jauntiness or bravado. Or, the meeting of parts can be done with such a sweep as to give the impression of gathering something in; or the parting can seem to scatter something abroad (flowers, seeds, money, good wishes). Or, the meeting can be a careful investigation; the parting, an abandonment of responsibility. These suggestions are not meant to be exhaustive, but may point the way to the discovery of further meanings. It should be noted that there may be a tendency to stress arm actions. Pupils should be helped to discover how significant a good movement in any part of the body can be: the flip of a shoulder, the turning of a knee, the drag of a toe can all be very expressive.

As in games and gymnastics, a part of the body can lead an action with the body following and a transfer of weight ensuing. For example, the action of rising might be led by an elbow, a turn led by a knee, a sinking action by a shoulder. The feeling that is occasioned by a particular body lead should be sought. The rhythm and the spatial design arising from the body lead should be appreciated.

The symmetrical and asymmetrical uses of the body in dance will not only create the same conditions of stability and mobility as occur in games and gymnastics but they may be deliberately selected for the purpose of conveying feelings of stability or mobility respectively. For example, suppose an abstract dance (i.e. nondramatic) is being created and a contrast between calm determination and agitated indecision is required. One group might arrange itself as a solid square facing in one direction. Each dancer might alternate rising movements with sinking movements of a firm, sustained quality. Body symmetry might be retained and the movements might be restricted to the door plane. The other group might be scattered rather widely, facing in random directions. They might use asymmetrical actions and body shapes, such as turning, twisting, leaping, or running with changes of direction. The contrast between stability and mobility would be clearly delineated and the choice of symmetrical and asymmetrical movements respectively, would be equally clear.

Sometimes, a movement theme may be best expressed through movements which give an impression of stability. Hence, symmetrical movements will be likely to dominate. For example, such ideas as majesty, forthrightness or determination connote a stable quality and may best be expressed by emphasizing symmetrical body movements. On the other hand, asymmetrical movements may be stressed if one wishes to create an impression of chaos, changeability or uncertainty because these conditions suggest a state of mobility. In themes concerned with such ideas as those of a squall, the rocking of a boat, the insecurity of a refugee or the erratic play of a child, asymmetrical movement of the body may be emphasized because these situations are characterized by mobility.

BODY ACTIONS

The stillness of the body or the absence of all action can be a very powerful statement in dance. Pupils should experiment with creating a contrast between phrases of stillness and phrases of action. It should be noted that it takes a great deal of control to "cease action and hold still." It also takes a considerable amount of courage because one senses that it is a highly noticeable part of the dance. Psychologically, there is a tendency to equate stillness with zero or nothingness. Thus, the performer who has stopped and held the still pose with an all-out effort unconsciously wonders if the observer appreciates the significance of his performance or if he has made a fool of himself. If the psychology of the situation is recognized, pupils can have a wonderful time experimenting with the idea. The experiences with stillness should help to clarify the beginnings and endings of dance sequences which are usually slurred or "thrown away" by beginners.

The body shape, the action preceding and following the phrase of stillness, the relative time values, the way the stillness is produced (suddenly from action or gradually by deceleration) are all possible variables which can be explored.

The meanings which stem from moments of stillness should be appreciated. Dances can be inspired by the ideas which are suggested by the use of stillness. For example, a favourite theme of junior girls is that of bringing a doll to life for a little while. Boys sometimes like to suggest the "vagaries" of machinery which stalls. Groups can have fun with ideas related to responses to traffic lights. Ideas of surprise, immobility, loss of power, sudden catastrophe can make use of the impact of stillness.

Locomotion has been mentioned in terms of foot patterns (p. 140) and its special significance in folk dance suggested. Creative dance often makes use of other forms of locomotion such as rolls, elevations, slides and step-like actions like crawling and other original ways of travelling. These latter forms are often done with a free rhythm, though they may make use of a metrical beat. The idea or feeling of the dance will dictate the rhythm and style of the action. For example, a fugitive may run low, slide suddenly to a long pause, slowly crawl a few paces before rising, running hard and finishing with a wide leap. For another example, the animals in Noah's ark may parade two by two using many different actions! Moments of exuberance are likely to use skipping, running or leaping. Moments of sorrow are more likely to be symbolized by walking or walking patterns, even rolling, sinking and rising while moving forward or backward.

Examples of gestures have been suggested in the section dealing with the use of the body parts (p. 140-p. 141). By definition, gestures are movements of the body which do not involve the transfer of weight. Hence, the hands can wave, the leg swing, the head nod, the shoulder shrug, the elbow jab, the knee lift (if that leg is not supporting the weight). It remains to suggest that the scope, meaning and use of gestures should be explored. The way in which the body parts are moved, and the rhythm and accent which they create are important in dance. The gesture is usually compatible with the main body attitude or movement as was explained on p. 139.

Turns are often significant in dance. Their spatial patterning and design may be important to the dance — however, they also may have a very expressive quality. Both of these characteristics should be explored. In design, the basic shape is circular, but a turning circle can create other beautiful and varied designs. The spiral, the in-turning, the out-turning circles, the rising or falling circles, the travelling circles, the shrinking or expanding circles all have lovely design possibilities. If an attempt is made to discover the expressive significance of turning, it might be found to convey impressions of: confusion, chaos, searching, joy, excitement, an embracing of all the world, a "turning one's back" on a situation. It is interesting to realize that multiple spins create a physical dizziness. Our own knowledge and experience of the phenomenon influences us to interpret certain forms of spins in a dance as expressing confusion and chaos or a dizzy abandon.

WEIGHTBEARING AND WEIGHT TRANSFER

It will be remembered that these operations are of prime importance in gymnastics and that it underlies efficiency in games. In dance, these matters are of importance to the extent that they help to increase the efficiency of the body as a tool for expression. In other words, if a beautiful jump with a knee gesture and a turn is required in a dance, hopefully, the dancer has the power to execute such an action and do it in excellent form. The ability to control the transfer of weight from one part to another is of prime importance to the *fine execution* of a dance. If one wishes to make a bright and breezy turn, giving the impression of carefree capering, the body must be able to turn without wobbling, without a great heaving preparation or a clumsy ending. This is what is meant by making an instrument of the body.

It should be mentioned here that the professional dancer is responsible for making his body a superb tool. We have other purposes in view for the child in school, namely, the cultivation of an awareness of himself and his world, the building of a security in expressing himself in movement as well as a suitable knowledge, understanding and control of his body. This points to the fact that techniques of movement should not take precedence over the larger scope of possibilities for learning. However, it must be clearly stated that an increasingly good body control is one of our aims.

Transference of weight

The awareness of how weight may be rolled from one adjacent part of the body to another is needed for control and balance. It is necessary to be aware that in walking the weight can roll from heel to toe in the foot and that a push-off is made in greater or lesser degree by the ball of the foot and the toes. This push-off increases until it becomes a spring in running, leaping, jumping. The pushing action should be taken through to the toes. Such a transfer of weight will be evidenced by the pointing of the toes when they are elevated off the floor. Body rolls, forward, backward, sideways, and asymmetrical ones on different parts of the body occur in dance. The ability to fall, often dramatically, requires that pupils know which parts (feet or hands usually) can meet the floor safely, accepting and controlling the body weight initially; and which ones (hips, shoulders et cetera) must receive the weight in transit.

This skill obviously has a close connection with gymnastics in that it is based on the ability to control the body weight in relation to the pull of gravity. By making references to the common problems a transfer of learning can be facilitated. After that the different expressions which are communicated by a fall or a roll will be the subject of examination in the dance classes.

Step-like actions, mostly those done by the feet, are part of this aspect of the work. The actual manipulation of step pattern naturally receives special attention in dance, particularly in folk dance where a polka, schottische, waltz or two-step are required. Once again, the kind of push-off, the part of the foot used, the inclusion of the bending of the ankles and knees in the preparation for the jump, and then the effective push-off which comes from the extension of the knees and ankles, all should receive attention.

The receiving of weight in landing from an elevation is mechanically the same in dance as it is in gymnastics and games. The initial action is a bending with some tension to kill the impact, followed by a stretching in the joints sufficient to direct the weight upward. This is followed by a repetition of the bend and stretch in diminishing size until the base is established. In dance this should appear to be easily executed. Thus the body will remain free to express the idea or feeling of the dance. Furthermore, jumps and landings will create rhythms and accents which will highlight the phrasing of the dance.

Body balance

Body balance of two types — stable (centre of gravity over the base) and mobile (centre of gravity outside the base) types — occurs in dance. If the impression being created is that of lifting a great weight, the stance will have to be taken over a broad base with legs and other parts of the body suitably bent. The mechanics of the lift must be correct. Stable balance will be needed. If the body is used in a flying and falling sequence, the centre of gravity must be moved outside of the base for the flight and remain there until such time as stable balance is again established. Frequently in dance, the body is poised high over a narrow base thus increasing the difficulty of balance. For example, to reach with both arms, fingers leading, as high above the head as possible, puts the weight in a narrow column above the balls of the two feet which are close together. The balance is very difficult. If the desire is to reach forward as far as possible, one hand (e.g. right) will be used, fingers leading. The weight will be on the ball of the right foot and most of the body will tend to be in the horizontal plane at the level of the hips. This too, is a very difficult balance. It is helped by using the left arm and leg and the head as *counterbalances* thus placing the centre of gravity over the base which is the right foot. It will be seen that when the weight is high over a narrow base even a stable balance is difficult to execute. This form of balance is commonplace in dance. The balance during turns often needs attention because the pull of centrifugal force, often centred in the head and shoulders, tends to relocate the centre of gravity. This is a feeling that needs to be experienced and the controls (positioning of head and shoulders) need to be developed.

In contrast to gymnastics, dance does not use balance as a self-testing competition. Dance attempts to overcome the difficulties of balance by means of superb control so that, as far as possible, the performer can do anything with his body that is required for what he is "saying" in his dance. Thus in the process of acquiring control, he must learn the laws of balance and practise until he can cope with meeting those demands.

BODY SHAPE

The shape the body makes is very significant to efficient games play because of the various functions the shaping can perform. For example, the wall-shape blocks the passage of a ball or an opponent, the screw-shape generates energy for throws, the pin-shape penetrates limited spaces without contact, the ball-shape gives mobility with power.

In dance, these body shapes can convey the same ideas symbolically. Therefore, in a theme of opposition wall- and pin-shapes may symbolize resistance and attack respectively. Fierce storms of action can be generated out of screw-shapes. Charging actions can be symbolized by the suggestion of a ball-shape. These are only a few examples of possible relationships between the shape of the body and the idea conveyed. Experimentation will reveal others.

The design of movement phrases may be created out of contrasting or changing shapes. These can be created by a single dancer or by small or large groups. For example, a group might move from a spearhead into a line, into a hollow circle. Or one dancer might assume a wall-shape and move in appropriate ways, more or less retaining that shape, while two others, with penetrating movements — one at low level and the other at medium level — opposed the obstruction. This might be an initial starting point for a dance for three based on some music — perhaps a specially composed "machine rhythm" or perhaps a selection of electronic music.

The idea that groups can form themselves into shapes, and that these shapes can continually reorganize themselves moving from one mass form to another is something quite new to most people. It is a theme that interests older children — eleven to fourteen years — and can be taken from the point of view of design or as an idea such as molding plasticine or nightmares or shapes on Hallowe'en. This theme can lead to the simulation of nature forms — cloud formations, ice floes or icebergs, changing scenery as viewed from a train window. There may be a tendency to become static. The idea should be used from the point of view of changing, melting and merging forms rather than from that of a tableau.

SPACE AWARENESS

Dance is a three-dimensional design that flows through space. Thus a knowledge of the rudiments of the theory of space should be cultivated and an ability to move well in space should be acquired.

What expressions are inherent in the various spatial components?

ORIENTATION

Directions

FORWARD. To move the body forward, to stretch the arms forward, to reach one arm forward, to kick the foot forward — not upward and forward, but forward — what is the meaning of the movement expression? It should be performed in an exploratory way in attempt to find the possibilities for expression. It will probably be found that the main feeling it to advance, to go to meet something. Therefore, according to how the advancing is done, one can portray greeting, intimidation, inquiry, search, pursuit and so on. The different possibilities will be revealed in the exploration.

BACKWARD is a retreat from something. Therefore, according to how it is done one can shrink, yield, withdraw, back up and so on.

SIDEWAYS. There are two possibilities because the body has two sides. If each side moves sideways in its own direction, the body is *opened*. The heart and vital organs are left relatively unprotected. Therefore, the action is a friendly one, an open, honest one, a revealing, exposing one. If each of the sides moves in the direction of the opposite side, the body *closes*. Thus the impression given is one of self-protection, privacy, secrecy, retention of something hidden. Other implications may be discovered by movement exploration.

UPWARD. If the body (or its parts) moves directly upward, there is a *rising* of the body or a focus upwards. This may be interpreted as a coming to life, an awakening, a resistance, aspiration, worship, or perhaps, intercession. Exploration will reveal other impressions.

DOWNWARD. If the body (or its parts) moves directly downward, a *sinking* action occurs. This may give the impression of settling down, of being finished, of terminating something. Or, it can be an obeisance, a submission to a greater force or authority.

If one reaches as far as possible in each of these directions in order, for example, from high to deep, then from right to left, and from forward to backward — one feels oneself moving through the axes of a triple cross which intersects in the centre of the body. One experiences the terminals of the movements as being six points located at the outer reaches of the body. The points which are established at the limit of one's reach (up, down, right, left, forward, backward) can be regarded as points of orientation in one's personal space (definition: Chapter Four, page 52). Various parts of the body may move in such a way as to pass through these points of orientation in a given order. For example, the right arm can lead the body into movement as it passes through high to right, to forward, to deep, to left, to backward, to high, making a circuit of the points. Other orders are possible which will encircle the body without retracing a pathway through any of the points. These pathways have been identified in Laban's writings. Other parts of the body, such as the head or knee, may lead the movement. As the body follows the leading part, it participates in the fluctuations into the different spatial directions. Each order of circuit will bring its own accents, rhythm, feeling and shaping. Each of these pathways and others developed by moving the body through a selected group of points of orientation (for example, from high to right to forward to high) could be regarded as a movement motif, which might be an interesting stimulus for a dance composed by pupils from Grade Seven or higher. See diagram at the end of this chapter on page 172.

Any of the motifs suggested above may bring about a dance characterized by changing shapes and rhythms and similar or contrasting movements between the participating dancers. In such cases, the enjoyment and expression is centred on these elements and the dance may be considered non-objective and non-dramatic. However, in other cases, the spatial aspects and relationship between the dancers may develop into a dramatic sequence. For example, rising and sinking can take on the dramatic expression of domination and submission; advancing and retreating can be linked with attack and flight. These motifs could inspire a dance drama or conversely, could arise spontaneously in the movement which expresses a dramatic sequence.

A movement may include a blend of two dimensions. For example, it may be a rising–and–advancing movement and it may be followed by a sinking–and–closing which terminates in a simple rise. Thus these blends, the following — rising–and–opening, retiring–and–rising, opening–and–advancing — and seven other combinations are possible. Exploration and movement studies related to these bodily orientations in space prove valuable and interesting. Movement of this degree of spatial clarity enriches dance studies in an immediately perceivable way. Even very young children may spontaneously incorporate two-dimensional movements in their dances. For example, occasionally young children decelerate a locomotor movement by travelling forward while sinking down to stop close to the floor. Or, they may start low down and travel forward as they rise. It may be possible to observe others who rise first and then move forward. Observation of contrasting ways of moving should stimulate interest in and awareness of the attitude to space which the individual may have.

So far attention has been given to movements which travel along the three dimensions or which arc about the periphery of the body, passing through the six points of orientation. Mention should now be made of movements which radiate inward or outward, to or from the centre of the body. These can be directed to or from the six points of orientation or (to) random points between them. Such movements as pushing, pulling and lifting tend to radiate out from or towards the centre of the body. The arms and legs are especially facile in describing radiating movements. In so doing, they create a variety of air patterns as, for example, when they move from high to the centre of the body and out into forward, right, left or back. Many such patterns are possible according to which part or combination of parts of the body are involved, and which starting and arrival points are stressed. Thus the body has the opportunity to collect itself after each expansion into or retraction from space. It may be noted that, in the above pattern, it moves from an elevation into a settling toward its centre and then into an advancing, opening, closing, or retiring movement. If both arms and one leg are engaged in leading movements out to the dimensional extremities, *chordic*[3] or *polylinear*[4] movements occur. Dance studies for three or more dancers, using a particular *chordic* movement or three sequences of radiating movements and their variations, can create particularly interesting spatial patterns and rhythms.

The chart given in Chapter Four on page 39 and pages 53 and 54 of the same chapter, mention the spatial orientations of the diagonals and the three planes. References[5][6] are given to Laban's books. Advanced

[3] Valerie Preston, *A Handbook for Modern Educational Dance*, Macdonald and Evans Ltd., London, 1963, p. 85.

[4] Rudolf Laban, *Choreutics*, Macdonald and Evans Ltd., London, 1966, p. 21.

[5] *Ibid.*, p. 14, p. 141-142.

[6] Rudolf Laban, *Modern Educational Dance*, Macdonald and Evans Ltd., London, 1948, p. 45.

dance study will take into account these and other spatial relationships. It is impractical to attempt to deal with these matters in this book, but at the same time, it is only proper to mention the importance of these aspects of space study and to encourage those who are interested to read and to seek instruction which will be of practical help.

Thus we become conscious of the association between the flux and flow of our movements, the constant and related change of body shapes and the interplay of pathways described by the different body parts in the course of their movements. In addition, we are aware that at times our movements extend beyond the original stance and we carry ourselves through forms of locomotion, off into the general space, describing various pathways, floor patterns and changes of direction. These patterns constitute much of the design and rhythm of a dance. In conjunction with changing relationships between dancers, the contrasting changes in spatial patterns may give a dramatic significance to the movement.

Dance studies may be improvised on space themes which are drawn from movements which relate to the dimensional cross or to pathways passing through certain points of orientation. In addition dance studies with a dramatic content may stem from spatial movements which provide contrasts or action and reaction relationships.

AWARENESS OF THE SPATIAL ENVIRONMENT

The movement of the body along the spatial dimensions represents changes of directions in personal space. That is, the sense of direction, or orientation, comes from the feeling within the body and the movements may be executed as described regardless of which wall of the room or part of the stage is being faced. Let us now consider the general spatial environment.

Space is all around us although it is limited by the floor or base on which we are supported. According to the way the movement is made — in effort quality and in spatial content — it is possible to *penetrate* space by moving through it with a very clear point of focus and perhaps with a quality that seems to convey the meeting of a certain degree of resistance. This can be done by a part of the body such as the pointing finger, or even the focussed gaze. Or, it can be done by the whole body which might rush in a straight line to stop at a seemingly chosen spot. A single dancer may do this or a group may be used.

On other occasions, the dancer may *expand into* space with leaps and turns and sweeping gestures. This may convey a feeling of freedom, liberty, generosity, social conviviality or the joy of having ample room in which to move. Conversely, the dancer may restrict himself in space, shrinking in body size and reducing his movements to a minimum. Exploration of this way of moving will expose other impressions which this attitude to space renders.

It is possible to *embrace* or *repel* space. In the first instance movements will be encircling, either in pathway or gesture, or both. In the latter case the movements will push away from the body in pathways which radiate out from a central base of resistance.

All of these attitudes towards space can be used as themes for dances or, if an expression of penetration or expansion is desired, it is possible that a spatial motif will convey it. For example, if a class wishes to compose a dance from the idea of "Born Free," the opening statement of the dance could be an expansion in space with leaps and turns and travelling to move into all parts of the available area, thus conveying the joy of unrestricted movement. Subsequent parts of the dance could make other statements about freedom, such as "freedom is the right to consort with people of one's own choice." This idea might be developed by using a relationship theme such as "meeting and parting" to give this impression of freedom of choice.

LEVELS IN SPACE

As dancers become sensitive to the space in which they move, and feel themselves a part of the ever-changing forms which exist in it, they become aware of the need to satisfy their sense of design, balance and proportion by moving in all three levels. Sinking and rising movements will necessarily carry them into the low and high levels respectively. However, in addition, they may become increasingly aware of the variety of movements which are possible to perform in close proximity to the floor. Rolling, sitting, kneeling, crouching, crawling, curling, twisting and, stretching in the horizontal plane, are possibilities which become apparent once the imagination is stimulated. Leaps, jumps, stretches, twists and elevations onto the balls of the feet and through the spine are characteristic of movements which take the body into the high level. They are often linked with exuberance and joyousness, and with light, gay moods. Movements which are associated with advancing and retiring, opening, closing and turning — the forward, backward, right and left points of orientation — are usually characteristic of the medium level in space.

In dance, more than in games and gymnastics, the teacher should attempt to help the dancers to become aware of themselves as entering into a flux and flow of change of body form which brings them into and out of the three levels of space. A variation of levels can give contrast and design to the dance movement. For example, the starting position of a group of three can be designed so that each started in a different level. Their movements can develop an interchange of levels and, according to what is selected, can meet in a common level at intervals.

The different levels can express particular ideas. Which would be used for dominance, for obeisance, for the meeting of two compelling forces? Light things rise to higher levels. Strength gathers at a low level, and is reinforced by a firm grip at the base of support which should be under the centre of gravity. Mobility comes in the medium level. The characteristics of movement at the different levels should become evident as the dancer finds himself increasing the versatility of his movement in space.

EXTENSIONS IN SPACE

The size of movements in space can help to convey ideas or it can contribute to the design of the dance or both. For example, a movement done as large as possible seems to indicate a great conviction. It dominates. It is impressive, flamboyant or swaggering according to the way in which it is done. A small movement is likely to be less impressive, less dominant, even cowardly, shrinking or insignificant. However, according to how it is done, it may become a very significant movement. In fact, a small movement, placed in contrast to a large one, may be all the more impressive. For example, the lifting of an eyebrow, the flick of a finger, a nod of the head can be very impressive indeed, especially if it occurs after a sweeping turn or run and an emphatic stop. However, in general, the possibilities are those stated above. It should be mentioned that the beginner is rarely aware of the possibilities of the size of movement as a form of expression. As a result his movements can become insignificant and the feeling it brings to him is dulled because of the evenness of the extension of his movements in space.

A little exploration of different ways of contrasting sizes of movements — the stride of a run, the rising of the body, the turning of the body, a closing movement — will give an idea of its value in the design and feel of a movement phrase. For example, one may start curled over a base which consists of the left foot and the right knee and leg. In rising one may come straight up to a full extension; or one may come up in three stages (a small rising and sinking; a larger rising with a diminished sinking; a full rise and extension). This can be done merely for the contrasting spatial design, for the rhythmic design or, according to the way it is done, for the feeling it gives of a reluctance to face a new situation.

The consideration of the extension of movement in space is an interesting and profitable theme for dance classes.

PATTERNS IN SPACE

Floor patterns or the designs of pathways are particularly significant in folk dancing. Circles, squares, two lines advancing and retiring and weaving patterns are found in the folk dances of almost every country. They are fixed by tradition and the dancers try to retain the authenticity of each dance, the formations being learned and executed as accurately as possible. Very often a dance which features complicated floor patterns has, by contrast, simple foot patterns. The American square dance is an example in point.

In such folk dances as *The Durham Reel** or *The Waves of Tory**, and in some creative dances, the spirit of the dance depends upon the precise linking of a change of direction with the accent which marks each new phrase of music. Thus the dancers may advance and bow to each other on the first phrase and retire precisely upon the accent of the second phrase. In like fashion, each new figure begins exactly on the accent of the appropriate phrase of music and an emphasis is placed upon the direction into which the dancer moves. These marked changes in the direction into which the dancer(s) moves brings about clearly defined floor patterns. They also bring about the meeting and separating of partners. The precision which is required adds greatly to the interest of the dance and it contributes a feeling of fun and challenge. In cases like this, the stress is upon the changing of directions in general space. These changes help to create the changing designs in the floor patterns and formations of the dancers. They do not often indicate a dramatic sequence wherein one partner advances upon the other who resists or flees, although in some folk dances such a relationship might occur in the miming of a flirtation.

Attention is drawn to the fact that the changes of direction described above do not constitute all or even the most important concepts of space theory. It is possible for pupils to incorporate spontaneous changes of direction in their locomotor movements. When the teacher observes this she may choose to clarify their adaptation to general space by means of observation, exploration and improvisation. However, attention should also be given to the orientation which is described on page 146 of this chapter. These concepts may also be approached through incidental teaching.

In creative dance, the floor pattern formed by the dancers usually supports the major idea. For example, if the basic idea demands the embracing of space, it is likely that the movement will describe circles. Movement which alternates between advancing and retiring is likely to create straight line patterns or radiations to and from the centre of a circle.

Occasionally the emphasis may be deliberately placed on the floor pattern. For example, to show a busy crowded street, it might be decided that each dancer work out an individual floor pattern which will take a given amount of time to execute. Since each floor pattern is different, the resulting impression is hustle and bustle and confusion, particularly if the movements are chosen to convey the idea of busyness. If ceremony, dignity and pomp are required, the floor pattern is likely to consist of straight lines and right angles.

In all art forms of dance, the air patterns described by the arm and leg gestures, and the accompanying trunk movements are significant. For example, the arc made by the sweep of the right arm overhead from left to right creates a striking opening movement. The sweep of the leg in a

* See Chapter Ten, p. 309.

turn emphasizes the rotation of the turn. The accompanying arm gesture in a bow adds flourish to a courtly movement.

A group of dancers can create some very significant air patterns by the power of repetition. A circle can open by the lifting, in unison, of a gathering of hands at a low position at centre; or it can open out from a starting point with an arm or leg gesture of each dancer in turn seeming to emphasize the peeling away of each part in succession.

The flow of shapes through and about the space creates a design in the air which constitutes a sort of melody of dance. It can be created by the individual dancer or by a group who together form a cohesive and related design. The effect may be harmonious or disruptive, smooth or angular, soothing or startling.

To summarize, the various aspects of the movement component, *space*, contribute both design and expressive elements to the dance. They should be given proper consideration in conjunction with the other three components of movement:

EFFORT QUALITIES OF MOVEMENT

The movement of dance is expressive. It may be a spontaneous expression of an individual's responses to a selection of music as may happen when one dances freely to music, improvising the movement as one goes along. On the other hand, it may be carefully selected and arranged to express a specific idea or mood as may be the case when a dance is being created.

The expression it communicates is determined by the particular balance which exists between the *time, weight, space* and *flow* factors which comprise the movement. The balance between these factors may arise spontaneously or they may be controlled deliberately. The first situation is likely to be true for young children and inexperienced dancers who are strongly motivated and deeply involved in what they are doing. The ability to select and control the nuances of movement requires a command of the *effort* qualities and will develop through *effort* exercise and study.

The discussion which follows is not intended to present a teaching order. It does attempt to indicate the types of experiences which may be used to increase the awareness and control of effort.

SINGLE ELEMENTS OF WEIGHT

If the pupils enjoy moving, it is likely that they will participate with enthusiasm and their movements will be energetic and, thus characterized by the quality of *firmness*. The experience of wholehearted participation in energetic movement can be enhanced by giving stimuli which encourage leaping, stamping, clapping and gestures of jabbing, pounding, stabbing or slashing with elbows, fists or knees. Energetic arrivals at a chosen spot, firm stops, perhaps with jumps or abrupt turns or low fierce crouches may be discovered or encouraged. Notice that word stimuli have been suggested: energetic, fierce, firm, pound, stab, stamp. Others will be found by the teacher which suit the situation in hand. Percussion stimuli — drum, cymbal, hardwood sticks used with suitable force — can be helpful. Dramatic situations such as an argument in movement perhaps starting with foot stamps and moving on to jumps and gestures may be useful. Dances dealing with forceful elements necessarily demand forceful action — thunder, pounding waves, explosions — the pulling or pushing of heavy objects may help to create the situation which will elicit or require *firm* movement. The teacher must judge the appropriate time, but eventually pupils should experience the feeling of firmness in the body as a sensitive awareness to that quality. This means, that gradually pupils should become capable of producing, at will, firmness in the whole body, or in selected parts of the body.

It must be stated that only very few repetitions of a movement quality can be executed without the relief of its opposing element. Therefore, after two or three fierce stamps, perhaps organized as a phrase, there should be a recovery phrase of light movement as for an example, a turning away and perhaps a short run in a circular path before coming back into the stamps again. Or perhaps, the stamps might build up to a fierce jump, the landing of which might move into a roll — a compensating relief of tension.

Fine touch quality requires that the tension of the body be eased. The feeling is that of being airborne, floating or gliding on the surface of the floor rather than driving into it. This will require an uplifting of the whole body but the centre of the uplift is in the sternum which is elevated. The rib cage may be raised and inhalation may be emphasized. The spine must be elongated. The head should be raised. The shoulders and arms tend to uplift themselves. The elevation in the upper trunk is manifested by an increased distance between the lower rib and the hip bones. Light-hearted actions such as skipping gaily, running freely and lightly may be used. Flying jumps that rise off the floor without straining for height or distance, high twirling turns can be done lightly. Leg gestures, particularly those which lift the knee and thigh upwards; arm and head gestures which are focussed upward or upward and sideways may be used to create a feeling of lightness, delicacy or fine touch. Word stimuli might include: lightly, gently, skim, skip, glide, float, drift, flip, tiptoe. Percussion instruments include bells, triangle, light taps on the rim of the drum, thumb-nail scrapes on the parchment. Dramatic ideas which require fine touch include such situations as creeping up on something, gaily dancing, a light breeze, rustling leaves, lullaby, sympathy, helping someone, dusting, securing a window, carrying a cup of liquid. Eventually, it will be possible to develop the awareness of the feeling of fine touch to the extent that it can be executed at will in the whole body or in selected parts of the body. Later still, it should be possible to control transitions between the extremes of firmness and fine touch. In all the early experiments, it should be realized that phrases of fine touch should be compensated for by phrases of firm movement, hence creeping can lead to a fierce jump, a gay skip can be accented by a stamping or clapping motif, a light breeze may have gusty moments. In this way, the control of fine tension can be restored.

SINGLE ELEMENTS OF TIME

Most children of primary and junior classes love the excitement and freedom of speedy movement and will respond enthusiastically to a challenge to "find ways of going fast." Older pupils may respond willingly, or they may be more inclined to find ways "which can start very slowly and then be used in a burst of speed." This is the quantitative use of time and it is the usual experience found in games and gymnastics. It is connected with getting something done in a hurry or being able to take one's time. It is the functional component of time. It can be used in contrasting fast and slow skips, gallops, arm or leg swings and even head nods. On the whole it puts an emphasis on the limbs. It can be approached as a challenge in contrasts or as acceleration or deceleration. As soon as the body is brought into a major form of movement such as a curl, stretch or twist, it becomes difficult to do a repetitive movement in fast succession and the tendency is to satisfy the urge with an explosive start or to gather momentum and then bring the movement to a sudden stop. This cannot be measured but it can be seen and felt. Pupils should be challenged to find ways of exploding, bursting into action, surprising themselves, finding that the movement has *already* happened. To retain the feeling of suddenness, it may be necessary to keep a trunk movement quite small, otherwise the suddenness will peter out into a sustained action. It is possible to get suddenness into the action of the limbs, or into locomotion. Staccato hand claps, jumps, sudden arrivals, stops, starts and changes of direction can be explosive. Sudden withdrawals into the centre of the body are possible. For example, one can lift a knee suddenly, slap one's chest or abdomen. The suddenness is easier to achieve if the action is coming in toward the centre of gravity. Again, it must be stressed that two or three sudden actions are about the limit of possibility before relief and compensation are needed from a sustained movement. The word cues which may be useful include: burst! explode! dart! flip! arrive! stop! go! Percussion instruments which are helpful include hardwood sticks, a *large* cymbal or gong which is hit and then muffled. Sometimes a maraca, if it is slapped against the free hand, can be used effectively. Dramatic ideas which could demand sudden qualities of movement include: firecrackers, a rocket launching, a dive for safety, dodging traffic, a ball or a bullet; a sudden decision; a movement of exasperation.

The opposing attitude to time is one of enjoying its endlessness and, hence, the action is done with sustainment. This is more than being slow. There is peace and contentment in feeling the movement progress. When a body part has moved as far as it can go in a given direction, it may carry on uninterrupted into another one. Or, the body weight may be transferred and a new body part will be free to move. Very young children find this rather difficult and it is probably wise to delay the teaching until sustainment appears spontaneously in their movement. Junior pupils and intermediates can experiment to find ways of moving with sustainment. Rising with sustainment from a crouch can involve the whole body in an uncurling movement. The choice of a wide base will provide good support and remove some of the problems of maintaining balance. Another experience is to start with two parts of the body touching and gradually to separate them. The sustainment could be continued in a movement bringing two other parts together. Sustained locomotion may be more difficult to achieve because the strain of maintaining the body balance may occasionally interfere with the ongoing movement. But it should be explored. Anyone who has observed a cat creeping up on a victim will have seen sustained transfer of weight. This might suggest some experiments in sustained crawling or rolling. In these cases, there are opportunities of selecting a broad base. Word stimuli (enhanced by sustainment in pronouncing the word) might include — go smoothly, go slowly, take a long, long time, there is no hurry, easy does it, glide, pull, press, slowly step. Percussion instruments can be useful, especially the large cymbal or gong — "Keep the movement going as long as the gong sound lasts," triangle, bells in certain cases, singing, humming or droning. Dramatic ideas could include: stalking a prey, being *very* sleepy, being adrift on a log or in a boat, dreamy, slow-motion performances, moving so that no one realizes you are moving. Music such as the *Berceuse, The Swan, Boating* expresses the mood and sensation of gliding or drifting and may be used to help children to move with sustainment. Once more, warning is given that most young children find suddenness and fast actions more compatible with their way of moving than sustained actions. Therefore, the latter should not be required too soon. Furthermore, fairly short intervals of sustainment should be relieved by phrases of suddenness. It may be that sustainment could be used as preparation for suddenness. For example, one creeps a couple of paces and then explodes into a leap or a series of frightening staccato stamps. One gradually raises an arm and then whips and slashes with it. As in the case of the other qualities, the teacher will try to help individuals to achieve a feeling of the qualities of time in the body or its parts. Eventually they should be able to control them at will and, thus, be able to give the required expression to their dance.

SINGLE ELEMENTS OF SPACE

If one pays strict attention to where one wants a movement to go in space and takes the movement there by the shortest path, that movement will be *direct* and will describe a straight line. Pupils may experiment with movement going to different places. For example, the right hand might touch a knee (which might be raised to meet it), the top of the head, or the opposite elbow. Similarly the left hand, a foot or the forehead, or an elbow might be used to touch or point to a given location in space. Always the intention being expressed is to get there directly. Older pupils will appreciate that they have to concentrate and give attention to where they are going. Younger ones may or may not be mature enough for such exploring since a location in space is an abstract idea and therefore difficult for them to comprehend. They may find moving like a mechanical doll, a wooden soldier or a piece of machinery a more comprehensible way to find "straightness." Helpful word stimuli might include dabbing, tapping, tagging, boring, tunnelling, penetrating. Percussion instruments such as the drum (the parchment or wooden rim), hardwood sticks, single staccato shakes of maraca, as well as hand claps may be helpful. Suitable dramatic ideas might include mechanical movements, making straight lines, arriving at chosen places by the shortest route, shuttling back and forth, miming actions such as pulling down a blind, poking a fire, toasting a weiner, tacking a picture, writing a figure in the air.

Flexible movements might be considered to swim or meander in space and the attention is not so clearly concentrated on the arrival point but rather more on enjoying "the trip." Words which might help are weave, wind, wander, stir, meander. The percussion sounds will have to be played with flexibility in mind. Therefore, the thumb nail may scratch in a meandering fashion on the parchment, the tambourine may be stirred or slashed to give a shower of rattles, the maracas may be similarly shimmered, and bells, especially several together, may be shaken to give a shower of sound. Vocal accompaniment may prove more suitable than percussion sounds. Moaning, sighing, squeaking sounds may be created to suit the movement. Dramatic ideas might include rubbing against something just like a cat, undulating like waves, mixing (glue), stirring (syrup). Moving the limbs in figures of eight which lie on different planes might be used, not as a dramatic idea, but as a form of experimentation.

As in the case of the other qualities, neither the direct nor the flexible way of moving can be produced without the compensating relief of using the other element. Hence it is likely that a direct arrival could be dissipated by a flexible phrase which could also form a preparation for the next direct action. Or, the undulating movements of the upper body could be collected to explode into a direct jump of the legs or a stabbing attack of the arm. While preliminary exploratory experiences of older children and the spontaneous uses of the qualities by primary children are accepted as initial forms of awareness, eventually the feeling and control should be built up to the point where the qualities can be produced at will and blended from one to the other element at will.

THE SINGLE ELEMENTS OF FLOW

Experiments in doing a movement while knowing that it may have to be stopped unexpectedly will give children an experience of bound flow. It can be experienced as a game with the teacher, a partner or a pupil calling the stop signal or using percussion cues. For example, rising, turning, travelling movements can be halted without a time lag if the mind is set to stop without warning. Gestures such as arm circles, bendings of the legs or trunk can be done with *bound* flow and stopped in midcourse upon a signal. Word stimuli might include: be ready, keep the brake on, hold the movement, keep in control. Percussion stimuli can include a skipping or galloping rhythm that is broken in mid-phrase by a strong accent followed by silence. A maraca, tambourine or bells could be used in a similar way. Hand-clap rhythms prove fairly satisfactory. A more difficult signal to react to is a silence or cessation of sound without the warning of a strong accent. Another free-flow experience might come from the challenge to link a series of actions together so that there is no pause at all in the doing of them. The cueing and advice can be directed towards joining different actions together with continuity. For example, one might skip, change to running, to turning, to sinking, to rolling, to moving backwards. Always there should be a preparation stage for the next movement so that one flows into the other with smoothness and continuity. Or, the challenge might be to move freely in the spaces with a feeling of keeping "going and being free to go." The tension of readiness builds up to a significant degree in the activities mentioned above and relief may be provided by giving a free time when the pupils may find their own way of moving, knowing they will not be interrupted. They are almost certain to use a *free-flow* quality as a "carefree break." If *free flow* is being used as a compensation for the concentration on *bound flow,* it is probably best not to analyze it with the class. However, on other occasions *free flow* may be created and examined. It may be helpful to have the pupils work from the challenge of travelling fast, filling up all the spaces in the room. The teacher may encourage the freedom of action and the freedom to find open spaces. Then, without warning, a stop signal can be given. The result can be discussed. The overflow of movement should be felt and even observed. This has to be done carefully and evaluated carefully to assess whether the movement genuinely had an overflow. Class observation will show how the action appears to stop upon the signal; but how the movement actually "runs on" before it settles into stillness. This is a form of "free-flow stop." Helpful words may include: enjoy yourself, move freely, be happy and carefree, move freely in all the empty space, lilting, bouncing, whirling, loop-the-loop. Sound stimuli may include skipping or 6/8 rhythms without a pronounced phrase accent, showers of sound to use for whirls, vibrations, fluttering, shaking movements, or circles built on momentum. The large cymbal can provide continuity with a regenerating accent which builds a new phrase of continuous sound. Dramatic ideas which might be useful include lashing, turbulent movement like stormy wind or water, whirling Dervishes, a merry-go-round, spinning (like tops, wheels, machinery).

It should be stressed that free flow is an ongoing movement, a continuity, but it is not complete abandonment and irresponsibility. If this is not understood, accidents may occur. Control of an ongoing movement can be achieved by guiding it into a free space. Alternatively, the movement may be controlled by changing the free flow to bound flow. Eventually, the awareness should be so acute that the merger from one kind of flow to the other is felt and can be produced voluntarily.

TWO ELEMENT QUALITIES

Sometimes dance movements make use of a blend of two elements of the quality factors. For example, a dance may require a bubbly, effervescent mood. In this case, the steps might be little light explosive skips accompanied by little shakes of the head to make the hair fly and sudden airy gestures of the hand. The qualities being used are *fine* touch blended with *suddenness*. Another dance might require *firm, direct* movements which might be expressed in firm steps which come from a high knee driving straight downward. It might work into a pattern of three large, firm steps forward followed by a large and a small jump on the spot. In this case the blend used is derived from the *weight* and *space* factors.

A brief outline of the possible meaning expressed by the blending of two elements of the different quality factors are suggested in the chart on page 160.

It is not expected that classes be directed through a series of lessons which would give experience in all these possible combinations of elements which determine the quality of a movement. However, people make use of such blendings without necessarily being aware of doing so. In the course of responding to percussion or developing an idea in movement, these mergers may sometimes be observed. It is possible, therefore, for teacher and pupil to recognize that a blend can, indeed, occur. The recognition of such blends gives evidence of a significant advancement in ability to observe and analyze movement. As blends begin to be recognized, so they can be subject for experimentation. They may be developed as a skill and come to the fore in the communication of particular shades of meaning or feeling in subsequent dance studies.

EFFORT ACTIONS

Junior pupils are particularly interested in working with *effort actions,* perhaps because they are still happy to be physically active and yet are capable of using intellectual inquiry and control in conjunction with physical movement.

Technically, *effort actions* result from a blend of three elements — one each of the *time, weight* and *space* factors. The analysis of these has been given in Chapter Four, p. 65. Their place in dance study will be the subject of the consideration which follows on page 161.

WORDS DESCRIPTIVE OF POSSIBLE BLENDS OF TWO ELEMENTS

Time - Weight

Sustained and Firm	Sustained and Fine Touch	Sudden and Firm	Sudden and Fine Touch
prolonged strong action	leisurely light action which feels airborne	bursts of strong action like hits and whips	effervescent, bubbly actions like darts, dabs, flicks

Space - Flow

Direct and Bound	Flexible and Free	Flexible and Bound	Direct and Free
careful and spatially economical	gay and flippant	cautiously weaving or knotted	whole-hearted participation with straight movements

Time - Space

Sustained and Direct	Sustained and Flexible	Sudden and Direct	Sudden and Flexible
persistent linear movements	contemplative or searching	pouncing or with flash decision	flashy erratic or short whips

Weight - Flow

Firm and Free	Fine Touch and Bound	Firm and Bound	Fine Touch and Free
strong swings	delicate and precise	tense and restricted	bouncy or springy

Time - Flow

Sustained and Bound	Sudden and Free	Sustained and Free	Sudden and Bound
careful persistence like stalking	abandoned and impulsive	carefree on-going movement	controlled impulsive or jerky movement

Weight - Space

Firm and Direct	Fine Touch and Flexible	Firm and Flexible	Fine Touch and Direct
strong and straight actions	light and spiralling	sinuously firm	gently straight or pointing

Exploration and experimentation which lead to an awareness and control of the eight effort actions (or a particular selection of them) may be a useful type of dance study particularly if the class has had a well-rounded movement background by the time this type of work is undertaken. In this case, the teacher may organize the lesson so that the pupils receive guidance for their explorations and suitable stimuli to help elicit desired responses. In general, it would be advantageous to experience the effort action in several parts of the body and eventually to discover them in various forms of familiar dance movements such as jumps, turns, foot patterns, arm gestures and other dance sequences.

THRUST (*sudden, firm, direct*): Thrust may be experienced in stamping, clapping, punching, stabbing, jumping and landing with a direct use of space. The fierceness of mood, the firmness of tension which were characteristic of the actions stressing *firmness* (p. 153) are needed here, but they must be applied in a direct way and they must happen with suddenness or be staccato. Therefore, pulling must be transformed into sudden jerks, pushing into sudden shoves. The knees can jab; so can elbows and shoulders, hips and even head and chins. Physical relief from the concentration required to control these qualities can be found in contrasting phrases of the pupils' own choice or the use of the contrasting actions of *floating*. The use of a drum or tambour should help to stimulate *thrusting* movements and if played in a light brisk way or rubbed slowly and lightly, should support the movement of the contrasting phrase.

DAB (*sudden, fine touch, direct*): Dab is related to thrust but the firmness has been replaced with fine touch. It can be experienced in little dabbing foot patterns especially those using crisp toe tapping and sharp little running steps, and in small bouncy jumps. Finger shakes, and head bobbings can be done with a dabbing quality. The knees and elbows can be used in little sharp jabs upward or outward. A dance in which this effort action is predominant will be lively, perky and obviously full of vitality. The drum or tambourine — used lightly and fairly softly — or the maraca, should offer a spirited and rhythmic accompaniment or stimulus. Musical compositions such as Arthur Benjamin's *Jamaican Rhumba* are often an inspiration which help to ensure that the movements are developed into a dance and do not remain at the exploratory level.

PRESS (*sustained, firm, direct*): Press is related to thrust but the sudden quality has been replaced by sustainment and, therefore, the strong, direct action is a prolonged movement such as a push with the palm of the hand(s) or the sole of the foot. If the action is directed toward the body, it can become a pull. The whole body can be pressed downward, or it may pull upward or backward against an imaginary resistive force. Dramatic actions such as plodding forward, as though pushing against the force of a strong wind can be expressed through the use of this effort action. The power of the body, stemming from the bent knees and the strength of the thigh muscles, is directed over an extended period of time in an outward or upward direction or it may gather itself together in an inward or downward direction. The dramatic possibilities of the movement may provide the needed stimulus. For example, the dancer may be miming the pulling of the yulelog, or one dancer may be pressing forward towards another who is resisting and retreating slowly. To become believable, the action will have to be firm, direct and sustained. Percussion such as the drum or cymbal could be used or selected musical compositions could be helpful. Pressing is very much a "working" action and will be used for movements based on lifting, carrying, pushing, pulling, squeezing, pressing or crushing regardless of which part of the body is used to do the work.

SLASH (*sudden, firm, flexible*): Slash is related to thrust but the direct quality has been replaced by flexibility and, therefore, this action whips and lashes about in all directions. The dancer may use it for jumps and turns that corkscrew about with sudden force. Gestures of arms and legs can whip and lash about. A stormy turbulent mood is engendered. All the movement is tremendously energetic. The spine whips, arches and twists. The whole body seems madly or joyously alive. Dramatic ideas which would probably require this action might include a wild storm, bucking horses, turbulent waves breaking on rocks, or a brutal beating with a whip. The dancer might find it helpful to carry his own percussion such as a tambour. Tambourine dances, if they include sufficient vigour, are likely to make use of *slashes*. Music such as Falla's *Ritual Fire Dance* or Kachaturian's *Sabre Dance* can also be used for this kind of movement. Phrases of vigorous slashing movements will probably be kept fairly short and compensatory phrases of glides, dabs and flicks may offer a chance to renew energy as well to supply a contrast in the dance form.

FLOAT (*sustained, fine touch, flexible*): Float is the effort action which has the absolute opposite effort qualities to thrust. While thrusting creates a feeling of fighting and resistance, floating has a feeling of dreamy contentment. Steps will be preceded by gestures of the leg which wind and twist gently and slowly before being placed for the transference of weight. The spine can bring the body into gentle twists and arches which form an accompaniment to the leg action. Arms, head and breastbone undulate, generally with the tendency towards uplifting the body. The feeling is one of unhurried, air-light undulations. There can be quite a dreamy, peaceful feeling generated. Floating may be necessary to such dramatic ideas as a slinky cat, a curl of smoke, a floating balloon, a ship at anchor, a drifting raft. In dances based on working actions, floating may be the rest between slashes or the preparation for hits or punches. Music such as Offenbach's *Barcarolle* or Fauré's *Berceuse* may be selected as a basis for a dance which stresses floating movements. In dances which feature air-pattern designs such as opening and closing circles, figure-eight patterns, twists and undulations, the effort actions of floating are usually observable. Of course, the principle of contrasts in design will assure that other efforts should be used as well, for contrast both in air pattern and in effort content. A large cymbal or gong can be played so that the tone undulates while the reverberations are sustained. This may be a helpful accompaniment or stimulus to floating movements. The voice can give a good accompaniment. Droning, moaning, squeaking are possible forms of suitable vocal sounds. Such movements should be relieved by contrasting efforts such as thrusting or slashing.

WRING (*sustained, firm, flexible*): Wring is related to float, but firmness has replaced the fine touch. Thus there is a firm tension or grip in the body. The feet and legs probably form a wide base. The knees may be bent to increase the firmness of the base of support. The movement may twist and screw around the body bringing the spine into twists and contortions. The movement of the upper body may be carried into the legs which may be forced to twist into a change of direction which would require a step or a transference of weight onto a knee or a hip. It may even bring about a contorted roll. Wringing may be made by several different parts of the body going into several different directions simultaneously, as, for example, in a great stretch which might be called a "body-yawn." Dramatic ideas which may be characterized by wringing movements could include forms of agony, ugliness and distortion, for example, of witches or gnomes; the destruction of iron scaffolding, the crunching of auto fenders, the onset of blight in a tree or of plague in man. Moods of grimness, agony, anger, wretchedness might be conveyed by wringing actions. Hard physical work such as unscrewing a fire hydrant or fastening a steel cable or handling heavy fishnets would probably need wringing actions if it was the theme of mimes or dramatic dances. Accompaniment on percussion might be invented by using gongs and large drums, creaking hinges, and scratch gourds. Selected mood music, particularly some of the electronic sounds might be found useful. A skilful pianist could improvise helpful accompaniment by using both the percussion and tonal possibilities of the piano. It is obvious that this is a very dramatic effort action. It is quite likely that interest in using the body in wringing actions would be sufficiently strong that accompaniments would not be needed. If this were so, each dancer would be free to work within his own body rhythms.

FLICK (*sudden, fine touch, flexible*): Flick is related to float but the sustainment has been replaced by suddenness and the movement is now cheeky, gay and flippant. Bright little curling actions pop out, particularly from fingers, wrists, head (and hair) and feet. Other parts of the body can be used for flicking actions. The most usual execution of the movement is to flick in an upward and backward direction *away* from the body. For example, this usually happens if we flick dust off our sleeves. However, the flick can also move in toward the body in an upward and backward direction. The action can be an expression of gaiety and flippancy, or it can carry a shade of irritation as in a shrug, or of nervous irrationality as in a series of twitches. Skips, jumps with flicking gestures of hands, arms, heads, shoulders, feet, heels can give a dance style. Hand claps and heel clicks can be done with the lightness and flexibility of a flick. Hips and shoulders can flick. Music used as an accompaniment should be light, gay and perhaps staccato in quality and perhaps syncopated in time. Chinese finger-cymbals, triangles, bells, the tambourine and maracas can be used by the dancer who makes his own accompaniment, or by a percussion orchestra or soloist. Moods of flirtation, insouciance, gaiety or enthusiasm might be expressed by flicking movements. Irritability and minor degrees of abnormality due to mental derangement might also be expressed by twitches and flicks. Electric currents, sparklers which twinkle, movement of insects, reptiles and fish, the twitches of tails and manes of animals might be portrayed in flicking movements. Flickering flames, sprinklers, gusts of wind or leaves scattered by such gusts, flapping flags, sails, sheets or clothes on a line could all be partially portrayed by flicking. This is an effort action which could perhaps be used in a mood of fun, exuberance or comedy. It has a lot of versatility!

GLIDE (*sustained, fine touch, direct*): Glide is related to float but the spatial factor has become direct. There is a smooth, continuous penetration of space which gives a serenity of feeling to the movement. Nothing is disturbed — neither the body through its action, nor the environment as the result of the passing movement. The gestures of the legs may be large or small, but they will move in the required direction in a penetrating way, though very lightly and with continuity. The transference of weight will not be done with a rise and fall, but with a gentle forward or backward progression. The head, arms and breastbone will tend to be uplifted, resulting in an airborne quality of movement. Music, melody, singing in soothing tones may be a good accompaniment or stimulus to this movement. Some sustained waltzes, such as *The Skater's Waltz* are particularly good. The Varsovienna uses a glide in parts. Large sweeping movements, if kept flat and direct, can be characteristic of glides. Glides, the chassée and glissade, have been part of court dances and ballet for many years. Smooth ballroom dancing features this effort action. Gliding action gives a wide scope for dance invention. Dramatic ideas can include such obvious ones as skating. Dusting, window cleaning, smoothing, lightly raking, and combing are working actions which are characterized by a gliding movement. Gliders and aeroplanes which bank, land, or fly, move with a gliding action. Elevators, the upward ride on a seesaw, swings, and escalators (provided very little power is required) glide. Rocking accompanied by a lullaby is a glide. A light breeze blowing or skimming a surface, if done with a continuity of action, will tend to use the gliding effort action. Percussion stimuli and accompaniments are rather difficult to find. Rubbing the parchment of a drum, tambour or tambourines with a gliding action is probably the most effective way of creating a suitable sound. A light tap on the triangle might be helpful but the sustainment of sound may be short-lived and force short gliding actions. Probably humming, droning and other uses of the voice would be a more suitable sound stimulus. Once again, it may be helpful to mention that the effort action of gliding needs the relief and contrast of other efforts such as flicking, thrusting, or slashing, and should not be used in too great a concentration.

The description of the eight effort actions and the discussion of what part they play in expression in dance should help to identify dance content.

If a dance is uninteresting or difficult to interpret, it may be possible to make improvements by clarifying the effort qualities which seem already to be suggested by the movement. When appropriate efforts are used, the mood or the idea can be communicated very convincingly. When suitable contrasts of efforts are selected, the artistry of the composition becomes evident and the dance can become very satisfying to perform and to watch.

RELATIONSHIPS

The relationship of one dancer to another is of great significance in determining what kind of dance develops. For example, is it a partner dance or is it a group dance? Is there a leader or are all dancers of equal status? Is there any form of grouping such as those who make arches and those who go through the arches? Is there a dramatic relationship between the dancers or do they contrast with each other in terms of the spatial or rhythmic design?

These alternatives suggest that an examination of the relationship between dancers should be considered in some detail.

It would perhaps be wise to stress that the term relationship implies interaction between people. If the negative situation is also included, then the question becomes, "What is the significance of the *lack* of interaction between the dancers?"

The various possibilities for relationships with people have been defined in Chapter Four, p. 70 ff. They will be examined here for the way these relationships can develop in dance.

ALONE

The solo dance represents one situation of "dancing alone." The dancer has the freedom to say what he wants to say in the way he chooses to say it. He is free to use the virtuosity of his "body-tool" according to his own requirements and his ability or his limitations. However, he is restricted in the sense that he has no help from a partner or a group of dancers. For example, if he wishes to show a contrast in levels, the high and the low must be shown by him in some way. If he were dancing in a group, some of the group could be dancing in the high level and others in the low level. Thus, the solo situation has its own freedoms and its own limitations. The interaction is, in a sense, between facets of his own being rather than with other people.

The soloist dances in relation to his environment. For example, there is an interrelationship between the soloist and the onlooker. In this case, there is a form of projection from the dancer to the onlookers. It affects, for example, the directions used by the dancer, the area used, the focus of the dance, the size and extension of the movements.

On the whole, the solo situation is the relationship situation least used in the dance education of young children; and this is probably as it should be.

Perhaps it had better be mentioned that "dancing alone" as a spontaneous expression of an inner feeling is quite another situation. One often sees little children literally dancing down the street. It may happen when they are thrilled and excited, as for example, when they are going to see a parade or going for a ferry ride or a picnic. In such a situation they are quite unconscious of those around them and, perhaps, even unconscious of their exuberant movement. It should be noted that the very absence of interaction with others has a significant effect upon the resultant movement.

ALONE IN A MASS

This is the usual situation in the school dance class, particularly in the primary grades. Each child responds to the stimulus in his own way. The relationship is that of "doing whatever is right for me so long as I do not interfere with others." Older children and adults have to be reassured, through experience, that everyone is so busy with his own situation that he has no time to assess what others are doing. Hence, no one is conspicuous and no one is in the "solo situation." This is an ideal situation for movement experimentation. It is used to a limited extent in dance forms. It can be used, for example, if a mob scene is required, or if the Pied Piper's pack of rats are infesting the scene. But in these cases, the dance is past the exploratory stage and each individual has selected his particular sequence and is capable of repeating it with all its nuances.

PARTNERS

Two people may develop several different forms of interaction. The result will always be that *both* are needed in the movement sequence.

Taking turns

This might be considered the transitional stage between dancing alone among others and dancing with a partner. It is rather likely to develop spontaneously if two children are asked to work with one percussion instrument. One may dance while the other plays. Then the roles may be reversed. It is possible that a short phrase of movement may be performed by one dancer and as he finishes his sequence and holds his final position, his partner will do a phrase of his own choosing. This rotation may be repeated over several interchanges. However, most children recognize that more interesting relationships can be developed with a partner. One which tends to be discovered very soon is:

Matching a partner

This way of dancing with a partner demands not so much the creative skills as the skills of thought and intuitive adjustment. To match a partner in quality of movement as well as in action and rhythm can make great demands on a performer. It can also bring movement experiences that might not have developed out of his own movement exploration. It is challenging, fun and companionable. It also usually increases the impact of the movement upon the observer by giving a repetition of the movement pattern or shape.

As one dancer finishes she holds her position while her partner moves.

Question and answer

This is a form of taking turns but there is a clear interaction between the two performers. It is as if a movement conversation is taking place. The movement of one partner requires a response from the other. For example, Betty might start things off by running lightly around Mary and finish by backing away slowly with a pulling action. Mary may interpret this as an invitation to follow. She may, therefore, spin once around and then with an advancing and sinking movement stop close to and in front of Betty. Betty may take over with a phrase of stamps. Mary might jump high with a half turn and finish low again — and so on. What one does in movement, is answered by the other in movement. This will tend to be resolved at the end of the dance, perhaps by one dominating the situation or perhaps, by the two melding their movement in some indication of agreement.

Action and reaction

This situation is an extension of the *Question and Answer* relationship but it has, perhaps, a stronger dramatic element and certainly a greater sense of interaction between the partners for what one does will determine what the other will do. For example, a slashing action aimed at the partner's feet must bring some reaction in his feet. He may jump to avoid the slash or kick back ·in retaliation. In dance, one partner's movement usually brings about a response, not by actual contact with the partner, but by allowing the quality, the spatial ingredients and the timing to clearly portray the intention. Hence, movements of pushing, pulling, enticing, repulsing, flirting with a partner should bring about suitable responses of resistance or compliance. Themes, such as "casting a spell," an "evil eye" (or hand), a "magic maraca" or "Mr. X" (who can intimidate others) may be used to give rise to dances which are based on dramatic interaction. The toy maker manipulating his puppet, partners sawing wood, rowing a boat or unloading a truck, pedestrians dodging each other, each of these situations presents movements that require a suitable reaction in movement.

Following a leader

While this relationship could grow out of the theme of "reacting to a partner," it really implies a more cooperative bond between two people. Indeed, it might develop out of the theme of "Matching a partner." However, the latter theme tends to develop into a face-to-face or side-by-side relationship. "Follow the leader" usually develops as a one-behind-the-other relationship. It has game-like overtones and, therefore, has restricted use in the dance situation.

Meeting a partner

This situation may be used as a theme in its own right. It gives rise to problems of:

1. Where do the partners start — far apart or fairly close together? What is the starting relationship — face-to-face, back-to-back, side-by-side, or facing in opposite directions?
2. What happens when they meet — pass right by, greet and then pass, move around (encircle) each other and separate, engage in movement (elbow turn, dance together, etc.) and withdraw, meet and merge (i.e. join forces and stay together), or meet and oppose each other?

These six relationships between partners — greeting, encircling, withdrawing, passing, merging, opposing — are the most obvious ones. Analysis will reveal that many folk dances are based upon one or more of these relationships. Original dance compositions based upon the theme of "meeting" will spontaneously make use of one or more of these relationships. However, participants are usually surprised when observation and analysis of their compositions reveal what relationships have developed between the partners. A clear awareness of the relationship will tend to give pupils the understanding which will permit them to capitalize on the situation. If, for example, they realize that they are really greeting a partner, this may give rise to bows, smiles and gestures of greeting. It may cause them to adjust the distance between partners or to adjust the timing of the greeting. The whole situation can be given a clear meaning and character.

GROUPS

If three or more dancers are participating in a dance, a group situation develops. The group is different from a mass or a collection of people. It has a common purpose and there is an interrelationship between the members. The group is incipient if the purpose is not yet accepted by all members. In this case, there may be a seeking among individuals for a common purpose and a unity of feeling will not yet have been achieved. The size of the group exerts considerable influence upon its nature and characteristics. For example, a group of three has potentialities which do not exist for a group of four.

Threes

Such a group is capable of varied formations: triangle, line, or circle. It may divide and regroup. It may stay together and change its formation without being shattered by the change.

The line formation is capable of moving in different directions as a line; for example, advancing and retiring or moving sideways right or left. The members of the line may interweave, or they may turn within the line. They may follow a leader while retaining the line. They have an option of two leaders.

As a circle, they may focus on the centre and advance and retire to or from the centre in different ways, with or without contact with one another. They may move around the circumference while remaining focussed on the centre, or they may abandon the focus at centre and place it on the circumference.

As a triangle, they have a less cohesive association. There is a possibility of a one versus two relationship, or a two versus one, or a one "looks after two" situation. For example, the latter situation is found in some folk dances where one man dances with a lady on his right and a lady on his left. It is possible to create different dramatic situations. For example, one might be rejected by the twosome, or one might be lured by the scheming of the other two. One might alternate his attention between each of the other two.

It becomes obvious that a grouping of three can set the stage for some rich experiences in relationships.

Fours

A foursome lends itself to a symmetrical arrangement of two pairs. This does not create as many dramatic situations as the asymmetrical grouping of three.

Fours may mass as a group or form a square, line, circle or triangle. It may divide and regroup or stay together and fluctuate between different formations, with or without physical contact.

As a massed group, forming an organic whole, it may have a particular group shape, a life and movement of its own, and a group purpose. The shape may be influenced by members who are working at various levels; it can be closely packed or loosely formed; it may be round, square or arrow shaped, etc. It may move to its own rhythmic pattern and its movement may rise, sink, advance, retire, turn, etc. Its purpose may be to remain a cohesive whole, or to send out probers, or to become more active, etc. All of these possibilities may be achieved with or without a group leader.

As a square, it may be formed by four individuals or by pairs inter-associated. It will tend to have a central focus similar to a circle and the movement is likely to stress advancing and retiring or meeting — with all the possibilities which were available to partners but with the complication of four people clashing in the centre of the square. There will be possibilities of movement available at the corners of the square. American square and "contra" dances are based on these relationships.

The line and circle formations offer the same relationship possibilities as the group of three, but on a slightly larger scale. The triangle formation is not so well defined because it has to develop out of a one versus one and a pair.

Fives

As a grouping made up of an odd number, a group of five permits very satisfying asymmetrical groupings, including the "V" shape. The line and circle formations are large enough to give a satisfying feeling to their movements. As a mass group, it permits good opportunities for dividing and regrouping, and for encircling and surrounding movements. Interweaving in different patterns is possible. The relationship of a leader and followers can be very direct. For example, the group may form behind the leader who may rise, advance, or sink, with such clear movements that the followers may participate in the action without the use of verbal cues. The group shape, life and movement can become very significant. For example, two at high level, two at medium level, one at low level will make an interesting starting shape. The movement life of the group may be concerned with cohesion, or it may deal with kinds of serializations where one member moves, another follows, a third follows until finally all are together again. They may work on variations of a two versus three grouping. A group of five is a very satisfying number for dance composition. The possibility of movement and shape are sufficiently varied that the grouping can be used often without fear of exhausting the variations available.

The situations so far discussed represent the most usual ones in which the experiences of true interaction may happen. However, some dance classes may acquire sufficient experience to move on to an even more complicated situation; the one in which one cohesive group reacts to the movement of another cohesive group. For example, one group may be massed, close together, low down with a focus just a little off centre. They may be concerned with a motive of gradually breaking free from that point of focus. A second group, clustered some distance away, at medium level, may be concerned with travelling as a group. The travellers may eventually discover the focussed group, who by this time may be less tightly drawn toward their focus. The mobile group may, by their very mobility, swoop and pass and advance and encircle with such surgings that their dynamics exert an influence upon the others and eventually draw them into mobility.

It will be seen that the groups assume the characteristics of a person and the two groups interact, one influencing the other, in much the same way as partners did in the *Action and Reaction* form of relationship. This may be considered the study and use of *Interacting Groups*.

The area of relationships in dance has not been discussed in its entirety in the foregoing passages, but certainly the situations which children may meet in even their earliest experiences have been identified. It is helpful for the teacher to be aware of the fact that relationships do arise in the movement and dance situations. When they occur, or significantly affect the work being done at the moment, they can be observed and the new awareness will give pupils a better grasp of what is happening. At the teacher's discretion, exploration can be done on relationship themes. Thus the totality of the factors which influence movement and dance can be appreciated and used by the pupils as they continue their work.

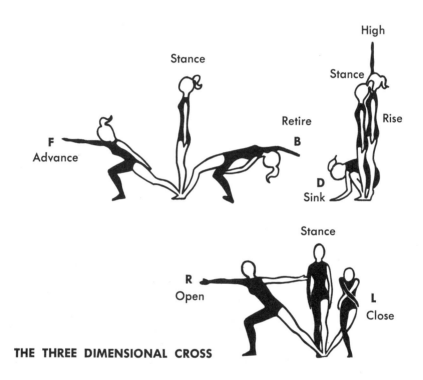

THE THREE DIMENSIONAL CROSS

EIGHT

THE TEACHING OF GAMES

In Chapter Five, the playing of games was examined in an attempt to discover how a knowledge of the concepts of movement which were presented on pages 36 to 75 could be used to upgrade the players' performance. In this chapter the purpose will be to suggest guidelines for the teaching of games to the various age groups of children. Particular attention will be focussed on the application of the movement concepts most relevant to the games skill or situation with which the pupils are working.

THE KINDERGARTEN

Teachers must keep in mind the needs of the class when making specific decisions as to the methods and materials to be used in a given lesson. In most cases even a lesson which has been planned with the needs of a particular class in mind will have to be modified during the course of presentation to make use of strengths and weaknesses, interests and abilities as they reveal themselves in the pupils' activities. However, it is necessary for a teacher to prepare a basic lesson, predicting the situation as best she can. It is this basic lesson which can be modified as the work proceeds. For very young children two different varieties of games lessons will probably take form: one for the activities associated with games equipment and the other for the activities associated with running and chasing.

ACTIVITIES ASSOCIATED WITH GAMES EQUIPMENT

The activities associated with games equipment will lay the foundations, in a very rudimentary way, for the ball games which are played by youth and adults. Junior kindergarten play equipment will also include vehicles which will aid their physical development and balance.

The equipment usually includes: balls of different sizes but especially the 7-inch inflated rubber ball; beanbags; paddle bats; plastic scoops, bats and hockey sticks with matching plastic balls; quoits; individual skipping ropes; hoops; Indian clubs or skittles; wooden blocks. Play equipment for Junior kindergarten may include: tricycles, wagons, scooters, seesaws, large blocks, skate boards.

The procedure may range from free play to a fairly well structured lesson. In either case it will be necessary for the teacher to work out with the pupils a suitable routine for moving to the play area, choosing the equipment, using the equipment in responsible ways (safe for themselves and for others), caring for and storing the equipment. The amount of talking and interaction, and the volume of noise which is permitted will depend on the teacher's purposes for the class and on the location of the play area in relation to other classes. If the teacher regards the session as a language and social growth period which is implemented through bodily activity, she will probably arrange to have considerable talking, planning and interaction take place. If she regards it as a lesson which is largely concerned with the growth of physical coordination, she is likely to guide the children toward the solution of individual movement problems. The first situation may occur when toys such as tricycles, wagons, building blocks are used. The second situation will probably develop when balls and the more traditional games equipment are used.

In both of the above cases, the teacher can influence the "content" of the "lesson". If she chooses to guide or interject movement concepts into the work, she will do so only after determining which ones are being used spontaneously by the children as they play. Once she knows what concepts are already in operation, she can help the children to become aware of their use. She may do this by commenting upon such features as the speed at which they move, the body part they use or the direction in which they go. Such remarks may precipitate the incorporation of that particular movement concept into the activity of the children who overhear the comment. If an immediate response is not evident, the remark may still enlarge their thinking and, over a period of time, contribute to what should eventually become a cohesive body of knowledge.

If the teacher deems it wise, she may influence the children's movement by adjusting the placement of the equipment. For example, they may be riding the tricycles in a clockwise direction which may give a particular stress in balance and work one side of the body more than the other. The teacher may initiate a change by placing a building block unit, a seesaw or a bench in such a way that the tricycles may reasonably move in a figure of eight. She may even influence the movement by stationing herself in a particular position in relation to the activity the children are doing. For example, by casually blocking a pathway to the ladder, she may cause the pupils to crawl under it before mounting. In other words, the teacher may assess the movement experiences offered in the play period and contribute to them in an incidental way.

If the balls are made available to the class, the usual working arrangement is to free the children to discover all the different things they can do with the ball. The pupils must be given to understand that reasonable things are implied and that they must choose activities which are safe for everyone. Therefore, if a boy wishes to kick a ball with all his might, he must find a good place to do it — perhaps against a wall.

Once again the teacher must observe and analyze what is being done. On the basis of what she sees, she will clarify the movement content, usually by moving among the pupils and praising them in specific terms. For example: "That's a good idea, Mary. You are *tossing* the ball *straight up*." "Good, Bill. You *kicked* it *forward* that time." If she decides to comment only on the *direction* used, she can very shortly have everyone thinking about the direction they are using and from that point it will be quite natural for them to explore the matter of directions and to discover ways of using two or three different ones. In this case she is guiding their experiences into a *movement theme*.

In the kindergarten, suitable games themes can be:

1. Becoming aware of the part(s) of the body which are being used to make the ball *go*; or *stop*. Exploring new possibilities.
2. Becoming aware of the actions which are being done with the ball, e.g. bounce, toss, roll, catch, etc. Exploring new ideas for the use of balls.
3. Discovering tricks which can be done with the body (while the ball is in play) e.g. clap hands, spin around, jump over it, etc.
4. Observing or finding ways of travelling with the ball; ways of working with the ball on the spot.
5. Discovering the different directions in which the ball can go; or, the directions in which you and the ball can go.
6. Finding things you can do with the ball while it is low/high.
7. Becoming aware of where the ball is; taking it from one level to another.
8. Steering the ball: in different pathways; with various parts of the body.
9. Sending the ball in a straight pathway (aiming).
10. Keeping yourself and the ball out of everyone's way (dodging).
11. Using the ball and the wall; ball and the floor; ball and the air; ball and a hoop; ball and a rope; ball and a bat, etc.
12. Discovering the things which are done with the ball which need strength; speed; suddenness; or fine-touch qualities in the action.
13. Making up a ball game of your own.

One of the most satisfying and profitable uses of the last half of the lesson is to arrange for pupils to play (or practise) at a series of games stations. Kindergarten pupils can manage very nicely in groups of four if each one of the four has his own equipment. This really develops into a form of parallel play.

The teacher may arrange the games stations according to her own discretion and the availability of space and equipment. Some suggestions are offered here.

1. Four soccer balls, an expanse of wall, a kicking line.
   Task: "Kick the ball against the wall. Do not cross the kicking line to do this."

2. Four Indian clubs (or skittles, plastic bleach bottles, weighted with a little sand) placed two feet in front of a wall. Bowling line 15 feet from clubs. Four balls or four beanbags.
   Task: "Bowl the ball (beanbag) from behind the line to knock the club over."

3. Four 7-inch playground balls. A gym wall with a chalk line 5 feet high. A throwing line 6 feet from the wall.
   Task: "Toss the ball against the wall above the line."
   Optional: "Find ways of catching it" (directly off the wall; after it bounces).

4. Four beanbags or balls. Two wastepaper baskets, cardboard cartons or hoops.
   Task: "Try to throw the beanbag into the basket."

5. Two Indian clubs placed in front of a wall at a width of 6 feet. Two plastic pucks or balls. Four plastic hockey sticks. Four players.
   Task: "Partners try to shoot the puck into the goal."

6. Four paddle bats and four balls. Four players and a wall.
   Task: "Bat the ball against the wall."

7. A row of six chairs lined up to make a tunnel. Four balls, a starting line. Four players.
   Task: "Bowl the ball down tunnel formed by the chairs. Run around to pick up the ball and return to the starting line." Repeat.

8. Four hoops laid out on the floor as stepping stones in a circle. Four balls. Four players.
   Task: "Bounce the ball in each hoop as you travel around the circle."

When they are ready, children of this age will begin to work together quite spontaneously. At such a time, the teacher may organize such stations as:

9. Four players on a court divided by a rope stretched between two chairs (or two high-jump standards). Two quoits, balls or beanbags.
   Task: "Partners throw to each other over the rope."
   Optional: "Throw and catch."

10. Four scoops, and two plastic balls. A court divided by a balance bench or a rope or line across the floor.
    Task: "Toss the ball to your partner in the opposite court."

The teacher may invent other games stations. Or after having had a number of lessons using stations, the pupils can be asked to lay out their own stations. In this case, the teacher must assume the responsibility of checking the pupils' arrangements for safety and of helping them to modify the layout if it is unsuitable.

If there are twenty pupils in the class, five stations may be laid out, the pupils being responsible for getting most of the equipment into the proper area. The teacher should check the layout and relative positions of the stations. Safety precautions should be observed to the extent that one station does not interfere with another. Pupils may start at the station they laid out. After perhaps five minutes, they may be asked to sit down. A rotation scheme should be arranged so that the groups move on to another station. It is usually helpful to have all pupils return to their original station at the end of the activity time. They can then put the equipment back where they found it. The next day they can lay out their own station again. If they work on it at all, it should probably be for a brief time. Then they may rotate to a station which is new to them. After several lessons, when they have visited all stations, they can start again at their original one. By that time they may show an improvement in skill or if they seem bored, the arrangement can be changed and/or a new task given.

Summary of lesson construction

The suggestions given on page 174 as a guide to the way the kindergarten lesson may be conducted would indicate that it falls into three main parts.

Part One

Free play with balls, beanbags or other games equipment. The teacher praises the pupils' efforts, checks the safety of all and observes the current level of skill of the pupils in relation to the equipment used.

Part Two

The teacher influences the children's activities by adjusting the equipment, by commenting on their activities and by questioning them about various aspects of their work. She may direct their activity into a movement theme related to games.

Part Three

a. The pupils may make up a game of their own, using the equipment they have been working with, or
b. the pupils may work at games stations.

Chasing and tag games are the delight of young children. They are an important part of every child's education because like folk songs, ballads, folk dances, myths and folktales, they are a part of the inherited treasures of mankind. Many of them are enjoyed for their strong dramatic content. Others provide the children with the freedom to run or the excitement of being chased.

These games require a fairly large group of players to give them meaning and character. They also require a large playing area and they are at their best when played outdoors.

To adults, these games appear to be so simple that it would hardly seem necessary to teach them. However, chasing games are highly exciting and contain a simple, but very significant form of competition, especially if they develop into tag games. Therefore, the teacher should weigh the demands of the game very carefully and try to select those suited to the current stage of development of the children. Very often, in the early part of the year, she must make up her own games in order to keep them simple enough for the pupils.

There are several ways in which a games lesson may be developed. The use of variety in planning the lessons should sustain interest and enthusiasm. Furthermore, sometimes one form of development may be more effective than another in forwarding the purpose of the lesson. For example, lessons in which the culminating activity is a running, chasing or tag game, are usually planned so that other parts of the body besides the legs are stressed in the activities at the beginning of the lesson. The lesson may begin with *free practice* using beanbags, hoops, ropes, skittles. These will probably be used with spontaneous stressing of the hands. Thus there is likely to be throwing, tossing and catching, chasing and picking up, bowling, twirling and so on. The teacher can accept these spontaneous reactions and widen the variety of things done, or, improve the standard of performance. In widening the variety of activities, comments should be made on the kinds of actions seen (throw, catch . . .), the concurrent use of the body (travelling while tossing, jumping to catch, turning until it is caught), the part of the body used (under the leg, with the foot, on top of the head), the use of space (direction of flight, level chosen), relationships (over the beanbag, between the skittles, around the hoop). In improving the standard of performance, the comments might be directed to the quality used (a quick run, a sudden turn, a strong throw) or to the efficient use of the body (landing softly, running on the balls of the feet, grasping with the fingers).

The lesson could then be directed toward *locomotor* experiences. The equipment could be placed on the ground and pupils could be challenged to find ways of travelling throughout the whole area while avoiding the equipment. Again, the comments may be directed towards increasing the variety of ways of travelling, but it can now also be directed towards bringing about an awareness of weightbearing, weight transfer and body actions. Some remarks about people who are using two hands and one foot, hands and knees, and so on can be helpful. Observations of children who roll, run, walk, slide, crawl or use other invented actions will help to establish a feeling for what locomotor actions are. Comments about pathways which twist or curve or circle or zigzag between the equipment will tend to awaken an awareness of floor patterns. Speeds, directions and levels can also be discussed.

A short time spent on *jumping* and *landing* is very profitable. This can easily arise if the challenge is given to remain near a piece of equipment and "move all about it." Or, perhaps it will be necessary to ask them to find ways of going over the equipment. This can be done by using jumps with one or two feet onto two feet or one foot. It can be done with or without a preliminary run. The distance covered in the jump, the development of a light landing, the use of markings on the floor for take-off or landing targets are all valuable themes which relate to games play. Variations can also be developed out of the consideration of the directions, levels or speeds used.

Another format for the games lesson has been found quite successful if it is decided not to use the equipment in the early part of the lesson. In this case, the free play and locomotion sections can be merged and the pupils can start by finding many different ways of travelling. Next they can find ways of taking weight on different parts of the body either as a means of travelling or as a method of stopping and holding a "statue" balance. This could be given a game content by the surprise with which the stop signal is given. Jumping and landing could be done as body actions (finding different ways to do it, or, finding how to jump high and/or land low).

It is valuable to give some attention to floor markings and to the concept of zones. This could be done as the introductory activity. For example they may:

1. "Run to visit all parts of the space between 'these' lines."
2. "Go anywhere in the space, but travel so that you are always on a black line." (Question: "How will you pass other people?)"
3. "Travel on all the lines that are of a chosen colour."
4. "Go everywhere without touching any line." ("How do you get over the lines — by being high, by being high and low, by jumping, or by stepping?")
5. "Find a 'red line.' Find many things to do which take you over or along it. Find a starting place a long way from it. Run fast to it; stop on it; cross over it and stop, etc."
6. Identify a safety zone line for the whole class. Have "all in" races to cross the line. Pupils can suggest the kinds of races: running, skipping, hopping. Actions which permit speedy travel are usually best. Try to stress the idea of crossing over the line and *then*

slowing down to a stop. Different kinds of "go" signals may be planned — some auditory, some visual.

Dramatic games which use the principle of racing to cross a safety line, or finish line, or zone line can be invented and named by the teacher. Some examples are listed.

1. Fire engine race.

Each pupil is a fire engine, parked in the station. Fire signal is: three loud claps and the word "Fire!"

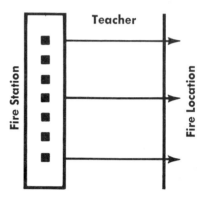

2. Ambulance.

Each pupil is an ambulance, parked in the garage. Red light flashes (red flag): all depart with siren going (an *outdoor* game).

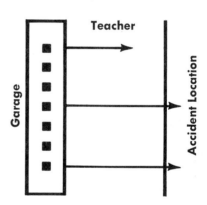

3. Telegraph boy.

It is agreed that the telegraph boy goes: down a street, around one block (his own circle), down another street, climbs six stairs (runs on spot with knees high) and runs to the door to deliver his message.

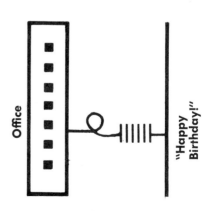

4. Statues.

"It" hides his eyes and counts "one, two, stop" and looks to see if anyone moves. Penalty for moving: two steps back. Finish by calling: "Go, go, forever." (Large outdoor area.)

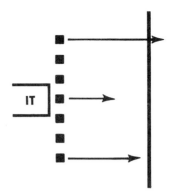

5. Fire on the mountain.
(Modified)

"Fire on the mountain — Run! Run! Run!" "Fire's out! Stop!"

Double circle, running in opposite directions. On signal "Stop" each pupil joins two hands with someone from the opposite circle and sits down. Identify first and/or last down.

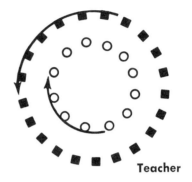

6. Magic wand. (Modified)

"It" has a magic wand. Class is clustered in a loose group, but must do what the wand says — e.g. mark time, run this way, jump, walk slowly etc. When the wand is dropped with a bang, all must run for safety across the zone line. If "It" gets there first all must lie flat on the floor wherever they happen to be.

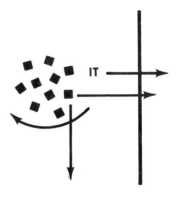

None of the above games has any declaration of a winner, although most could be altered to include that added competitive feature. Usually the teacher will be "It" until the children thoroughly understand the game. Pupils may eventually take over the "It" role. It may be necessary to encourage the pupils to emphasize the dramatic and suspense elements when they become "It."

The next progression from the running and chasing games is to add the element of tag. This is a highly charged situation and children can take it very seriously and become very excited. The young ones usually don't understand the concept of "tag" and want to "capture" or "grab" the runner. Preliminary experience with tapping actions should help to prepare them. Situations which might be useful include:

1. Tapping with the toe: first one side, and then the other side of a line.
2. Jumping to tap the wall as high as possible.
3. Jumping to tap a ruler or rope held over the head.
4. "Ten Trips" — reduced to three or four, or whatever seems reasonable. "Run to tap a line with the toe and return to the starting base." At the discretion of the teacher this could be changed to "tap the wall."
5. Explorations of tapping two parts of the body together (two hands, forehead and knee, foot and knee, foot and head.)
6. Tagging games, done in the classroom, where those tagged may go to sit by the piano, put their coats on, or go to the work centre. In these cases, there is no competitive pressure and the starting situation is usually stationary.

Active games using the tagging element may be invented by the teacher to fit the situation. However, many of the traditional tag games can be used in their original form or may be modified to make them more suitable. A few are suggested here and on the next two pages, but other sources should be used for more material.

1. Frog in the sea.

(A game of teasing and daring.)

Chant: "Frog in the sea, can't catch me." Repeat until "It" calls "Yes, I can!" and chases.

The players usually skip and dart about while chanting. "It" may be seated or standing.

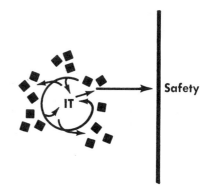

These games and others like them bring up the problem of what to do with those caught. For obvious reasons, it is not suitable to have them eliminated. So probably all that is needed is to state: "Four were caught that time. Let's try again." Then a new game can be set up with new "Its." It is probably best to choose the "Its" at random rather than as a penalty

2. Mother Bird.

(A game with a danger zone, safety zones and a loose team and leader organization.) Canaries and Bluebirds fly freely in their own areas. (Various bird activities can enrich this movement.) Mother Bird calls them home in turn. The Hawk tries to tag them as they pass by.

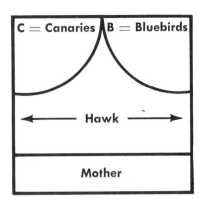

3. Hill Dill.

(A game with a danger zone and an "It" who calls the play.)

Chant: "Hill Dill come over the hill
'Else I'll catch you
Standing still. Red!"

Reds must try to cross safely to the other side.

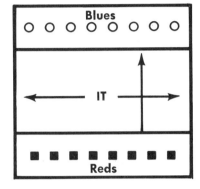

Variation:

All must come at once.

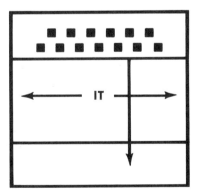

for being caught. Very young children regard the role as a privilege and thus sometimes try to get caught if it means becoming "It."

This characteristic behaviour of the young child which is rooted in his egocentric outlook, casts doubts upon the suitability of these games. Some experts feel that if the game has to be radically modified, or, if it must be

4. Chinese Wall.

(Runners must cross a danger zone. Several defenders guard the zone.) It can be played without a signal or the leader of the runners can call "Go."

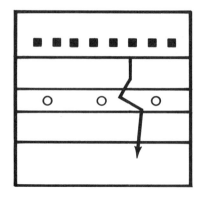

taught by the teacher rather than being evolved from a challenge set by the teacher, it should be considered incompatible with the aims of modern education. Teachers, then, must make a judgment, weighing the fun and excitement implicit in the game against the possibility of it being too complicated for the child to comprehend. Perhaps the solution would be to reserve these games for recess or party play.

THE PRIMARY DIVISION

The suggestions made for teaching games in kindergarten will apply in many ways to the games program in the primary classes, especially if the six-year-olds did not go to kindergarten. The teacher's responsibility is still to assess the needs of the children and to select and modify the games to meet these needs. The games program may include the traditional running and chasing, and tag games, some dramatic games, and a variety of other simple folk games. It will also give a good deal of attention to activities associated with games equipment. An understanding of movement principles may be achieved concurrently with the acquisition of the experience and skill in the body management which is needed for skilful player performance and the various skills related to handling the equipment. Conversely, what is known of movement principles should be applied to the execution of playing skills. Thus the standard of performance should be raised. These two aspects of the games program will be considered next.

ACTIVITIES ASSOCIATED WITH RUNNING AND CHASING, AND TAG GAMES

The analysis of games given in the kindergarten section should be studied. It will indicate that running games are easiest if, upon a known signal, all must flee across a long base line. This is still fun for the six- and seven-year-old. It is also fun for the eight-year-old if a winner is declared or if the last man over has to pay a penalty before re-entering the game. The penalty should be a constructive activity, not a punitive one.

Two trips across the width of the field or twenty-five rope skips or ten stationary dribbles with each hand might be a suitable penalty for an eight-year-old.

Games with freer chasing patterns can be managed by the eight-year-old. For example, several "Its" can be used simultaneously, or runners can come from two different directions to cross the danger zone. Greater demands can be made on memory, alertness or ability to adjust, or upon physical strength. Three examples are given here, and on page 186.

1. Circle Partner Tag.
(Memory involved)

Partners form a double circle facing centre. Inside circle place hands on each other's shoulders and slide clockwise while outside circle join hands and slide counterclockwise. On the signal, outside circle scatter while inside circle try to find and tag their original partner.

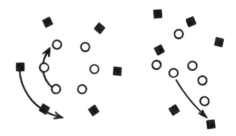

2. Ring Tag.

Groups of two pairs of partners are arranged so that three join hands in a ring. The fourth player, standing outside the ring, tries to tag his partner on the back. The ring swings around to protect the one who is to be tagged.

The scheme of the lesson which devotes much of its time to a running and chasing or a tag game should include some preliminary activities which put stress on parts of the body other than the legs and which provide for an increased awareness of movement principles. This may be done with or without the use of small games equipment. The scheme which was outlined for kindergarten children could be used in primary classes with suitable adjustment of the challenges used. In other words, the lesson will probably include a simple, vigorous *introductory activity*. It might be a free play

3. **Squirrels in Trees.** (Adapted)

(Running in random directions. Converging on a small area at a time of tension.) Two thirds of the class are in partner formation with hands joined to form an arch. The other third, plus one or two extras, are running freely in the space between the "trees." On the signal, each "squirrel" tries to get into a hollow tree. The last one (or two) will be left out and will be "recognized". After a reasonable number of turns, "squirrels" should change places with one of the partners forming the tree. After the new "squirrels" have had some turns, a third change will be needed.

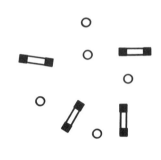

interval with balls, hoops, balls and bats, beanbags, scoops, and plastic balls. It might be a time to practise a body skill, such as running to fill up all the spaces, or making your own pathway. It might be participation in a very simple running game, for example *Odd Man Out*. (In this game all run, skip, etc. in their own pathways until the signal is given. Then all rush to sit back to back with a partner. The one who has no partner is recognized as "Odd.") This part of the lesson would be brief. The next challenge would be to *travel* in many different ways — "Try to make other parts of the body work and let the feet have a rest." After this has been developed through exploration, observation, and adding variations such as changes in speed, direction or level, the challenge would be changed to a consideration of some aspect of *jumping*. This might be concerned with "Jumping and landing lightly, or low down, or letting your knees bring you down, or turning so that you land facing another direction." If hoops or beanbags are available, the task could become — "Relate the jump to the equipment in some way." This might develop as a jump over or around the target, or it could be jumping to catch the beanbag, or to skip using the hoop. The *weightbearing* part of the lesson may feature actions which are done on the spot or which are locomotor. The challenge should be set so that the concern is focussed on "The part of the body which is on the floor" or, for eight-year-olds, "that takes your weight." So the explorations can be concerned with:

- "different parts used when travelling"
- "parts which push you upwards"
- "parts which touch the ground first when coming down."
  (Caution: this has to be worded carefully. The feet are the most effective, hands and feet are possible, hands only are difficult, and other parts of the body have a very restricted use.)

- "how the feet and legs help you to stop or change direction; how the rest of the body helps."

It will be noted that these general forms of activity give a good deal of exercise to the whole body and demand alertness and thoughtful consideration. They are not specific to games activity, but help to bring about general control of the body and a degree of body management.

Most games include a lot of locomotion. Therefore, as the pupils become more skilled it would be beneficial to set tasks which require the joining of several actions together in a highly mobile phrase of movement. For example, the class could observe someone who travels fast between the hoops, and turns and lands in each hoop in succession as he returns to the starting line. Then they may try to find their own ways of joining their actions together.

As indicated before, the categories of activities suggested above — introductory, locomotor, jump and weightbearing — will comprise the first half of the lesson. The second half can be devoted to running, chasing, or a tag game. This sort of lesson is particularly suited to the outdoor program.

ACTIVITIES ASSOCIATED WITH GAMES EQUIPMENT

The analysis given to this section of the work in the kindergarten should be studied because it will probably become the starting point for work with six-year-olds. On the whole, the same equipment is used in the primary grades. However, volleyballs, soccer balls and softballs may be added in Grade Three, but the teacher should carefully observe the way children use them. Sometimes it will be necessary to suggest the use of a lighter ball for pupils whose performance is being disturbed by the weight, say, of a soccer ball. Some schools may choose to add softball bats to the supplies. Again in this case, the teacher should check to see that the bat is a suitable length and weight. Pupils should not develop poor habits through using unsuitable equipment.

Lessons may start with free practice using a piece of equipment made available by the teacher, or with free practice of a body-management skill such as running with changes of direction. According to what the teacher chooses to comment upon and to use for observation and analysis, the lesson can follow a theme which will help the pupils to become more aware of the use of a movement skill. As the lesson progresses, opportunity should be given for pupils to select a particular problem and to practise until an improvement in performance is achieved.

SOME SUGGESTIONS FOR THEMES FOR GAMES LESSONS FOR YOUNG CHILDREN OR INEXPERIENCED PLAYERS

1. Discovering the variety of activities which can be done with a given piece of equipment. (Bounce, toss and catch, roll it, push it, jump over it, etc.)

2. Refining and practising a particular skill such as throwing and catching.

3. Discovering that various parts of the body can be used to control equipment, or to make it go. (Fingers, hands, feet — inside, heel, knee, head, nose, tummy, etc.)

4. Discovering what part of the body can be used to stop the ball. (Hands, whole body, feet, arms, tummy, etc.)

5. Discovering that a ball can be controlled as it is taken through the space (i.e. using it in a locomotor situation).

6. Discovering that it can be used on the spot in different ways.

7. Discovering the contrast between "travelling" and "on the spot."

8. Finding ways of doing body "tricks" while continuing to work with the equipment. (Clapping hands, turning around, touching the floor, etc. before catching the ball or skipping the rope.) Some children regard "tricks" as a way of making their work harder or more challenging.

9. Becoming aware of the concurrent action of the feet (or other specific body parts) while carrying on the main action. (Feet may be still, sliding, running, hopping, or doing special foot patterns while the ball is being bounced.)

10. Becoming aware of the direction(s) into which the ball or equipment is being sent. (Forward, upward, down, down-and-up, up-and-down, to the right, etc.)

11. Discovering the directions in which *you* can go while you work. (Forward, turning, up, sideways, backwards, etc.)

12. Becoming aware of the level(s) at which you can work.

13. Discovering that the equipment can be at one level and the performer at another. (A ball is tossed high while the player touches the floor.)

14. Exploring ways to change between two levels.

15. Discovering the pathways made while working with equipment. ("Do you travel in a circle, a box, a straight line, a zigzag, etc?")

16. Discovering that some actions are done very quickly (or slowly, or suddenly).

17. Discovering that some actions require a strong (gentle) way of moving.

18. Exploring ways of showing a contrast between fast and slow actions (or sudden and slow; or strong and gentle).

19. Discovering that one can use the equipment on the floor, or in the air, or against the wall, or a combination of two of these.

20. Discovering that some players work in relation to markings on the floor, or the wall.

21. Becoming aware of ways of working with a partner.

22. Discovering a way of scoring actions. (Counting how many, seeing how fast, seeing if you can, seeing if you miss.)

23. Making up a game: "Your game is to include — e.g. working with the foot, the ball and the wall between these marks."

Games stations

Simple games stations have been suggested for kindergarten. These may be used as a beginning situation for any of the next three grades and modified according to what seems to be needed. Sometimes the starting line can be moved further away from the target; sometimes a different kind of ball can be used; sometimes the challenge can be made more difficult. The teacher must be prepared to think of new situations which will take into account the increasing ability of the pupils or a closer alliance to a specific game. The children are capable of arranging the equipment and players in ways which will give them a satisfactory play situation.

Original games

As the pupils advance in Grades Two and Three they become increasingly able to make up a game with rules and a scoring pattern. They should probably start with a partner or a group of three and should perhaps be asked to work in groups no larger than four. If the major theme of the lesson has been concerned with specific ball handling skills, these should probably be included in the games they invent. Similarly, if the stress has been on changes of speed, they should be asked to invent a game in which changes of speed are required for good results.

SAMPLE LESSON PLANS

The lesson plans given below are an attempt to indicate how the teaching of these three kinds of games lessons might be organized.

SAMPLE LESSON PLAN ONE: Games lesson based upon a theme and culminating in an opportunity to make up a game using some aspect of the theme

GRADE: One, Two or Three

THEME: Awareness of directions being used

SUBTHEMES: (These are not all stressed in the plan, but may need some attention during the lesson.)
  1. Actions: e.g. toss, kick, catch
  2. Relationships: the games situation

INTRODUCTION:
Challenge: "Get yourself a ball. Spread out in the space. Decide on your own things to practise."
Teacher moves among them. Praises. Verbally identifies some of the things being done.

DEVELOPMENT:

Observation: Two performers show what they have been doing. Teacher gives an observation question *before* they perform: "In what direction do their balls go?" (Tossed *up* and dropped *down*. Kicked *forward*.)

Challenge: "Do your own work again. Find out in which direction your ball goes."

Observation: One-half of the class watches the other half work. Observation question: "See if you can find anyone sending the ball in another direction besides up, down or forward." If necessary, the other half of the class is observed.

Challenge: "As you work with your ball, try to make it go in different directions."
Teacher moves among them. Praises. Verbally identifies some of the directions used.

Challenge: "Choose two of the things you have found to do. Make sure that your ball goes in two different directions. Practise, so that you can do these things very well."

Observation: "All the people who have chosen 'up' in their work, do yours now."
All the watchers will see if they can find the upward direction. Possibly two categories can show their work and have it checked. A third group should include all those who have not yet shown their work. The teacher should make a quick comment about them.

CULMINATION: The class is divided into four even groups. Each group is given a working area. Each member of the group is given the challenge to make up a game which includes certain specifics.

1. Individuals. Ball and hoop each. Game is to stress **down.**

2. Individuals. Ball each. Share the use of a wall. Game is to stress **forward.**

3. Partners, sharing a beanbag. Game is to be for two and stress **up.**

4. Partners, sharing a seven-inch ball. Game is to be for two and stress **backward.**

At the discretion of the teacher, the groups may rotate and experience more than one situation.

SAMPLE LESSON PLAN TWO: Games lesson based on a theme and culminating in the use of *Games Stations*

GRADE: One, Two or Three

THEME: Ball handling actions

SUBTHEMES: Ball actions, relationships — e.g. to floor, air, wall

INTRODUCTION:
   Challenge: "Get your ball. Find a good working space. Practise something that you want to improve (i.e. do a little better)."
Teacher moves among pupils. Praises. Discusses individual actions. Coaches.

DEVELOPMENT:
   Observation: Two or three show what they have been practising. Observers are asked to decide *what* the three have chosen to practise (e.g. catch, kick, bounce).

   Challenge: "Everyone try to do two or three different things with the ball."
Teacher encourages and verbalizes actions being done.

   Observation: Two or three pupils are chosen because their balls are used in relation to the floor, or the air, or the wall. Observers are asked to decide *where* the performers are sending their balls. Or, they are asked: "What do the balls touch?"

   Challenge: "Everyone try to use the air, or the floor, or the wall, or each one of them."
Teacher coaches for safety and concern for others.

   Observation: All observe two pupils; one of whom uses the floor, and the other the wall. Observers are asked to decide *what happens* to the ball after it hits the floor or the wall. (It bounces back.)

   Challenge: "Try to find ways of making your ball come back to you."
The teacher must decide whether to show the results of this step, or to accept the work and move the lesson on.

CULMINATION: Games Stations. Approximately four pupils work at each station.

1. Seven-inch inflated ball each. Four hoops placed on the floor as stepping stones.
Challenge: "Make up a game which uses the ball and the hoops."

2. Seven-inch inflated ball each. Four skittles or Indian clubs. A starting line.
Challenge: "Bowl the ball to the pin."

3. Three-inch bouncing ball each. Wall space.
Challenge: "What can you do with your ball if you use the wall?"

4. Two ring quoits. Two sets of partners.
Challenge: "Play a catching game with your partner."

5. Seven-inch inflated ball each. Four players. A section of floor with some lines on it.
Challenge: "Use the lines in an interesting way as you play with your ball."

6. Seven-inch inflated ball each. Two sets of partners.
Challenge: "Make up a game with your ball and your partner. Use the floor too."

7. Seven-inch inflated ball each. Four skipping ropes placed on the floor.
Challenge: "Make up your own game using the ball, the floor and the ropes in their position on the floor."

8. Two three-inch balls. Two chairs. Two sets of partners.
Challenge: "Make up a game using the ball. Have one player on each side of the chair."

The groups may remain at one station, or may rotate. Perhaps Grade One will take quite a long time to organize themselves and should remain at one station. On the other hand, their short attention span will have to be considered. Probably Grade Three will rotate two or three times. On the other hand, their games may become sufficiently complicated to require a fair time to develop to the full.

The teacher should probably move from group to group and toward the end of the lesson comment upon the ways in which players are getting the ball to return to them.

These games stations may be used as the culmination of a series of six or eight lessons depending upon how quickly the groups are rotated.

SAMPLE LESSON PLAN THREE: Games lesson based on *Running, Chasing and Tag Games*

GRADE: One, Two or Three

THEME: Space awareness; moving freely in an area

SUBTHEMES:
1. Body awareness: forms of locomotion, awareness of body parts touching the floor
2. Chasing game

INTRODUCTION:
    Challenge: "Travel fast all about this big space. Visit all the places." "Good! Some are going down the side; some are going across the middle; some in the corners. Here's someone who has found a way to go close to the ground. Good! Here's a boy who goes away up in the air."

DEVELOPMENT:
    Observation: "Watch these people. What parts of their bodies touch the ground as they travel?"

    Challenge: "All of you find different ways to travel. Find out which part of you touches the ground."
Teacher observes and states which parts are being used on the ground. She may note (aloud) that some ways of travelling have to be *slow*.

    Challenge: "Can you do the very opposite? Can you find ways of getting yourself right off the ground for a moment?"

    Observation: One half observes the other half. Reverse roles. Question: "What do most people do?" (Probably jump.)

    Challenge: "Try again. Get yourself right off the ground. Be sure you know which part will touch the ground first when you come down."

    Observation: All watch two or three individuals to see which part of them touches the ground when they *land*. They should notice that the feet are very important. They are strong enough to help in a landing.

    Challenge: "Try jumping and landing on your feet." (Since this is a form of recapitulation, it is possible to close off at the end of a few practices with a comment of assessment.)

CULMINATION:

Activity: *Crows and Cranes* (Simplified).

"Everyone put their toes on this line and sit down."

Teacher will explain that the centre line is a starting line. One zone line is for *Crows* and one zone line is for *Cranes*. If she says "Crows," all run there, etc. etc. She should test out the sound "Crrr—ows!" and let them notice that they must listen to the end before they run.

Play the game, the teacher giving as much help as is needed. The scoring for Grade One may simply be a show of hands of those who went the right way.

Note: Grade Two will probably be able to play the regulation game. Grade Three certainly can.

Crows and Cranes.

Simplified Version

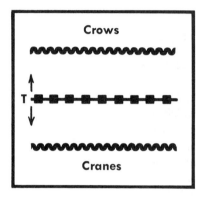

Regulation Game

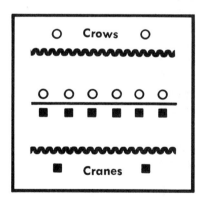

In the regulation game, teams start with even numbers. Each team's safety zone is behind its starting position. If a team's name is called, the players flee for safety to their own zone pursued by the opposing team. Anyone tagged must join the tagger's team. The team which has the most players at the end of the session is the winner.

Note: 1. No time has been spent on the concept of tagging. If this needs attention, the teacher may deal with it as an opportunity to understand a concept. The discussion on p. 182 will probably help the teacher plan for this understanding.

2. While the lesson plan has been given in the form of implicit instructions the lesson for the teacher, in actual fact, should develop from the movements which are being used by the children. The instructions are intended to indicate that the teacher praises often; verbally identifies many of the desirable actions of the pupils; sets precise questions to guide the observations, and follows the observations with a challenge which makes use of what has been observed. Certain routines and organizational procedures are stated in the imperative. The teacher should not be alarmed if the original plan is subject to considerable change as a result of making use of the movements which the children invent while responding to the various challenges.

THE JUNIOR DIVISION

Children of ages nine, ten, and eleven will do most of their games work with the skills associated with such major games as soccer, softball, volleyball, and track and field. The skills will be used in competitive situations which arise in simple games based on these skills. For the most part the games will use six to eight players on a team. The teacher should try to arrange for maximum participation for all pupils. There should be a minimum of waiting or taking turns. The general planning should assure that, for a considerable part of the lesson, each pupil or each set of partners has a ball or whatever basic equipment is being used. That is to say, volleyballs should be used when the skills of that game are being learned and soccer balls should be used for the development of soccer skills. However, the seven-inch inflated ball should be used if needed to give everyone an opportunity to be active. In this case, the balls should be exchanged often so that all pupils have a chance to work with the regulation ball.

The following five themes should give a fairly thorough experience in the skills of any of the games. All experiments should be done in accordance with the strategy and rules of the specific games being developed.

SOME THEMES FOR USE IN DEVELOPING SKILLS ASSOCIATED WITH THE MAJOR TEAM GAMES

1. Themes concerned with the development of a specific games skill: high volley, soccer dribble, overhand throw, two-hand pass, broad jump take-off, etc.

2. Themes concerned with body management in games: going to meet the ball, jumping for better play, keeping on the move (with or without the ball), using the eyes, working by feeling (kinesthetic sense), using body turns, stopping under control, variations in speed of movement, good balance on feet, making the knees work for you, getting strength with accuracy.

Body management is important in basketball.

3. Themes concerned with space work: lining up with a ball to receive it, spreading out on the playing area, looking for open spaces, running into open spaces, sending the ball into open spaces, changing directions (with and without the ball), using a change of levels (for self or for ball), judging distance (near and far).

4. Themes concerned with teammates and opponents: passing to a partner, receiving from a partner, passing and receiving, taking a partner's rebound, changing places with a partner, keeping an even distance from a partner, working in your own zone, helping your teammates to fill up the whole court, dodging an opponent, watching an opponent to anticipate his moves, intercepting, taking rebounds, making yourself an obstacle in his space.

5. Themes concerned with games strategy: making up a game according to .simple requirements, finding ways to score, finding ways to start a game, deciding on fair penalties, making rules for safety, making rules to

keep the game manageable, devising special systems for scoring, planning the defence.

LESSON PLANNING

In planning the games lessons for juniors, it should be remembered that a transition is being made from general ball handling skills and active ball games to skills which are particular to a major game. These skills are governed by the rules of the game concerned, and are or will be executed in accordance with or adapted from the requirements of the regulation game. This will probably mean that considerable emphasis will continue to be placed on general body management.

SAMPLE LESSON PLANS

The lesson plans given here are an attempt to show how the challenges and the observations can be directed towards the requirements of the game being dealt with.

SAMPLE LESSON PLAN ONE: Games lesson

GRADE: Five

THEME: Soccer skills: — stressing trapping
                                    — reviewing dribbling and kicking

SUBTHEMES: Games strategy: attacking and guarding

INTRODUCTION:
    Soccer (or substitute) ball each.
    Challenge: "Warm up and improve skills by alternating dribbling, passing and kicking with vertical flights of the ball off different parts of the body." Teacher moves among them. Encourages. Coaches.

    Observation: Two or three carry on as above. Observers watch to see which parts of the body can put the ball in vertical flight: e.g. parts of one foot, grip of two feet with a jump and a flip, knee (if the ball is high enough to get under it), also shoulder or head.

    Challenge: "Work again on the same challenge. Try to improve the control of the ball."

    Challenge: Balls placed on the floor. "All run and dodge in the spaces between the balls. Pause and repeat with increased speed. Pause and repeat concentrating on nimble footwork."

Challenge: "Run. Choose a convenient ball as a target and jump *high* over it. Land and continue to run and jump for height."

Class observation: All watch one jumper to see what shape is made by the body in the air.

Challenge: "Everyone work again. Try to make an *arched* shape in the air."

DEVELOPMENT:
Challenge: "Dribble in a clockwise direction. Pass-kick the ball against the wall or fence or line of players. Retrieve it and continue to dribble, pass, kick and retrieve."

Although this is review, attention may be drawn to the part of the foot used for passing, which foot is used, strength of kick, part of the foot used for retrieving, or the flow of one action into the next. Practise in the reverse direction.

Challenge: "Dribble in towards the wall, fence or line of receivers. Send the ball with a low, hard kick to the wall. Control the rebound. Practise freely as a review." Teacher coaches by questioning: "What kinds of kicks?" (Short, sharp, hard.) "What part of foot?" (Top of instep.) "How are the feet used?" (Both equally.) She draws attention to the balance required, and the position of the supporting foot in relation to the ball when kicking.

Class Observation: All watch a good performer to see how he controls the ball as it comes off the wall, fence or receiver. Some questions may be: "Which parts of the body are used — for high balls and for low balls? How does the player handle the impact to avoid injury?"

Challenge: "Return to your own work and concentrate on trapping the rebound or pass."
Teacher observes, and coaches individuals.

He will probably have to encourage pupils to kick hard enough to make the rebound forceful, or to reach the receiver with force.

CULMINATION:
Groups of threes having one Indian club and one ball between them.

Challenge: "Make up a game of 'Club Guard' which stresses the trapping skills which have been learned. Keep the play open." There may have to be some restraining lines for kicking and guarding. Work out a rotation so that all get experience in trapping.

Note: When a line of receivers is used instead of a wall, the teacher will have to arrange a suitable exchange of roles at reasonable intervals.

SAMPLE LESSON PLAN TWO: Games lesson

GRADE: Six

THEME: Volleyball: — stressing ball control in the vertical plane, i.e. the volley

SUBTHEMES: 1. Space: upward direction
            2. Body parts: stressing use of hands, and mobile feet

Volleyball: "Explore ways of stressing the vertical flight of the ball."

INTRODUCTION:
    Challenge: "Using a seven-inch rubber inflated ball, warm up by finding ways to control the ball while you keep on the move — e.g. toss and catch, bounce, toss against the wall, volley upward."

    Observation: "Try to name two different actions which people use while working with the ball."

    Challenge: "Work again. Be able to name the different actions you can use. Keep yourself on the move."

DEVELOPMENT:
    Observation: "Watch these two players. Find out how they use their hands (to toss, and catch; to volley)."

"What is the difference in the use of the hands?" ('Catch' is 'seizing,' see Chapter Five, pages 78 and 89; 'toss' is 'getting rid of,' see Chapter Five, pages 78 and 89, 'volley' is 'getting rid of' with no 'seizing.')

Challenge: "Using a volleyball, stress getting rid of it."

Observation: "Watch this player. In what direction does he send the ball?" (Upward)

Challenge: "Continue your work, stressing 'getting rid of' and 'upward.' "

Relief Break: "Put the ball on the floor and make your feet work very quickly all about the ball without touching it."
Teacher encourages speed, all forms of jumping and nimble footwork.

Challenge: "The ball can roll and bounce. Use the ball in any convenient way *while* you make *yourself* roll or bounce."
Teacher praises and names some of the good ideas.

Challenge: "Find a partner. Put one ball away. Pass the ball upward and over to your partner without catching it."
Teacher encourages a high arc, "Getting rid of it."

Observation: "Watch these two couples and find the difference in the way they use their feet." (One couple is stationary; the other mobile.)

Challenge: "This time, keep the ball passing with a high arc, but keep your feet very mobile."
Teacher encourages a great deal of foot movement, even movement in a half circle, or forward/backward for a distance of three feet.

Challenge: "Change your work into a game by placing the ball for your partner so that he has to travel to reach it. Choose two lines on the floor which will indicate where the ball will be placed."

Challenge: "Form groups of four with one ball. Play 'Keep-Up.' See which group can keep it up for the greatest number of volleys in one minute."

CULMINATION:

Station three groups of four on each side of the net. Each group of eight has one ball. Play "Keep-Up" over the net. Extra groups can play "Keep-Up" over a bench.

Rules: The side which allows the ball to touch the floor gives a point to the opponents. There is no limit to the number of volleys between team

---

members, but stress should be placed on volleying the ball over the net in the hope that the opponents will allow it to touch their floor.

"KEEP-UP"

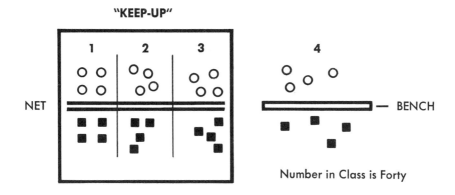

Number in Class is Forty

THE INTERMEDIATE DIVISION

The teaching of games in the intermediate division should progress from the work done in the earlier grades. Therefore, the various skills should be approached as review work and analyzed for weaknesses, worked on for improvement and used in increasingly demanding games situations. This will necessitate attention being given to body-management skills which will support the specific games skills. In addition, the fitness of the body should be given attention so that the stamina to run and the strength and speed with which the skills are performed will meet the requirements of the game. A good deal of attention should also be given to team strategy and to the effect of the rules upon it.

Some suggestions are made in two areas from which specific activities can be drawn to increase the standard of play in various team games. These areas are:
1. skills of body management, and
2. the skills of individual and team play required in games.

SUGGESTED ACTIVITIES FOR DEVELOPING SKILLS OF BODY MANAGEMENT

1. *Locomotor Skills*: Run, walk, step, jump, hop, step-hop, slide, side-step, cross-step, etc.

Each game should be analyzed to determine which types of locomotion are characteristic of its play. The actions selected may be practised in conjunction with changes of direction, levels, floor patterning. They may be varied in the manner of execution by being done sometimes with strength and vigour, and at other times lightly and easily; sometimes fast, sometimes with suddenness, sometimes slowly, occasionally with sustainment, sometimes in a twisting, curving manner, but more often with directness. They can be done with ongoing, free flow intention, or with restraint in expectation of having to stop. They can be done with or without the equipment, and with or without teammates or opponents. They can be used very profitably during the warm-up part of a lesson.

2. *Non-locomotor Skills:* Landings, pivots, turns, jumps, twists, reaches, bends, varying forms of balance.

The particular form that these actions take should be determined by the game being practised. For example, in the basketball season, jumps could be related to the centre jump and be done with one hand leading. In the soccer season, jumps could be related to heading and done with the head leading.

Jumping practice may be related to the centre jump in basketball season.

These actions can also be varied according to the suggestions made for the locomotor skills, that is, in terms of *space, effort quality,* or *relationship* to equipment or other players.

SUGGESTED ACTIVITIES FOR DEVELOPING SKILLS OF INDIVIDUAL OR TEAM PLAY

1. Using and/or improving a specific type of skill: e.g. underhand throw, two bounce dribble, bunt.

2. Aiming at different kinds of targets: e.g. narrow, bull's-eye, open goals, containers.

3. Aiming at moving targets.

4. Making use of rebounds: e.g. ball must ricochet off the wall before it can be aimed at the target.

5. Bringing a ball down a big court by passing it among teammates. Shooting after crossing a shooting line.

6. Breaking for open spaces to receive a ball on the move.

7. Receiving a ball and changing direction *before* passing it.

8. Stressing a special quality of movement: e.g. suddenness, strength, or bound flow — as a variation of a body management or a games skill being practised.

9. Working with a bat (or other equipment) and a specified number of players: e.g. one partner, a group of six.

10. Working a ball between two planes: e.g. from vertical into horizontal and into vertical again.

11. Player and ball moving in different directions: e.g. passing right and running left, tossing ball up while travelling forward or backward.

12. Using *any* part or one *specific* part of the body for stopping the ball.

13. Combining speed with changes of direction as a form of control in body management or games skill practice.

14. Working on floor patterns with a specific number of players in a game context, e.g. basketball forwards.

15. Making up a game in accordance with certain specifications: e.g. "Use four players, the wall and a ball," or "Use three players, the basket and a ball. Stress locomotion."

16. Using a two-part sequence: e.g. "Send the ball to the base before sending it home."

17. Finding ways of scoring when two teams are doing different things: e.g. one passing and the other running.

18. Finding fair ways to start a game.

19. Finding ways of giving everyone a turn.

20. Stressing mobility: e.g. as many players moving as much of the time as possible.

21. Finishing *on* a base or line.

22. Overrunning a base or line.

23. Using "chasing" as a theme. Finding forms of defence such as fleeing, dodging, taking advantage of a crowd.

24. Play based upon use of a specific piece of equipment: e.g. bat, racquet, stick, scoop.

25. Play based upon the use of a net, rope, crossbar, wall or other obstruction.

26. Play based upon some aspect of a specific major game: e.g. a basketball jump ball, the volleyball serve, the soccer dribble, the softball underhand pitch.

27. Play based on the strategy required in a major game: e.g. plays for out-of-bound throw-ins for basketball, soccer or field hockey, or the starting plays for these three games, or court passing plays in volleyball.

28. Opposition themes: one player aiming while the opponent deflects, one team taking prisoners while the other recaptures them, one team filling a container while the other empties it.

29. Speed themes: e.g. which group can accomplish a task (within the rules) first.

30. Quantity themes: e.g. which team can accumulate the most runs, most balls, knock over the most clubs, etc.

SAMPLE LESSON PLANS

The lesson plan given below is an attempt to show how body management skills and game skills including game-like situations can be presented to a class of thirty-five players in a physical education period of thirty to forty minutes.

SAMPLE LESSON PLAN ONE: Softball

GRADE: Seven

THEME: Using a specific skill: improving batting skill

SUBTHEMES: 1. Using a specific skill: good base-running technique
2. Making up a game according to certain specifications

INTRODUCTION:
Challenge: "Warm up by alternating jogging with short distance speed runs."
Teacher evaluates the suddenness of take-off and speed of run. Relates the practice to base-running by coaching the pupils to check distance of speed-run and to try to make it the same as a base-length.
Partners, starting a base-length apart.
Number 1 runner — runs full speed to partner's base and stops on it. No overrun allowed.
Number 2 runner — jogs to starting base and repeats the base-run.
The whole sequence is repeated several times.
Teacher gives general evaluation and coaching. The partners give personal evaluation and coaching.
Warm-up for throwing. Partners with one ball.

Challenge: "Alternate an underhand pitch, a rolling grounder, an overhand throw. Time it so that the fielder can run in towards the grounder for the pick-up and return throw, but has time to return to position to receive the pitch."

Coaching Hints: Make sure that the players get equal practice.

Carry on, but increase *speed* and *distance.*

Check the pitching form.

Take the necessary time for wind-up and delivery.

Use the feet in the legal manner (see rulebook).

DEVELOPMENT:

Working on batting skills. Partners with one bat and one mush ball.

Challenge: "Warm up arms with some easy swings, stressing the bat coming through parallel to the ground. Check the grip and location of the trademark (up)."

Observation: Preparatory stance. Players take turns practising or evaluating partner for:
— foot positioning — feet astride, weight on back foot
— elevation of elbows at the end of the backswing, ready to swing through
— eyes on pitcher.

Challenge: "Swing."

Observation: Pupils check following points:
— retain parallel swing
— put strong force into swing
— shift weight forward to put power of body behind the swing
— keep eyes on the ball (mime).

Challenge: "After five or six swings, partners change roles."

Teacher checks individuals and gives individual and group coaching, including directed observation.

Challenge: "Repeat, hitting mush balls. Continually check points stressed previously."

CULMINATION:

Make up a softball-type game using the equipment. Arrange it so that all players have as much variety as possible in the different skills. "Work-up" would be a good example.

NOTE ON METHODOLOGY.

Directed observation may be used when techniques need upgrading. Problem-solving may also be used as for example: "Find the effect of a parallel swing, a down-cut swing, an up-cut swing" or "Find the effect of a short, long or medium grip on the bat." The observation and evaluation of the games which are developed in the last activity will allow good ideas to be shared.

NINE

THE TEACHING
OF GYMNASTICS

In Chapter Six an attempt was made to analyze the ways in which an understanding of certain concepts of movement can contribute to an increase in body control and management in gymnastics. In this chapter, consideration will be given to how this knowledge of gymnastic movement can be organized for the benefit of children in different levels of the elementary and junior high schools.

The deciding factor in lesson planning must always be the needs of the pupils and, therefore, each teacher must arrange the lesson in the light of his knowledge of his pupils. Even so, a plan which is prepared with the needs of a particular group of children in mind may still have to be changed as the pupils' ideas and performances are taken into account during the lesson. However, certain expectations can govern the initial planning and form a basis from which these modifications may spring.

Generally speaking, a major part of the lesson will be devoted to floor work, that is, movements of the body such as locomotion, jumps or balances performed on the floor without any equipment. The other major part of the lesson will be concerned with movement done in relation to apparatus, such as the wall climber, vertical ropes, various types of vaulting boxes, balance beams, tumbling mats and so on. Small equipment, such as hoops, canes and ropes, is often used as a partial substitute for the apparatus named above. This may be done as a way of preparing the children for activities on the climber. Or, it may be used to supplement the large apparatus if that is in short supply. Work with partners or members of a small group, usually without small equipment, is another common aspect of the work. In the simplest sense, the partner may be a substitute for apparatus, as he is in leapfrog, for example. On the other hand, the problem may be one of group relationships. In such a case, partners are necessary for its solution.

Thus the lesson may proceed from individual floor work, to a secondary stage where small apparatus and/or a partner are involved,

The last part of the lesson is concerned with movement on large apparatus.

to the final stage on large apparatus. Another alternative would be to start with free practice using small equipment, proceed to floor work and conclude with work on large apparatus. The second alternative is often very helpful for the primary classes because the small equipment provides a strong stimulus to movement. The teacher, by observing the movement arising from the use of the equipment, can discover the needs of the pupils and develop the subsequent stages of the lesson to fulfil these needs.

In deciding upon the procedure to be followed in developing the lessons, it will be necessary for the teacher to consider the use of four vital tools, namely: challenges, observation, small equipment, large apparatus.

• *Challenges* are verbal stimuli which establish the problem to be solved in movement. According to how they are worded, they can set a broad problem which will involve a good deal of exploration, or they can set a more specific problem which will tend to require a fairly precise or a very specific modification of the movement. In the early stages of any movement study, the broad, exploratory challenge will probably be needed in order to allow the pupils to discover for themselves as much about the movement as possible. For example, if the teacher wishes the pupils to become aware of the nature of locomotor movement, the challenge may be as broad as: "Use the first few minutes to warm yourselves up. Use many *vigorous* movements." Such a challenge is likely to give rise to activities which are done on the spot, and movements which take the performer around the room. Hence, by the contrast, *locomotion* can be identified as movement which causes you to travel.

If, on the other hand, *locomotion* is already understood as *travel*, the challenge might be as precise as: "Find several different ways of using the feet for travelling." This could lead to the identification of such foot actions as run, gallop, slide. In this particular case the study would be concerned with the relationship of one foot to the other — a Body Awareness challenge. As soon as this is clear, the challenge is stated equally precisely: "See if you can find any other relationships between the feet in travel actions."

The great necessity is that the teacher maintains a logical succession of challenges which delve into the nature of the movement. It is not a matter of simply keeping the pupils active by asking them to find more

Small equipment may be used as a partial substitute for large apparatus.

examples of the movement theme under consideration. Rather, it involves a seeking for the identification of the actions.

The *observation* of contrasting movements helps immeasurably in the identification process. For example, if the teacher wishes to have the pupils become aware of locomotion, the observation of one boy who warms up by running on the spot plus the observation of one who runs around the room makes it relatively easy to discover the chief difference in the runs. Once it is observed that one form of running makes the boy travel through space, the basic definition can be established.

Thus the observation of contrasting movement elements is a great help in the process of analyzing movement.

In using observation as a teaching technique, the teacher must guide the pupils by giving them something specific to look for. For example, to observe a run and a gallop the question may be: "What is the difference in *the way the feet are placed*?" The italicized words give the observer something very definite to look for. This will give a clarity to the teaching and give the pupils considerable security, because they know what their responsibilities are.

Within a lesson, different forms of organization may be used for the observations. For example, one half of the class may observe the other half. This may be used to show the great variety of possible actions as a means of encouraging individuals to widen their own scope of activity. It may be used as a quick check to be sure that everyone has found a way of travelling. It may be used as a quick way of searching for an exceptional variation, as, for example, walking on the hands. The observation of two performers who are using contrasting elements of movement is often employed because it gives a clear basis for comparison. Three performers may be observed. For example, if a runner, jumper, and galloper are chosen, the observation question could be: "In what different ways are the feet used?" Or, for another example, if a runner, galloper, and slider are used, the question could be: "In what way does the runner use his feet which is different from the way the galloper and slider use theirs?"

Thus, observations of contrasting actions are indispensable when an analysis is required. When large groups are observed, variety, the unusual or the general effect are picked out.

Immediately following an observation interlude, the class should be given a challenge which allows them to use their observations to identify or modify their own work.

• *Small equipment* may be used as a stimulus to movement. If it is used for this purpose, the teacher must select it carefully so that the movement elicited is the movement which is required for that lesson. For example, if the teacher wishes to deal with the curling and stretching of the body, she may start by allowing the pupils a few minutes for free play with hoops. The subsequent observation may be made using pupils who have chosen to go through the hoops. The observation question can be directed towards watching the action of the body as the performer goes through the hoops. The body will curl, at least partially. In this way, hoops have been used by the teacher to elicit a response which she needs as a starting point of the lesson.

Small equipment may be used as a substitute for large apparatus. When pupils work on the climber, the benches, the vertical rope and other large apparatus, it is necessary to avoid overcrowding. For the sake of safety and for the sake of growth and improvement, each child should be provided with working space. There should be a minimum of waiting for turns. Hence it is often necessary to improvise apparatus to accommodate the number in the class. Hoops, ropes, beanbags, clubs, blocks, canes or staves can be combined with mats, benches and utility boxes to provide more apparatus stations. It is usual to work in relation to these pieces as they are placed on the floor and not to pick them up and use them as manipulative material. Thus they are used in relatively the same way as the large apparatus is used and become a substitute for it.

• The *large apparatus* provides a new environment for the child and presents new opportunities for movement. For example, the hands and arms are used extensively in climbing, hanging and swinging. Inverted positions of the body are possible in a great variety of circumstances. Challenges to balance and to muscular strength are presented. Control of the body in descending from a height is a major area of experience permitted by the use of large apparatus. Depending upon the needs of the children, the teacher may arrange to use the apparatus as a stimulus to movement, or as a tool which will facilitate certain combinations of movement. In the first case, the children are rarely given a specific movement challenge, but the teacher gives them a purpose by saying "Find something to do which is safe for you and safe for others." In the latter case, they usually work on developing a specific movement theme on the apparatus. When they do this a challenge such as "Develop a short sequence in which a change of speed is a significant part of the action," may be presented.

Details of the types of apparatus used for this work are given in the Appendix.

LESSON PLANNING

The details of lesson planning are affected by the individual class and by the general level of experience and maturity of the individuals in it. Nevertheless, certain other factors must be considered by the teacher at the lesson-planning stage.

The first consideration has to do with the teacher's purpose and its bearing on the balance between the physical demands of the lesson versus the understanding of the nature of movement. Presumably, the teacher will attempt to give a reasonably even balance to these two aspects of the work in the overall effect of a year's work and, therefore, will usually keep the two balanced within any one lesson. However, sometimes the search for meaning in movement may interrupt the vigour of the lesson. At other times, the vigorous participation may overshadow the analysis of what is being done.

With this dual responsibility in mind, it is usual to plan a lesson around a movement theme and to try to bring the theme into a sufficiently varied number of situations so that a thoroughly vigorous lesson results. This should mean that respiration has accelerated — perhaps through loco-motion or forms of jumping; that the trunk, including the spine, has been brought into action and that there has been some weightbearing done by the arms and shoulder girdle. It will be noticed that all the points mentioned above fall into the Body Awareness aspect of the movement con-cepts. This may be safely considered to be required in every gymnastics lesson. The use of apparatus in the latter part of the lesson will also mean that the relationship to the apparatus must always be considered. In addition to these two mandatory considerations, there will be a par-ticular point of emphasis chosen for the specific lesson. It may be selected from any of the four components of movement, viz., Body Awareness, Space Awareness, Effort Qualities of Movement or Relationship.

Thus a lesson is usually designed to have a *major theme* and two *subsidiary themes*. A theoretical example is given below. With alterations to suit the individual class, it should be reasonably functional. It is given in abbreviated point outline showing the expected results of observations and subsequent challenges.

SAMPLE LESSON PLAN

The sample lesson plan illustrates theory discussed. Its purpose is explained in the paragraph immediately above.

SAMPLE LESSON PLAN: Adaptation of a plan to meet the needs of a first lesson

GRADE: Five (limited experience)

THEME: Use of hands

SUBTHEMES: 1. Pathways
2. Relationships to apparatus

INTRODUCTION:
Challenge: "Run — fill up all the spaces — stop on clap."

Observation: One-half observes the other half: "Are they able to fill up all the spaces?"

Challenge: "All try again. Think about the kind of pathway you use."

Observation: One-half observes the other half: "Watch one person. Try to find a word to describe his pathway." (Curving).

Challenge: "Use *curving* pathways, but choose your own way of *travelling*."

Observation: "Find two or three ways of travelling. Be prepared to name the parts of the body which touched the floor — e.g. hands and then feet, hands and stomach."

DEVELOPMENT:
Challenge: "Continue with your own way of travelling, but find out which parts of your body are touching the floor."

Observation: "Observe all those whose hands touched the floor. Find out one way in which the hands were used — e.g. pushed against the floor, pulled; both hands together, one hand and then the other."

Challenge: "Explore ways of using the hands to assist *locomotor* movement."

Challenge: "Work with a partner. Stress the use of hands for *locomotor* movement. Use your partner to *help* your locomotion."

Observation: "Observe pairs who show varied use of hands — e.g. gripping, pulling, pushing (ungripped), interlocked hands (open, closed), et cetera."

CULMINATION:
Groups of four. "Arrange apparatus," (arrangement designed by teacher to elicit varied pathways and to give opportunities to use hands in varied ways).

Challenge: "Try out the apparatus, finding a pathway which includes all the pieces. Check your safety."

Challenge: "As you travel, stress the use of the hands. Arrange your pathways so that all four people are working all the time."
The work may follow these stages:
a. Exploration and invention.
b. Select a given pathway and specific actions.
c. Practise the sequence, improving details of bodily control. Strive to be clear in the use of the hands.

d. Selected groups are observed. Use of hands is analyzed. Pathways and activity of all members is recognized.

QUIET ENDING

1. Housekeeping — each group puts away the equipment which they set up. Everything is carried. Nothing is dragged across the floor. Everyone works until all items are put away. The teacher supervises except in primary classes where he may assist the pupils with the heaviest pieces of equipment.

2. Quiet time — young children lie on their backs "like rag dolls." The teacher checks the relaxation of individual pupils. Older pupils sit and discuss the successes of the lesson and may plan for the next lesson.

LAY-OUT OF APPARATUS STATIONS

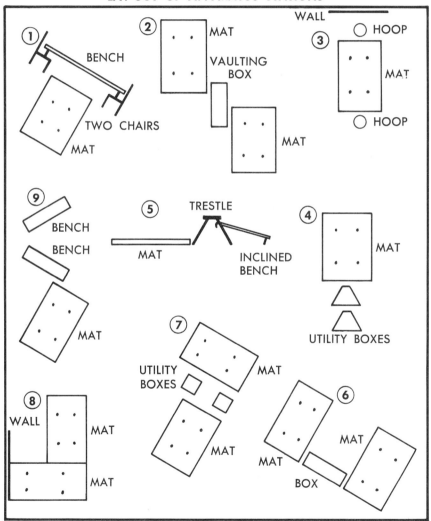

PROMOTING GROWTH AND PROGRESS

According to the grade level and the experience of the children, the teacher will guide their growth and progress in gymnastic movement through certain well-defined stages.

1. EXPLORATION OF THE PROBLEM. This is the first essential stage of diffused responses and trial and error efforts. In very young children this stage is very protracted. With older children, it is usually much shorter. In somewhat familiar situations it tends to be fairly short. In radically new situations it tends to be lengthy. It is a mistake to omit this stage or foreshorten it. It is one of the arts of teaching to judge the correct moment for moving on. If the teacher moves on too soon, the work will lack scope and understanding and in the case of the use of apparatus this could lead to accidents. On the other hand, if the exploration phase is retained too long, children become bored and lose interest in and respect for the activity.

2. IDENTIFICATION OF WHAT HAS BEEN REVEALED BY EXPLORATION. This identification process usually needs to be a class endeavour helped by the teacher. It is done by observing several pupils' exploratory work to discover the contrasts of movement which have been uncovered. These contrasts will reveal a principle at work. For example, if one child is turning clockwise and another turning counterclockwise, the principle being examined is spatial and it is specifically a matter of direction.

There will usually follow a period of study which fluctuates between exploration (what other directions can be found?) and identification (forward and backward turns in the wheel plane — as in the forward roll — et cetera.)

3. SELECTION. At this stage the performer should settle upon some material in order to work on it and refine it. Usually it is necessary to ask the pupils to select, perhaps, three actions which can be joined together in a sequential flow. It is not until the performer experiences a participation in the flow of movement, controlling the pauses, accenting certain movements, having suitable ways of connecting the various actions, that he really feels the exhilaration that movement can offer.

Beginners do not recognize the unity or phrasing of their movements. They rarely have any comprehension of the beginning, the selected actions and the conclusion of their phrase of movement. This is one reason for specifying the number of actions to be included. However, as soon as they begin to show a sense of phrasing the teacher should leave them free to compose their own sequences.

4. REFINING THE SEQUENCE. This may necessitate slight changes to accommodate the flow of one movement into another. However, it should soon be spent in working on the dynamics of the movement sequence

By changing from one part of the apparatus to another, a sequential flow of movement may emerge.

(see page 118). There should be an awareness of using one movement (unaccented in time and weight) to prepare for a major movement (accented) which in turn will be followed by a recovery movement (usually unaccented and perhaps quite brief). Attention should be given to an appropriate beginning and a logical ending. An effort should be made to control the body with great precision. For example, if the body moves from stretch to curl, the dimensions of the stretch and the curl should be considered. Does the stretch need to include toes, knees, head and neck, and fingertips?

5. MASTERY. At this stage the movement sequence should be under the complete command of the performer. It should be remembered in all detail. The actions, the accented and unaccented parts, the exact use of the body, the flux and flow of the entire sequence should be at the command of the performer. He should enjoy his mastery over the problem. He should be secure enough to be able to show it to a partner, the teacher, or the class.

In terms of long-range development, the teacher needs to evaluate what has been selected by the pupils for their sequences. If, for example, the theme is based on the *time* factor the teacher should know whether all the pupils are gaining mastery over both of the contrasting elements of fast and slow.

It probably is safe to say that the teacher should set the exploratory challenge at the point of difficulty which is compatible with the pupils' abilities. Some of these challenges may prove useful:

- "Travel, using your own choice of actions." (Observe fast, and slow.)

- "Travel, showing contrasting speeds." (Observe the contrasts.)
- "Travel, showing sudden changes of directions." (Observe the suddenness of the change.)
- "Find a sustained mode of travel. Relieve it by contrasting it with sudden actions." (Observe the stress on sustainment.)
- "Use rolling actions. Emphasize the sudden quality in some way." (Observe to see that a roll is used and to see how the suddenness has been used.)

It will be noted that the first challenge allows the *time* factor to reveal itself spontaneously. The second challenge assumes that there has already been some background acquired in the use of the *time* factor. The third challenge indicates that *suddenness* is already part of the movement vocabulary and can be controlled at will. The same is true of the fourth challenge. The fifth challenge indicates that *rolls* and the *time* factor are parts of their movement vocabulary.

The teacher must be aware of the demands made by the challenges and safeguard against demanding material which is not yet part of the pupils' vocabulary. Conversely, in order to make true progress, the pupils need challenges which make demands upon their movement vocabulary.

When work is being applied to the large apparatus, the teacher should set a broad challenge.

It is dangerous to demand a specific action unless the teacher is sure that each pupil is capable of that particular response. For example, "Take the weight on hands only" may be too specific to be safe for some children if applied to action on: the bare floor; the vaulting box; the window ladder; the vertical rope. A safer challenge might be: "Stress the use of the hands in your sequence related to your apparatus." In this case the use of the hands has not been limited to weightbearing.

DRESS

Suitable dress is required for safety, efficiency and hygiene. The minimum requirement for work on the climber should be barefeet or rubber-soled gym shoes, bare legs and arms. This will allow for freedom of movement and the "grip" necessary for safety. If possible the children should wear light tops and shorts rather than slacks. The health rule is to strip down for activity and cover up afterwards to avoid colds. The advantages of going barefooted are described on p. 111 in Chapter Six. They are, briefly, that the foot can grip and push, and become alive and active if it is free to move, but it remains relatively inactive encased in a shoe. Medical advice, the support of the principal and a suitable explanation to parents and children will be needed. This standard will have to be optional, but it should be implemented if at all possible.

The safety of the pupils is always a matter of concern for the teacher and proper provision must be made for it. The number of pupils working on the climber and apparatus stations should be limited to avoid over-crowding. An attitude of responsibility should be expected of each individual. He should concentrate upon the task in hand, thinking and planning before moving. He must choose to do things within his own capabilities and which will not endanger those working near him. He should be expected to put forth his best effort. If the teacher finds that he has no confidence in a particular child, it would be in order to take him off the apparatus, explain clearly what is expected and have him consider his behaviour. If

In special circumstances the pupil may ask the teacher to help.

he is prepared to work safely, he should be allowed the chance, but should be watched carefully. Otherwise, he should be put on simpler apparatus or given a special task.

The general rule is "Do the things you can control. Plan how you intend to finish." Spotters or assistants are not encouraged. Each child should take responsibility for his own safety. In special circumstances pupils may need to ask the teacher for help.

It is usual to require no talking when working on the apparatus. Talking interferes with concentration and it may lead to pupils giving poor advice to one another or daring each other. There should be no element of competition. Observations are used to evaluate the response to the challenge, not to show the "best feat." Therefore, no one should feel forced to do a particular movement or climb to a particular height or use a particular speed.

Certain routines may be developed which will help to create a safe working environment. When the attention of the class is required, it is advisable to say, "Finish your work and come down," and supplement this with an arm gesture. Those closest to the teacher will respond immediately and the others follow suit as they become aware of the situation. This avoids any shock situation which might arise if the whistle signal is used. If the pupils sit on the floor during observations and before rotating to a new station, the teacher can see that all are safe and no one is tempted to carry on working on the apparatus after the stop signal. As soon as they rotate, they should be able to start work immediately without any loss of time. The teacher should stand where he can see all the stations at a glance and thus be able to control any situation which might be unsafe.

It is worthwhile taking time to establish routines for arranging the apparatus. The apparatus should always be carried and never dragged across the floor. There should be a sufficient number of helpers for each piece. All directions should be given before anyone starts to get anything out. The stations should be well placed to avoid collisions and to be clear of the walls. All apparatus should be checked for proper assembly and all fasteners should be locked. The teacher must have an overview of all the stations and see that the work is done properly. The final check of assembly, locks and placement is the teacher's responsibility.

The material given so far has been somewhat general in terms of conducting gymnastics. It will now be necessary to consider what specific adaptations need to be made for teaching gymnastics to children in the different grade levels throughout the school.

THE KINDERGARTEN — JUNIOR LEVEL AND SENIOR LEVEL

In the Kindergarten, Junior Level or Senior Level, distinctions between games, dance, or gymnastic movements are rather vague. One moment the child seems to be playing a game with a rope, the next moment he may be lassoing in cowboy style — a form of dramatic play. The next moment he may be bunny hopping over the rope. Hence, it is the teacher who will recognize the spirit or intention behind the movement and who can guide its direction by the comments she makes or by the stimuli she provides.

JUNIOR KINDERGARTEN

In Junior Kindergarten, the teacher may make available equipment which is likely to encourage gymnastic-type responses. Ropes, hoops, individual mats, beanbags, and building blocks are most likely to be used in a self-testing situation in which body management seems to be the prime purpose. Large climbing apparatus such as jungle gyms, ropes and benches, and even playground slides will encourage body management activities. Thus one of the major functions of the teacher is to make gymnastic-type equipment and apparatus available. She should manage the situation in such a way that the number of pupils using the apparatus is small enough to ensure safety and ample activity. She should then take an interest in what the children choose to do. She should show approval of their ideas and efforts whenever this is possible. If she feels it is wise, she may make a comment which helps the child identify what he is doing. For example, she may remark: "You have found a very interesting way of *going along* that bench," or, "That was a good jump," or, "You used both feet that time!"

The teacher of very young children is apt to worry if she notices a child repeating a movement over and over again. "How long shall I let the child do this?" she will ask. Teachers cannot really know for certain, but, fortunately, the child seems to know what is best for himself. Teachers may take comfort in the fact that he is gaining something from the repetition or he would not continue with it. He will try something else when he becomes bored with what he is doing and when curiosity stimulates his interest in other things. The teacher may consider having a little chat with him about it, or she may pass by with a smile, making sure that she has provided many stimuli which will attract the child at the appropriate growing time.

Teachers will do well to remember that there is a distinguishable cycle which governs the learning of a skill. It follows this pattern: A stimulus arouses interest — initial responses lead to discovery — there is a selection of a satisfying response — repetition of it — which brings mastery — then it becomes boring to repeat and therefore — it is embellished or used as a tool to achieve something else. For example, Jim may discover that he can jump both feet off the floor at the same time. So he jumps, jumps, jumps. When it is done so easily that he doesn't have to think or worry about it, he is likely to become bored with it. At this point he may abandon it, or he may embellish it and you may find him jumping with a bang (which could be an incipient dance action) or jumping across the room. He may boast or show-off (which could be an incipient competitive situation related to games). Then he might use his jump in getting over an object or coming down from a height (and this would bring it back to a gymnastic, body management situation).

Hence, for the very young child the gymnastics "lesson" really consists of providing a spacious area, and selecting the equipment and apparatus which will be made available. Then the teacher should begin to distinguish the kinds of responses the pupils make. She will support their ideas and efforts whenever this is possible. She will use her comments to guide their awareness of what they have discovered as-and-when she feels this awareness is appropriate.

In considering the matter of guiding the actions which children may choose to do, certain physical coordinations should receive attention. Current research [1] [2] seems to indicate the need to establish certain bodily coordinations before reading skills can be achieved. These skills are creeping (on hands and feet), crawling (on hands and knees), rolling like a log to the left and to the right and attaining balance in the upright posture, as, for example, is necessary for walking, running, jumping, hopping and so on. There is a need for the child to distinguish inwardly, through nerve-muscle connections, the right and left sides of his body. These bodily activities can certainly become part of his gymnastic activity period. The teacher needs the conviction that these basic coordinations are really fundamental to the child's physical and mental growth; and, then she will be conscientious in encouraging these activities when they arise spontaneously and arranging the environment so that these responses are elicited. Each day, rolling, crawling, running, walking, jumping, and hopping can be worked into breaks, games, rhythmic responses as well as physical education periods. The development of the awareness of the right and left sides of the body can be helped if the teacher will give opportunities for use of:

1. *Both* hands — as for pulling, lifting, lowering.
2. *One* hand and *then* the other — as for climbing, crawling, changing a beanbag from one hand to the other.
3. *One* hand stressed in a repetitive action, later the other hand stressed as for stunts such as a lame dog carrying his paw, or using the hoop with one hand.
4. *Both* feet — as for jumping, raising both legs up, lowering both legs, dragging both legs.
5. *One* foot and *then* the other — as for climbing, crawling, running, walking, stepping stones, peddling.
6. *One* foot stressed in repetitive action, later the other one stressed — as for hopping, slip-step sideways, toe tapping, leg kicking or swinging.

[1] Kephart, Newell C., *The Slow Learner in the Classroom*, Charles E. Merrill Books, Inc., Columbus, Ohio, 1965.
[2] As outlined in diagnostic reports and prescriptive programming under the direction of Dr. Samuel Rabinovitch, Director of Perceptual Motor Learning Clinic, Children's Hospital, Montreal, Quebec.

7. Rolling to the *right* or to the *left* — playing with the alternation of these directions.
8. Using right leg and right arm — as in a "bear walk," a "pacer" horse.

Other valuable activities include those associated with balance and those which make the child aware of the size, shape and location of his body.

Situations which provide experiences related to balance include:

1. The playground slide — climbing the steps, sliding down the chute.
2. "Riding" a big barrel.
3. Playing on a plank, especially if it is inclined or set on a low block which gives it a slight seesaw action.
4. A skate-board.
5. A balance beam — on the floor or two to six inches above the floor.
6. Stepping stone tiles of different colours which may be arranged by the children themselves.
7. Scooters.
8. Jumping onto a sack filled with scrap foam rubber.

Situations which provide experiences related to achieving an awareness of the body image include — any apparatus which will define a space through which the child may go. For example:

1. Hoops of different sizes.
2. Barrels with the ends removed.
3. Plywood cubes with different shaped and sized entry holes cut in five of the surfaces.
4. Window ladders on the climbing frame.
5. A tunnel improvised by lining up three or four chairs.

A word should be said about designing and securing apparatus. Colours may be used to enliven the play material and they may also be used to define the pathway of the expected action. For example, movable stepping stones may make use of one colour for the right foot and another for the left foot. The teacher should examine the condition of the apparatus for splinters and for general sturdiness. It would probably be wise to plan the design and acquisition of the apparatus with the help of the principal or the physical education advisor, since the school officials are usually held responsible for the selection and maintenance of apparatus to ensure the safety of the children who use it. Some provision will need to be made for its safe storage. The movement and arrangement of the apparatus should be included in the routines of the class. The children should participate fully in getting it out, arranging it and storing it. This should be considered a very valuable part of their total educational experience.

In summary, gymnastics for the very young child appears to be a very natural response to a play environment. However, the teacher has given her professional attention to the structuring of the environment. She has a clear conception of the nature of gymnastics as a matter of body management and knows that certain coordinations such as crawling, rolling and running are of the utmost importance to the optimum development of the child. On the basis of this knowledge together with her assessment of the children's needs, she provides the necessary stimuli in terms of apparatus equipment, verbal comment and attitude of support and guidance.

SENIOR KINDERGARTEN

The work of the five-year-old should lead on from his experiences in Junior Kindergarten. However, not every child has been to Junior Kindergarten. Therefore, it may be necessary for the teacher to study the material which was written for the four-year-old and use whatever seems valuable to her pupils. As is true in all phases of teaching, professional judgement must be exercised in adapting whatever work is used so that the needs of the children are satisfied. The work suggested on p. 220, having to do with coordinations which prepare the child for reading, is recommended for consideration. Some of the apparatus such as hoops, blocks, canes and balance beams will be needed in the kindergarten. However, the teacher should negotiate with the principal for a share of the time in the gymnasium and thus begin work on the wall climber, the tumbling mats, and vertical ropes as well as the other standard apparatus such as the vaulting box. These, of course, will be arranged and used in ways which are useful to the five-year-old without any compulsion to consider their traditional uses in the gymnasium.

While it has been stressed that physical education in the Junior Kindergarten is largely a spontaneous response to an environment which has been deliberately arranged by the teacher, the children of the Senior Kindergarten can learn in a slightly more structured situation. In other words, much of their work will stem from a response to the equipment or apparatus which has been selected by the teacher with an expectation of the responses which will be elicited. The rest of their work will arise as a response to verbal stimuli which are given in the form of movement challenges. For example, they may be asked to, "See if you can find some ways of going around the gym using your hands to make you go."

Movement challenges are very difficult to word. This is partly because they should be brief — briefer than the example given above if it is possible. It is also because they must be as concrete as possible since very young children are limited in their comprehension of abstract ideas. For example, "low" is fairly difficult for them to judge; but "as close to the floor as possible" is much more concrete and it is reasonably easy for them to relate themselves to the floor. However, if the latter challenge is used, a further step must still be taken, namely, to discover that the part close to the floor is "low" or that the body itself is "low."

Furthermore, challenges directed to the actions of the body are difficult to keep broad enough to provide for extensive explorations and discovery. For example, the challenge, "Put the rope on the floor in a V-shape. Find as many ways as possible of using your feet without touching the rope,"[3] leaves room for many ideas to develop and yet is concrete enough that most children can respond to it readily. The body action challenge, "Go in your own pathway. Find as many ways of travelling as possible" leaves great scope for invention but the prerequisite is that pupils understand what is meant by "travel" and "pathway."

Because these difficulties are found in setting challenges in gymnastics, many teachers find it easier to start the work by using selected items of small apparatus, perhaps for free play. While the children concentrate upon using the hoop, the teacher can draw attention to the use of the body. For example, in free play with hoops, different pupils may crawl through the hoop, jump in and out of it, hop around it. This gives the teacher an opportunity to allow the class to observe three body actions — crawl, jump, hop — some of which will be locomotor. The next challenge can lead towards a search for other types of locomotor actions while the hoops are the focal point. A little later, the hoops may be put away and the class can use some of the locomotor actions they have discovered for travelling around the room. Thus "travelling" as a body action is beginning to take meaning.

The teacher must then decide how far it will be wise to develop this concept at this particular stage. It would be possible to examine the various ways of travelling which are being used and to label them in terms of the action — run, hop, crawl, and so on. It would be possible to modify their work by drawing attention to:

1. Where they are travelling — i.e. weaving pathways.
2. Their relationship to others — i.e. keep out of other people's way.
3. How the actions are done — i.e. fast, vigorously (firm).
4. The spatial aspect of the actions — i.e. forward, low.

The decision as to the amount of development attempted at any one time must remain with the teacher.

However, it is usual to reserve part of the lesson for the use of the large apparatus. The challenge can then be, "Find many different ways of travelling along the bench." This will likely bring about an application of the locomotor actions discovered earlier either with the hoops or during the work on the floor.

Thus through combining the use of equipment and apparatus with verbal challenges, the children are given a variety of experiences which grow out of their own spontaneous reaction to the equipment and which are all related to one movement concept, in this case "locomotion." The

---

[3] In the teaching situation, the oral challenge would probably be, "Make a V-shape with your rope. What can you do with your feet without touching the rope?"

breadth of the experiences is kept large enough to include adaptations to the apparatus and the floor and thus secondary themes are included.

It may be helpful to see a schematic summary of the lesson. Such an outline follows.

SAMPLE LESSON PLAN

GRADE: Senior Kindergarten

THEME: To help pupils form a concept of "travelling"

SUBTHEMES: 1. Relating one's action to equipment or to the floor
2. Moving in a "pathway"

INTRODUCTION:
Individual free play with a hoop.
Teacher circulates among pupils, praising the work and identifying aloud all the *actions* being done.

DEVELOPMENT:
Observation:
A short class observation of three pupils moving in different ways in relation to the hoop — e.g. running around it, jumping through it, hopping in and out, and around it.

Observation question: "What way does each one move?"

Challenge: "What ways can you move? Find out."
The teacher praises and labels actions, seeking to label various step-like actions, jumps, rolls (See Chapter Six, p. 114).

Challenge: "Put hoops away. Travel about the gym all by yourself."
The teacher praises those who start first, labelling the action used. "Good Mary, you are running. Bill is using big jumps. What other things are people using? Oh, a walk on tiptoes. Here's someone crawling. What a lot of good ideas!"
Teacher coaches: "Have you thought about *where* you are travelling? Make a pathway of your own. Visit the centre of the room, the corners, the sides."

Observation: Half the class may watch the other half.

Coach: "See how well they can curve about, making their own path and keeping away from others."

At the discretion of the teacher, the groups may reverse roles and/or the challenge is restated.

Challenge: "Everyone make a winding pathway. Fill up all the spaces." The teacher coaches: "How do you travel? Hop? Crawl?"

CULMINATION:
Groups of six, with each group using a bench and a tumbling mat.

Challenge: "Find interesting ways to travel."
The teacher praises and coaches, labelling the actions being used on the *bench* or on the *mat* or on the *floor*.
At the discretion of the teacher, the comments or observations may be directed towards finding activities which are particularly suited to the surface being used; e.g. sliding along the bench, rolling along the mat, jumping along the floor.

CONCLUSION:
"All put apparatus away. Stand in scatter formation. Stretch tall and thin. Gradually droop lower and lower, and limper and limper until you are lying out on the floor like small, limp blobs." The teacher may test limpness by lifting a foot or a hand.
All lie limp for a minute.
"Quietly come to life. Sit. Stand. Walk off floor."

Even if the lesson includes the use of the large climbing apparatus it can still begin with free play with selected equipment. Or it can begin with a verbal challenge such as "You may start with a good run today. Keep out of everyone's way." Next, each pupil can choose his own mode of travel. This can be developed into an exploration of some movement theme such as finding ways of moving which stress a curling of the body if one or more pupils are using a curl in their forms of locomotion. The latter half of the lesson can be devoted to work at apparatus stations, one of which would be the climber. It is necessary for the teacher to decide how many children can work safely on the climber at one time and, therefore, what other stations are required to accommodate the rest of the class. The table on page 226 shows some ways of organizing the class.

For children of kindergarten age, it seems best not to carry the theme of the lesson on to the work on the climber. Nor does it seem advantageous to apply it to apparatus stations when they are varied in nature. In this respect, the work in Senior Kindergarten resembles the work in Junior Kindergarten. The apparatus at different stations provides a very stimulating environment. It seems wise to allow the children to react spontaneously to the environment. The challenge most often used is, "Find things to do which are safe for you and safe for your neighbours." It will be a matter

Climber	Other Stations	Rotation Needed
1. One half class	2-4 groups: benches and mats	One
2. One third class	⅓ benches and mats; ⅓ hoops and blocks	Three
3. One quarter	¼ benches and mats; ¼ hoops and blocks; ¼ utility boxes	Four
4. One sixth (A)[4]	⅙ B; ⅙ C; ⅙ D; ⅙ E; ⅙ F	Three rotations in each of two lessons

of great interest to the teacher to observe whether the children make a voluntary application of the movement theme to their work on the apparatus. If they do, this may be verbally recognized by the teacher, but she must make a judgement as to whether this will be done privately to individuals or aloud to all. The deciding factor will be its effect upon safety.

The general rules for dress, safety and the routines for arranging equipment which are suggested on page 216 are applicable to the work in kindergarten. Some modifications may be made for moving the apparatus. Since it must be carried, not dragged, children may need to ask for help. They should wait until it arrives. Methods of carrying benches and mats can be codified. For example, one person must be at each handle on the mat. The teacher should help with especially heavy pieces. It will be wise to assign certain pupils always to get out and put away the apparatus used in a given station. Thus they learn exactly how it is to be done.

The teacher may want to start by using only one type of large apparatus at a given time so that the problem of teaching the children how to get it out is simplified. For example, all the benches can be used. If they do not accommodate all the children at once, half the class can work with hoops on the floor. One rotation can be made during the lesson.

LESSON THEMES SUITABLE FOR THE FIVE-YEAR-OLD

A. RELATIONSHIP THEMES:

1. Free play with equipment.
2. Working alone.
3. Keeping out of other people's way.
4. Choosing things to do which are "safe for you and for others."

---

[4] Letters represent any suitable type of apparatus.

5. Finding many different ways of using a piece of gymnastic equipment — hoop, rope, block, small mat.

6. Putting the equipment in a position and "finding all the things you can do without touching it."

7. Free practice on the large apparatus. "Finding things which are safe for you and for others."

8. Finding ways of moving the apparatus onto the floor (and putting it away).

9. Putting two or more pieces of apparatus together so they are safe and interesting to use.

10. Learning to listen, and to follow directions. (This is a relationship to the *authority*. Some people regard it as discipline or the learning of routines. But in the age of T.V., radio and other distractions, listening, hearing, recognizing directives, reacting to signals are more accurately regarded as relationship skills.)

11. Recognizing and using such relationships as: Going along, going through, going up or down, going around or over, being close to, avoiding contact, etc.

12. Coming down or off apparatus safely. This may include a specific awareness of reaching the floor with the feet first.

13. Adapting to apparatus — i.e. finding that the floor or a bench surface is good for sliding along, but that a mat surface is not.

B. *BODY AWARENESS.* (For details see Chapter Four, pp. 39-40 and Chapter Six, p. 104).

1. Recognition of "travelling."

2. Finding different ways of travelling.

3. Recognizing and/or performing specific actions — run, roll, crawl, hop, swing, bend.

4. Ways of moving body while staying in one place — bend, stretch, swing, jump.

5. Recognizing and/or performing the basic body functions — curl, stretch, twist.

6. Recognizing and/or making a part of the body "important."

7. Doing "tricks" with the body and/or parts of the body — heel clicks, touching two parts together, e.g. head and foot, travelling in stunt fashion such as on knees only.

8. Becoming aware of the parts which touch the floor.

9. Using the body symmetrically or asymmetrically. See coordinations described on p. 220 for Junior Kindergarten.

10. Using the body in situations which require balance. See p. 221 for Junior Kindergarten. This will probably remain at the participation stage and not be taken into an *awareness* of balance.

C. *SPACE AWARENESS.* (For details see Chapter Four, p. 49 and Chapter Six, p. 123).

1. Travelling in your own pathway.
2. Scatter formation.
3. Working on the spot.
4. Changing between working on the spot and travelling.
5. Awareness of moving forward — and whatever other directions are spontaneously used.
6. Awareness of up — i.e. feet are up; tummies are up.
7. Awareness of being "low" if this is being used spontaneously; parts being high if it arises spontaneously.

D. *EFFORT QUALITIES OF MOVEMENT.* (For details see Chapter Four, p. 56 and Chapter Six, p. 118).

Any of the following if they arise spontaneously:
1. Going fast.
2. Doing actions — fast or slow.
3. Going sometimes fast, sometimes slow.
4. Moving lightly or strongly. (Many strength situations should be provided for boys.)
5. Finding light actions or strong actions.
6. Wiggles, twistings, wavy actions.
7. Sharp, jagged actions.
8. Go and stop — stopping in different ways, i.e. suddenly, gradually — stopping yourself — making statues.
9. Getting ready to start — holding a starting position.

Material from these themes may be chosen and developed into a lesson in somewhat the same way as that illustrated earlier in the chapter on page 224. More detailed ideas for arranging large apparatus are given in the Appendix on page 321ff.

THE PRIMARY GRADES

The work in Grades One, Two, and Three should progress in a logical manner, being built upon the foundation given in the kindergarten. Whereas, a considerable amount of work in those years developed as spontaneous responses to the use of equipment and apparatus, in the primary grades an increasing use may be made of verbal stimuli. However, the equipment and apparatus continue to play an important role.

The discussion of the use of challenges, observations, small equipment and large apparatus which is found at the beginning of this chapter on page 206 — should be read carefully and applied to the work in these grades. The lesson planning as outlined there can be used for these classes. Growth and progress will tend to be found at the exploration and identification stages (see pages 214-216) for Grade One or primary classes with limited backgrounds. Pupils in Grade Three, and sometimes in Grade Two, can begin the selection stage (see page 214) and can put two or three activities together. However, the connections between the actions, the flux and flow, accents and climaxes in the sequence will not be characteristic of their work.

The themes suggested for Junior and Senior Kindergarten may be used at the discretion of the teacher. It is characteristic of this work that children respond to a challenge in accordance with their level of maturity and physical ability. Hence, challenges used in earlier grades can be carried through to later grades and the responses examined for signs of progress. Throughout these grades there should be an increasing awareness of the body and its parts in action. The pupils should know with greater clarity which part is being stressed, whether they are curling or are curled, whether or not the legs are apart or the knees are straight. There should be an increasing comprehension of the good mechanics of movement (see Chapter Six page 111) and by Grade Three there will be many spontaneous efforts to cope with balance. Hence, this should be given attention in the lesson.

Their work on the apparatus will show a greater clarity in the actions used as the pupils progress towards Grade Three. They will begin to join actions together in simple sequences. There may even be some awareness of the start and finish of a sequence.

In their work on the floor, with small equipment and on the apparatus, there will be some ability to vary an action by selecting the spatial or effort factors. For example, a child may have chosen to crab walk along the bench with his feet leading. Midway across he may elect to turn over and crawl backward for the remaining distance, thus showing variety in the use of the spatial factor. Another may have chosen to roll across the mat and may bring about a change of speed in his execution.

Because these spontaneous uses of movement elements give the clue to their readiness to explore those elements more fully, the teacher must study their work carefully and select the themes of the lesson wisely. In this way the work will develop at the children's rate.

SUGGESTED THEMES FOR PRIMARY GRADES

A. RELATIONSHIP

Check those listed for kindergarten and use them if they are suitable. Add to these the following possibilities:
1. Finding actions suited to large apparatus — hang, swing, climb, hold, grip, balance, reach, pull, push.
2. Applying general themes to the apparatus — stressing the use of hands,

feet, knees, etc.; discovering when you are stretched, curled or twisted during your movement; travelling on or along apparatus in appropriate ways; ways of getting on, ways of getting off — landing on feet (p. 111); other parts.

Getting on and off equipment with different parts of the body taking the weight.

B. BODY AWARENESS

Check those listed for kindergarten and use if suitable. In many themes, the stages of "recognition" and "use" may be advanced to the stage of "becoming aware of." This is particularly true of:
1. Awareness of specific actions — run, roll, jump, etc.
2. Awareness of curling, stretching, twisting actions.
3. Awareness of stressing a particular part of the body.
4. Awareness of parts touching the floor and taking the body weight; special stress on hands, or hands and another part taking the weight.
5. Awareness of good mechanics for landing from a jump.

(The last two points are especially important. The teacher should check Chapter Six for details which may be considered in developing the awareness.)

C. SPACE AWARENESS

Use the challenges listed for kindergarten. They may be developed more fully in lessons since they will be used more extensively in spontaneous responses.

D. EFFORT QUALITIES OF MOVEMENT

The themes suggested as possibilities in kindergarten may now be developed as subthemes (i.e. as adding variety to actions) and possibly as themes for exploration. Contrasts in effort qualities may be developed if the teacher feels that the class is ready for this development. The discussion about challenges on p. 207 of this chapter and the description of the first two stages of growth and development found on p. 214 should help the teacher.

SAMPLE LESSON PLAN: Children with good background

GRADE: Two

THEME: Awareness of moving into a curl

SUBTHEMES: 1. Pathways
2. Starts and finishes

INTRODUCTION:
Challenge: "Take a hoop. Get into scatter formation. Put it on the floor and practise going over it or landing in it."
Teacher circulates, checks spacing for safety. Coaches. Praises good ideas, good techniques including soft landings.

DEVELOPMENT:
Observation: Observe three children who use a body curl in their work — e.g. full knee bend upon landing, curled bunny hops to get over it, high jumps with knees tucked up during flight.

Observation Question: "What shape do all these people make in their work?"

Observation Question: "How do they make the curled-up shape?"

Challenge: "Do your own work. Find out if you curl any part of yourself during your work."

Observation: "All those who find they have a curl do the work now."

Observation Question: "See if they are really curling." (N.B. if all are active, have the observation done in manageable groups.) Pick out one or two with the most complete curl to repeat their demonstration. Discuss the curl briefly.

Challenge: "Use your hoop in any way which will help you use a big curl."

Teacher circulates and praises suitable efforts. Conclude the activity with a verbal comment of assessment.

Challenge: "After you put your hoops away, travel in your own pathway. If you find yourself using a big curl as you travel, try to remember what you were doing."

Teacher coaches — checking on spacing, speed, direction; and observing all uses of curl.

Challenge: "Bring your work to a stop. All of you choose one kind of travelling to do now. If you found yourself curling as you travelled, try to remember what you did. Do it again now. Good. There were a lot of different ways of curling that time."

Challenge: "Now, something different . . . use fast runs and high jumps for travelling. Make your own pathway. When you hear the clap, sit in groups of four."

CULMINATION:

Challenge: "On the signal, each group of four will place a mat and a bench close together. Move in and out of the holes under the bench. Use the top of the bench and the mat. Choose pathways which will allow all four people to work all the time. Start as soon as you are ready."

Teacher checks location of stations for safety — good spacing in relation to other stations and to the walls. Teacher observes explorations. Comments on pathways, safety, appropriateness of actions *plus* any uses of the curl.

After time for an exploratory period, pupils may be asked to choose a starting place and to decide on a finishing place, and then to choose a way of getting there. They should think of how they use the apparatus and where their pathway goes. They should try to remember what they do and repeat it.

Teacher circulates during this phase, ready to make the occasional comment, and attempting to select a group to demonstrate for the rest.

Observation: After a few minutes, work is stopped and one or more groups, or individuals are watched.

Observation Question: "Can you see any curls being used? Did they use both the bench and the mat? Was there a good start and a good finish?"

CONCLUSION:

"All put apparatus away. As you finish, skip about the empty space. Skip to a scatter formation and rest. Stretch up high." With the teacher leading, "Curl fingers, hands, arms, head, trunk, knees; curl down on the floor. Find a comfortable curled shape and rest quietly . . . . Uncurl gradually. Walk to the door and wait until all are ready to leave."

OTHER LESSON FORMATS

As has been mentioned earlier in this chapter on p. 206 and p. 207, the lesson may be organized in the following ways:

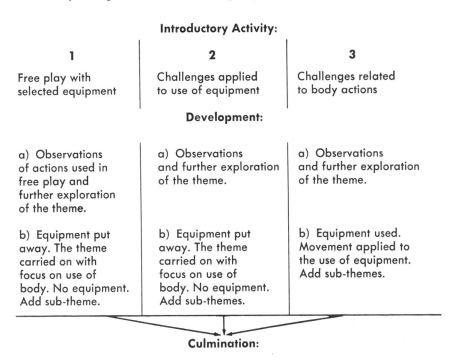

Introductory Activity:

1	2	3
Free play with selected equipment	Challenges applied to use of equipment	Challenges related to body actions

Development:

a) Observations of actions used in free play and further exploration of the theme.	a) Observations and further exploration of the theme.	a) Observations and further exploration of the theme.
b) Equipment put away. The theme carried on with focus on use of body. No equipment. Add sub-theme.	b) Equipment put away. The theme carried on with focus on use of body. No equipment. Add sub-themes.	b) Equipment used. Movement applied to the use of equipment. Add sub-themes.

Culmination:

Choice of:
a.) Small groups of four to six pupils. Each group using the same apparatus, e.g. mats or benches, or mats and benches, or mats and two hoops, etc.
b.) Small groups four to six pupils. Half the group on the climber. Half the group with selected apparatus, e.g. mats. Rotate.
c.) For other forms of rotation see page 226 and for suggested arrangements of apparatus stations see the Appendix.

In the primary grades, the theme of the lesson *may* be carried on to the apparatus. In the sample lesson given for Grade Two, the apparatus was selected to elicit a curl but the verbal challenge did not refer to the curl. However, the teacher recognized it orally as it was used and the final observation was directed towards it. At the discretion of the teacher, the theme can be carried over into the challenge for the work on the apparatus station. This will likely happen in Grade Three. When the climber is used, it may not be appropriate to stress the theme. The main consideration may have to be, "Find safe ways of using the apparatus."

Routines, Dress and Safety

The standards which are described and recommended for Senior Kindergarten pupils on p. 226 should be carried on throughout the primary grades. The children should become very competent in handling the apparatus efficiently, but the final responsibility for checking details must remain with the teacher. As the children advance into Grade Three, there may be a tendency to work with a partner. This may give rise to talking and planning. The teacher must take a definite stand on the behaviour which can be accepted. Partner work may be used as a theme, if it begins to arise spontaneously or it may be delayed until Grade Four. The pupils should understand what the rules are for their particular class.

THE JUNIOR DIVISION

The work in the junior division will hopefully build upon a good program carried out in the primary grades. In such cases, the children will have a good background in:
1. Using large apparatus in many combinations
    — freely relating their movements to the environment created by the apparatus
    — applying some themes to different pieces of apparatus
    — beginning to join different movements together in a rudimentary sequence of movement.
2. Awareness of their own body movements
    — curling, stretching, twisting — perhaps being conscious of moving from curl to stretch, etc.
    — specific actions — locomotor — run, skip, roll, hop, slide — on the spot — jump, bend, swing, etc.
    — stressing a particular part of the body
    — being aware of the parts which touch the floor, perhaps knowing that they support the body weight
    — knowing a limited amount about the mechanics of jumping and landing.
3. Facility in moving forward or backward, taking parts up or down, turning, moving sideways
    — moving at a low or high level
    — pathways — "their own," curving, etc.
4. Using such qualities as
    — fast, slow, sudden in certain situations
    — strong actions, light or gentle actions
    — wavy, wiggly movements

— sharp, jagged movements
— stopping in different ways
— joining actions together.
5. Some experience in composing sequences.
   The work in the junior grades will be concerned with:
   1. Weightbearing, weight transference, balance, overbalance.
   2. Partner and work in small groups.
   3. Sequence building with attention to beginnings and endings, to the dynamics of flow within the sequence.
   4. Work on apparatus will be demanding in terms of adapting the bodily actions to the possibilities afforded by the apparatus.
   5. Awareness of bodily form should be significantly improved; i.e. awareness of pointed toes, straight knees, arched back, etc.
   6. Movement themes will be carried through from the floor work to the work on large apparatus.
   7. The challenges can be more abstract and, therefore, less use may be made of the small equipment.

LESSON THEMES SUITABLE FOR JUNIOR GRADES

A. BODY AWARENESS

1. Taking the weight on different parts of the body
   — finding bases — different sizes and shapes
   — selecting a base and using it as a support while doing varied gestures.
2. Transferring weight
   — examining the nature of locomotion: steps, rolls, jumps, and slides
   — transferring through a series of adjacent parts — rocking and rolling
   — transferring to non-adjacent parts — steps made by different parts of the body; arches.
3. Arresting the transfer of weight
   — building a base and holding a balance — exploring the influence of the shape of the base, speed of movement, height of the centre of gravity above the base.
4. Bringing the body weight down from a height
   — meeting the floor with the feet; i.e. landing from a jump
   — meeting the floor with the hands
   — dissipating the force of impact, e.g. through a roll.
5. Taking the weight up
   — jumps and springs — away from the floor or apparatus
   — mounting the apparatus — hands and then feet; other safe ways.
6. Using the body "curl-stretch" action.
7. Using the body "twist-counter-twist" action.
8. Moving the body or its parts into stretches.

9. Controlling the body parts during any action; i.e. straight knees, pointed toes, etc.

10. Themes of the teacher's choice according to the needs of the pupils.

B. RELATIONSHIPS

With people:
1. Partners — taking each other's weight
   — sharing your weight with your partner
   — matching with a partner
   — mirroring a partner.
2. Three's — matching
   — sharing your weight or strength.

With apparatus:
1. Mounting in different ways
2. Dismounting in different ways
3. Using the apparatus as a support
4. Using the apparatus as an obstacle — going under, over, around, etc.
5. Phrasing the movement to use more than one piece of apparatus in a continuous flow
6. Working out a movement theme on the apparatus.

C. SPACE AWARENESS

1. Moving the body in a variety of directions: up, down, forward, back, right, left
2. Being aware of different parts moving in a specific direction — e.g. in the headstand; feet stretched upward; legs in forward/backward splits
3. Being aware of using definite body shapes — e.g. during flight of a jump: arched, tucked, forward/backward stride, etc.
4. Changing levels with ease and safety.

These topics should probably be used as subthemes. The bodily movement should be determined and the appropriate quality for efficient performance searched out and emphasized — e.g. elbowstand into handstand into a walkover. The appropriate effort quality is likely to be a sustained press into the elbowstand, a sudden-strong thrust upward into a handstand, a sustained-firm balance continued into a walkover, a sudden-strong push to stand. This is safer than trying strong actions when the performer doesn't realize how the action will terminate.

D. EFFORT QUALITIES:

1. Changes of speed
2. Sudden jump for take-off
3. Sustained recoveries — e.g. lower legs from a headstand
4. Strong actions, firm grips
5. Efficient use of lightness — e.g. landings, running.

E. SEQUENCE WORK

1. A good functional starting position and a logical ending position
2. The transition between two movements should be well designed; the flow suitably controlled
3. The sequence should have a climax, contrasts, and accents of stress (perhaps arising from time-weight factors).

As the children move from Grade Four to Grade Six, there should be more purpose to the practice and refinement of their sequences. It will probably be wise for the teacher to allow several lessons to be devoted to one major project. The project could be a theme such as "weightbearing stressing the hands." Perhaps it would be wise to allow the pupils to choose the apparatus they wish to use and concentrate on it for three or four periods.

Another type of organization might be as follows: a fairly lengthy time spent on the apparatus which is the performer's first choice, perhaps ten minutes; and one rotation with a short length of time (five minutes) on a second and quite radically different station. This could be done over a series of lessons, thus allowing work to proceed in depth at one station and simpler sequences on a variety of other stations to broaden the experience.

Some sample lessons are included to give some indication of how these themes may be implemented. Teachers should redraft them to suit the needs of their own classes.

SAMPLE LESSON PLAN ONE

GRADE: Four, Five or Six if adapted

THEME: Stepping and rolling

SUBTHEMES: 1. Transferring body weight — adjacent, non-adjacent parts of the body
2. Adaptation of steps and rolls to selected apparatus

INTRODUCTION:
Challenge: "Warm up by travelling about the room, in your own pathway. Find several ways of travelling."
Teacher circulates among pupils and encourages their efforts, labelling their actions, commenting upon speed, strength, and pathways.

DEVELOPMENT:
Observation: Two performers: "A" crawling, walking or stepping in some way; "B" rolling.

Observation Question: "What parts of the body take the weight in A's work? in B's work?"

Observation Question: "What is B's action called? What kind of action does A take?"

Challenge: "Do some of your own travel action again. Find out if you take steps or if you roll."
Teacher circulates. She may ask a few students what action they are using.

Observations and group checks:
a. "All those who have a step-like action, do it now. Observers, do you agree?"
b. "All those who are rolling, do it now. Observers, do you agree?"

Challenge: "Find one step-like action and one rolling action which you can do well. Practise."

Challenge: "Feel your body parts on the floor. Find out the difference in the feel in the two actions."

Observation: Watch one performer and discuss the difference in weight transference between steps (non-adjacent parts) and rolls (adjacent parts).

Equipment stations are ready.

CULMINATION:
Groups of four. Equipment stations made up of two pieces of apparatus e.g. mat and bench; mat and utility box; vaulting box and mat; cross beam on climber and mat; rolled mat and flat mat.

Challenge: "Use both pieces of apparatus in your sequence. Include step-like and roll transference of weight in your sequence."

CALM ENDING
"Equipment away. Scatter formation. Use slow, large steps with feet making a square pathway of your own."

SAMPLE LESSON PLAN TWO

GRADE: Four, Five or Six if adapted

THEME: Body arches

SUBTHEMES: 1. Body parts bearing weight
2. Transfer of weight from one non-adjacent part to another (Chapter Six, p. 106)

INTRODUCTION:
Challenge: "Warm up by practising weightbearing on different parts of the body — e.g. hands only, hands-then-feet, head-and-hands, forearms, etc. Use locomotion or balance."
Teacher circulates, advises, coaches, checks safety.

Challenge: "Release tension: phrases of quick runs accented by high jumps and low landings."

DEVELOPMENT:
Challenge: "Choose two of your weightbearing activities used in the warmup which can be joined together in a sequence."

Observation: Two or three pupils demonstrate examples of arches. "Name the parts bearing the weight. Note their placement on the floor — non-adjacent. Note the arch made by the body."

Challenge: "Experiment with making different kinds of arches."

Challenge: "Move from one arch form to another. Discover how this is done." (*Step, roll, spring.*)

Challenge: "See if it is possible to travel while retaining the arch. Find many variations."

Challenge: "See if it is possible to move from a balance into an arch or vice versa."

Observation: Pupils demonstrate the use of strength or changes of timing which aid the movement.

CULMINATION:
Select apparatus, e.g. vaulting boxes, climbing frames, beams, and rolled mats.

Challenge: "Work out a sequence which is built around arches and the movements which lead into or out of them. Be sure your choice is a sensible and safe use of the apparatus."

CALM ENDING:
"Apparatus away. Scatter formation. Alternate between slow log rolling and stillness in a curled shape."

SAMPLE LESSON PLAN THREE

GRADE: Six

THEME: Weight onto hands from another part of body

SUBTHEMES: 1. Taking some or all of a partner's weight
2. Sequence work

INTRODUCTION:
"Warm up by using rolls in different ways — e.g. several in succession for travelling; as a way of coming out of balance; as a way of getting into a stretch."

DEVELOPMENT:
Challenge: "As you work, notice when you take the weight on the hands."

Observation: Watch two performers. Discuss the use of the hand(s) for weightbearing.

Challenge: "It isn't necessary to limit yourselves to rolling. Find different ways of getting the weight onto the hands."

Observation: "Look for different ways of getting the weight on the hands."

1. Steps — cartwheel, walkover.
2. Springs — catspring, handspring.

Challenge: "Take a partner who is your own size. Find ways in which you have part of your weight carried by your partner."

Observation: "See what ways this can be done."

1. Partially carrying the partner — as in wheelbarrows.

1. WHEELBARROW
(barefoot)

Hold by knees

2. Sharing weight — each pushing or pulling equally — as in a Chinese sit-up.

2. CHINESE SIT-UP
(barefoot)

START
Hips/shoulders touch
Elbows linked
Sit back to back

STAND
Back to back
Elbows linked
Heels touching

3. Acting as a support — as in leapfrog shown at the top of page 242.

Challenge: "Continue your experiments."

3. LEAP FROG
(barefoot)

Side view of supporter   Front view of jumper

CULMINATION:
    Challenge: "Devise partner sequences which include
           — weightbearing on hands
           — weight-taking between partners."
The work may follow these stages:
a. Exploration: observations if required.
b. Selection of actions to be done by each individual and/or partners.
c. Modification: starting, finishing positions, transitions between actions.
d. Refinement: rhythm, climax, excellence of body control.
e. Practise.
f. Showing.

CALM ENDING:
"Slow curling and stretching starting close to the floor and finishing in
a good standing position."

THE INTERMEDIATE DIVISION

The work in Grades Seven, Eight and Nine will have to make a good
deal of allowance for individual differences in growth patterns. Also, the
pupils may have had varied backgrounds, especially if they have graduated
from several elementary schools into a district senior school.

The teacher will need to build routine procedures for working, and a
standard of performance, dress and behaviour which will set the stage for
happy, progressive learning. The boys and girls will probably have separate

classes and to some extent pursue different forms of gymnastic activity. For example, the boys are likely to include more strength-demanding actions than the girls. Their floorwork generally includes more handsprings, head-springs, round-offs, press-ups, sustained levers up or down, and greater height on the leg springs than the girls. More boys than girls seem to enjoy speed within their sequences or as lead-ups to their sequences. On the other hand, girls' work seems to be much more flexible than that of the boys. They get a wide range of movement out of the hip joint and the spine. They have much less strength in the shoulders and may find climbing and hanging, swinging and arm presses very difficult. They seem to have greater initial interest in the form of the movement.

In spite of these variations, based on the responses of boys compared to girls, or based upon individual differences within one sex, the same movement themes can be considered. The teacher must deal with these differing responses in the light of the needs of the individual and the best possible outcome in movement. Some themes may seem to repeat what has been used in lower grades. It should be emphasized that movement challenges have so many ramifications that they can never be considered "taught," "finished" or "achieved." Therefore, it may be necessary to go back to pick up ideas and skills which were missed previously owing to a lack of maturity or to a lack of time to get the best out of the theme. No work should be needlessly repeated. The most important aspect to be considered is that gymnastics is concerned with the ability to transfer the body weight under control. While there is a primary need to develop sufficient strength in the arms and shoulders to carry the body weight, and the proper mechanical use of the legs in receiving the body weight, all work should be integrated to produce greater understanding of movement and of self.

SUGGESTED THEMES FOR GRADE SEVEN, EIGHT AND NINE. BOYS AND GIRLS

A. BODY AWARENESS

1. Bodily efficiency: mechanically correct use of feet, knees, legs in take-off, landings, for running and jumping (Chapter Six, p. 111); strength of muscle groups — arms and shoulder girdle for taking body weight; for springs; flexibility of spine, hip joint, legs and ankles. (It is more interesting and realistic to develop this in floor sequences than by calisthenic exercises).
2. Excellent use of body actions in a great variety of combinations — *steps*, e.g. feet onto hands; hands onto feet; various other parts used in conjunction with hands or feet; *rolls*: symmetrical — forward, backward; asymmetrical: shoulder rolls, side rolls; *rocks* — used as partial rolls to get momentum for a subsequent action, *jumps, springs, elevations* (i.e. *flight*) — control of body shape in flight; variety of take-offs (i.e. part of body used) and landings; *turns* — in flight or in conjunction with weightbearing.

Effective control of the body in action: awareness of a full stretch.

3. Weightbearing; transfer of weight; balance — the ability to move into and out of a wide variety of "on-balance" positions; use of *gesture* actions while in the "on balance" position; knowledge and ability to manage the "overbalance" situation, i.e. how to fall safely by rolling, arching, spring-ing, etc.

4. Awareness of body parts — good form and good mechanics resulting from suitable control of the parts of the body (knees, hands, head) as related to the whole body action.

B. SPACE AWARENESS

1. Using changes of direction as a means of providing variety or proving one's control.

2. Taking the body through a variety of levels as proof of control of body weight and balance.

3. Composition of sequences which show good control over the use of the activity area. Pathways to be well designed.

C. EFFORT QUALITY OF MOVEMENT

1. Good use of: *sudden-strong* qualities — e.g. in spring take-offs; in sudden twists or pushes; *sustained-strong* qualities — e.g. in press-ups; in gradu-ally lowering or raising the body or parts of it; *sudden-fine touch* qualities

---

— e.g. in bounces when taking weight momentarily on feet or hands as for example in some vaults or landings; *sustained-fine touch* qualities as in gestures or in the conclusion of some forms of weight transfer, for example the walkover.

2. The control of flow — *bound* flow to hold the movement in a balance, to prepare to land on a given spot, to hold a starting or a finishing position; *free* flow to acquire continuity within a sequence; to blend take-off, flight and landing; to use combinations of *bound* and *free* flow as contrasts within a sequence, e.g. run, jump into a cartwheel, into a handstand, into two forward rolls and a finish.

3. An understanding, through exploration, of the following aspects of an action or a series of actions: the preparatory phase, the action phase, the recovery phase. For example, the cartwheel begins with a backward counter lean, the downward swing is part of the transfer of weight, the recovery is the binding of flow to halt in the attention position. The weight-factor sequence required is fine-(firm)-fine. The time-factor sequence is usually a transition from sustained-(sudden)-sustained.

D. RELATIONSHIPS

1. Partner work: weightbearing — taking all or some of a partner's weight; aiding the flight of a partner;
   — no contact relationships: matching actions; complementing partner's actions, e.g. "A" rolls while "B" does a stretch-jump over the roll
   — using a partner as an obstacle
   — composing a sequence for partners.

2. With apparatus: Ways of getting on or off apparatus — flight onto or off; one part of the body leading onto or off — e.g. two hands, one foot, etc. using the apparatus in more than one way before coming off: sequences built around mounting and dismounting in several different ways; taking the action from one piece of apparatus to another (e.g. vaulting box to mat; mat to vaulting box).

Note: in all cases consideration should be given to the suitability of the action to the apparatus.

Sequence Building. This is a skill which may be applied to any theme. Thus three selected actions may be built into a sequence. Or, a sequence may be composed to illustrate changes of direction or the use of bound flow or adaptation to a vaulting box. Apart from the skill with which the theme is used, the sequence should be evaluated for: the start, the finish, the use of climax, variety, and/or contrast. The overall control of flow and continuity, good body mechanics and aesthetic alignment of body parts should all be given critical consideration. The skill of the individual performer will determine the degree of difficulty of the actions used, but the pupil should be encouraged to strive to achieve a standard consistent with his ability.

It should be noted that once a performer can execute a given action, such as a headspring, its inclusion in a sequence doesn't necessarily indicate a significant growth in that performer's work in gymnastics. This may need to be considered if attempts are made to grade and evaluate work for report cards.

SAMPLE LESSON PLAN ONE: A class with a good background

GRADE: Seven, Eight or Nine

THEME: Flight

SUBTHEMES: 1. Quality of sustained lightness
2. Two partners assisting a third member

INTRODUCTION:
"Warm up. Practise a series of movements which take you from one level to another."

The teacher encourages individuals; coaches, especially the mechanics of bringing the weight down to the floor.

DEVELOPMENT:
Observation: Observation of those using any form of flight, e.g. jumps, springs onto hands. Short discussion on ways of landing safely.

Challenge: "Free practice of different forms of flight."

Teacher coaches them to establish safe landing practices and then to give attention to the flight.

Challenge: "Try to sustain the flying. Feel a moment of suspension. In that moment, try to glide with no more effort than is required to hold the body shape. Feel the descent. Determine the moment when you must move into the landing action."

Practice time is allowed. The teacher coaches, using vocabulary suggested above: suspension, glide, lightly, no effort, hold it, elongate it.

Observation: "Note the moment of glide and suspension. Try to follow the rhythm. Note the strength of take-off."

In pairs. One utility box or one mat for each pair.

Challenge: "Use the box for a take-off for flights of your own invention. Remember the landing is onto the floor," or, "Use the mat for a landing from a flight, especially for landing on hands."

Exchange apparatus stations.

CULMINATION:
Groups of threes; one mat per group.

Challenge: "Explore ways in which one performer may be assisted into a higher flight than could be executed alone."
"Conclude with a sequence for three. Include some unassisted flight and some assisted flight. Determine the climax."

CALM ENDING:
"Mats away. Scatter formation. Slow stretching alternated with a body curl. Start low and arrive in a good standing position after three phrases."

SAMPLE LESSON PLAN TWO: A class with a limited or a traditional background

GRADE: Seven, Eight or Nine

THEME: Locomotor Actions

SUBTHEMES: 1. Pathways
2. Relationships — Threes; adaptation to apparatus

INTRODUCTION:
Challenge: "Warm up by running counterclockwise."
The teacher checks speed and style of running — i.e. on the balls of the feet, long strides, easy use of arms.

DEVELOPMENT:
Challenge: "Run in your own pathway, going into open spaces and keeping out of others' way."

Challenge: "Keep the idea of individual pathways. Invent your own ways of travelling. Try to find four different ways."

Observation: One half of class observes the other half. "Are their pathways good? Name several actions being used for travelling." (Hopping, rolling, crawling.)

Challenge: "Try some further ways of travelling. Remember you can use other parts of the body in addition to the feet."

Challenge: "Choose two of your discoveries and join them into a short sequence."
Teacher observes the work and coaches: "Plan the movements which

will take you from one action to the other. Keep the repetitions short. Know exactly what you are doing. Check on your starting position. Hold the finish."

Observation: In twos. Each partner checks the other's work. The performer does the sequence twice. "Were they exactly alike? Was there a clear beginning and ending?"

Class should observe a good performance and note the points being stressed.

CULMINATION:*

Groups of threes. Each group has one mat or one bench.

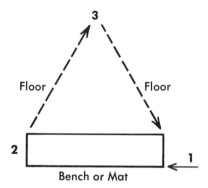

Bench or Mat

Challenge: "All three are to work all the time. Each must find three different ways of travelling — two ways for the floor and one way suited to the apparatus."

Teacher uses observation and/or coaching to help the group to time their work so that they arrive at the apex at the same time. Coach them to distinguish actions suited to the mat or bench as compared with actions suited to the bare floor. Coach for a good standard of execution.

CALM ENDING:

"Equipment away. Scatter formation. Make up a short pattern in which the body is opened and closed while kept close to the floor."

---

* Note: This uses a very simple situation for the first experience of inventing one's own movements. The culmination can be made more challenging by using more difficult apparatus or by combining two pieces of apparatus, but it will be necessary to add "Choose locomotor actions which can be safely done on the apparatus." The lesson could also be made more difficult by requiring one phase of locomotion with weight on hands, or hands and one other body part. The teacher must judge the safety factor involved in the challenge.

SAMPLE LESSON PLAN THREE: A class with a background in movement education

GRADE: Seven, Eight or Nine: Boys

THEME: Twists

SUBTHEMES: 1. Qualities: strong-sudden; strong-sustained
2. Weightbearing and non-weightbearing parts

INTRODUCTION:
"Warm up using floorwork which combines runs, jumps, landings and rolls. Work on control in making one action merge into another."

DEVELOPMENT:
Observation: Observe any sequence taken from the Introduction which includes a twist. Observe and assess *why* the twist was included.

Challenge: "Work on your own sequence so that it will include a twist."

Observation: One or two pupils demonstrate such sequences.

Observation Question: "Where was the weight placed immediately prior to the twist? What happens in the body to create the twist?" (Base remains fixed while a non-weightbearing part rotates about it.)

Challenge: "Explore different twist situations resulting from establishing the weight on different bases. *Follow* the *twisting part* and establish a new base."

Challenge: "Explore the possibility of controlling the speed of the twist." (Sudden twist out of a handstand can bring about a round-off; a sustained twist out of a shoulder roll into a headstand.)

Challenge: "Explore to discover how a twist can be executed during the flight of a jump."

CULMINATION:
"Compose a sequence, without the use of apparatus, which features one or more twists. Use a good variation of timing," or, "Work out a sequence on apparatus which features one or more twists. Use a good variation of timing."

CALM ENDING:
"Scatter formation. Start with weight on hands and feet. Remain on the

spot while making a pattern which brings the feet and hands alternately close together and far apart." (Timing: slow.)

SAMPLE LESSON PLAN FOUR: A class with no knowledge of movement education

GRADE: Seven, Eight or Nine: Boys

THEME: Symmetrical and asymmetrical uses of the body

SUBTHEMES: 1. Stressing hands and feet
2. Slow and fast speeds

INTRODUCTION:
Challenge: "Warm up by changing from running to sliding sideways to running to jumping on the spot with a double take-off and a rebound."
a. Change at the signal of the teacher (e.g. phrases of eight counts).
b. Repeat the same actions but every boy decides the order of the items and the number of repetitions for each.

Observation: Observe one example chosen by teacher. Pupils should name the order and name the length of phrase. The teacher may give a verbal evaluation of good form.

DEVELOPMENT:
Challenge: "Everyone, do your sequence again and decide in which action(s) both sides of the body are used in exactly the same way."

Observation: Observe one boy. Discuss the problem.
(Note: The particular jump described above is symmetrical. Running uses both sides of the body in a like manner but at different times and, therefore, is not truly symmetrical. Sliding is clearly asymmetrical since one side of the body leads throughout.)

Challenge: "Find other body actions you can do in which both sides of your body are used in matching movements."

Observation: Pupils demonstrate, e.g. forward and backward rolls, handstands and headstands, (only if double footed take-off is used); catsprings; dives; jack jumps; tuck jumps; stride jumps; rocking; press-ups.
"Notice that the parts of the body involved are both hands, both feet or the spine."

Challenge: "Find actions which start on one side of the body and lead the whole body into action."

Observation: Pupils demonstrate side rolls, shoulder rolls, cartwheels, turns, twists. Notice that these are very often original movements with no particular name.

CULMINATION:

Groups of four. Selected apparatus,* — mats, utility boxes, benches, vaulting boxes, high beam, *plus floor space.*

Challenge: "All four must work all the time, but keep out of each other's way." (Therefore, there will be a good deal of floor action.)

"Compose a sequence (or routine) in which symmetrical and asymmetrical actions are featured. Stress one and use the other as an unaccented preparation."

Note: If no apparatus is available the challenge may be: "With no apparatus, each boy should make up his own floor sequence combining symmetrical and asymmetrical actions. One type should be accented. Polish the sequence, working for controlled starting and finishing positions and a continuity within the sequence."

CALM ENDING:

"Scatter formation. Lie on the back. Slowly sit up and slowly lie down. On each sit up touch two parts of the body together — e.g. forehead and knees."

* All groups may have the same apparatus, e.g. one mat and the floor. Or, each group may work with a different piece.

TEN

THE TEACHING OF DANCE

The material to be presented here will deal mainly with the selection of content for dance lessons and with some aspects of the methods used in teaching dance. Creative dance and folk dance content and methods will be considered separately. However, the teacher will be in a position to draw upon either type of dance according to the needs or desires of the class. This will mean that the two forms of dance may be integrated or may retain their separate identities when the teacher develops the program. The particular requirements of the class will determine the details of the course.

CREATIVE AND MODERN DANCE

It has been said earlier (p. 37) that the purpose of this book is to help the teacher to apply the teachings of Rudolf Laban to the presentation of physical education in all its areas but with particular emphasis on the work in games, gymnastics and dance. Much of Laban's work was done in the field of dance, and the dance program in many schools is based on the teacher's interpretation of his research, writings and teaching. The materials which follow are based upon experiences derived from attempts to implement the recommendations laid out in *Modern Educational Dance*.[1]

THE URGE TO DANCE

The impulse to dance seems to be natural to man; there is evidence[2] that he has danced from earliest times. Why? Sach says that "In the ecstasy of the dance man bridges the chasm between this and the other world, to

---

[1] Laban, Rudolf, *Modern Educational Dance*, Macdonald and Evans, London, 1948.

[2] Sachs, Kurt, *World History of the Dance*, W. W. Norton and Co. Inc., The Norton Library Series, New York, 1963, pp. 207-208; 258.

the realm of demons, spirits, and God. Captivated and entranced he bursts his earthly chains and trembling, feels himself in tune with all the world."[3]

Man creates rhythmic patterns in the timing of his actions; spatial patterns and forms with the placement of his movement. Out of his imagination or from his experience of living he creates an interpretation or a reaction to the forces in his world. For a short time he is removed from the monotony of everyday existence and participates in the lively harmony which permeates the rhythmic motion of a body made free of the practical demands of the usual work actions.

The urge to dance, then, is the impulse to express oneself in movement. Laban has said, "The world too deep for speech, the silent world of symbolic action, . . . is the answer to an inner need of man."[4] He also reminds us that "the most deeply moving moments of our lives usually leave us speechless, and in such moments our body carriage may well be able to express what otherwise would be inexpressible."[5] Laban has also identified two other needs which are probably satisfied by dance.

First, he suggests that dancing can be used to relieve the discomfort which is experienced when man's actions are limited, repetitive and concentrated in two or three specific joints.[6] This discomfort arises because the other joints tend to be held immobile and the inhibiting impulses build up strong tensions. Dancing allows the whole body to participate in the flow of movement. In short, children and adults will enjoy dancing for the freedom of movement which it permits.

Secondly, he points out that dancing calls forth very complicated blends of efforts.[7] For example, a coordinated series of efforts might start with pressing, merge into thrusting which might become flicking, and then blend into floating. The smooth coordination of the transitions from one effort into another gives rise to a pleasurable sensation. Thus the adult or child dances with enthusiasm because it feels good.

THE VALUE OF DANCE IN EDUCATION

Dance can contribute in several ways to a sound and rich education.

For one thing, if creative dance is part of the curriculum, the child is given an opportunity to participate often. If it is omitted from the curriculum, he is likely to dance only rarely and may, therefore, lose confidence in his ability to move freely. The feel of the flow of movement through the whole body may be lost. The result will probably be feelings of self-con-

[3] *Ibid.*, p. 4.
[4] Laban, Rudolf, *The Mastery of Movement,* Macdonald and Evans, London, 1960, p. 91.
[5] *Ibid.*, p. 91.
[6] Laban, Rudolf, *Modern Educational Dance,* Macdonald and Evans, London, 1948, p. 17.
[7] *Ibid.*, p. 18.

sciousness and uneasiness when he is asked to dance. It is almost as if the individual becomes a stranger to himself and he is alienated by the unusual feel of a total body stirring. Therefore, it may be inferred that dancing can bring about a form of self-realization and thus make a special contribution to the total development of the individual.

Dance also provides a counterbalance for the stress placed on intellectual activity in our schools. Not only does it promote the ability to move well, but it also provides opportunities for using the imagination and for developing aesthetic appreciation. The selections of rhythms and spatial designs, the appreciation of the relationship between motifs and their variations or between contrasting elements of movement, all help to foster a sensitivity to beauty in nature and in the arts.

Dance has a special contribution to make to the all-round development of the child. It can offer a full training in the efforts and in the shape patterns of movement. Effort and shape patterns are important because they reflect the inner attitude of the mover; and, conversely, the combinations and blends of effort elements and the various blends of movement shapes which comprise dance movements stimulate the mind. This being so, the study and acquisition of control over the efforts and movement shapes should be considered part of the total education of the child. Dance can contribute to this part of his education as no other activity can, because dance is concerned with movement as an end in itself. Games and gymnastics cannot make the same contribution because, in each case, the movement is subordinated to the end product. That is to say, dance is movement for movement's sake and therefore, all the blends and combinations of efforts and shapes can be fully explored. But the movements of games are selected to achieve a win, and the movements of gymnastics are selected to prove the control of the body in the presence of the pull of gravity. Therefore, the movements practised in these areas are fairly selective and it would be unlikely that all the effort and shape combinations and transitions would be considered part of the curriculum.

Furthermore, dance contributes to the development of the actions needed in the work life of the individual. The efforts and the shape patterns used in dance are the same as those used in working actions except that they are organized in a slightly different way. This means that the efforts and the shape patterns which occur in dance activity can be used in daily life. For example, in dance the foot might be pressed into the floor as a part of a movement sequence. In work, the foot might press a spade into the ground in the course of doing a job of work. The effort actions of wringing or thrusting occurring in expressive movement are the same as those of wringing a cloth or hitting a nail except that the resistance to the action comes from the body rather than from the cloth or the nail. Therefore through dance, the child gains greater control and range of the effort elements which he will be able to use to master the specific skills needed in other situations.

One more value must be mentioned. Since a dance is often an expression of the dancer's ideas, attitudes or knowledge, it may consolidate what he has learned in other subjects. It also may inspire him to seek further knowledge. For example, one class felt the need to visit the zoo to study the movement of animals before they could compose their dance for the story of Noah's Ark. Another class, who chose to compose a dance about refugees, did a lot of soul-searching, a lot of reading and studying of pictures before they were satisfied that they understood the feelings of a refugee. Dance can become a vivid, real and personal experience and as such, it becomes a very valuable form of education.

SOME CRITERIA FOR DANCE LESSONS

In each dance lesson the teacher should try to achieve the feeling and flow of dance in the movement of the pupils. In other words, the movement must not stop at the level of an exercise or a technique but should involve the inner participation of the individual. This will happen when the pupil feels the flow of the movement and enjoys dancing. For example, the dancer may involve himself in the situation: "I am running quickly away from something which frightens me, but I fall suddenly to the ground here because there is danger ahead too," or he may merely run fast and stop suddenly, falling into a crouched position. The first movement, expressive of inner feeling, will have a very distinctive quality. The second movement could be merely a well executed phrase of movement composed of two distinct parts. However, by feeling the flow of the movement between the parts, the pupil could immerse himself in it and it could become, for him, a dance phrase. The teacher should aspire to having the dance quality in all of the pupils' work.

Each pupil should feel that he has the freedom to work out his ideas and reactions in his own way. This does not imply a lack of discipline. The discipline is fostered by the expectation that each pupil will make a sincere effort to solve the problem at the best level he can achieve. It is reinforced by the evaluation process which causes the pupil to examine his response in the light of the principles of dance. In other words, in the best situations the pupils submit to the discipline of the art of dance rather than to the discipline of the teacher. The teacher tends to become the guide who helps him to meet the requirements of dance form and offers him assistance when he requires it.

SOME QUOTATIONS FROM LABAN'S *Modern Educational Dance*[8]

From page 23. "Dance training from its earliest stages is principally concerned with teaching the child to live, move and express itself in the

[8] *Ibid.*

media which govern its life, the most important of which is the child's own flow of movement."

From page 24. "Older children feel the need for finished dances and the feeling of working towards something definite, while the younger children's foremost need is for effort exercise."

From page 92. "Rhythmic music is an incentive to rhythmic movement, but it is only when a fully developed flow of movement, including a definite composition of shapes, has been built up around the rhythm that one can speak of dance proper."

TERMS USED IN DANCE EDUCATION

Dancing is a participation in the flow of total body movement.

Dance techniques are the practical skills required in dancing, such as pointing the toes in certain leg gestures.

Dance studies are the equivalent of *études* in music. They are miniature dances which are created, usually by the dancer(s), for experimental purposes, or to gain command over a principle or theme, or to find a mode of expressing an idea.

Dance sequences are miniature dance studies. They are characterized by a distinct beginning, an action or actions, and a definite ending.

Dance is an art form which is the result of selecting, refining and balancing movements to create a cohesive statement in movement. The result is the communication of an idea, feeling, mood or story.

The recommendations which will be made for the teaching of dance will stress that the children's movements should qualify as dancing. Dance techniques will not be stressed as specific and selected movements but will develop through clarifying the movement in terms of the four components of movement — effort, space, relationships, the use of the body. Dance studies will generally be the culminations of the lessons and will probably be regarded as "dances" by the pupils. Dances as works of art, produced for purposes of performance before an audience, will not be considered as part of the dance program. However, special interest groups may receive their impetus from the dance lessons, and they may go on to production work in the extra-curricular organization of the school.

THE DANCE LESSON

Even though pupils have a basic urge to dance, they will need to be motivated to do so when the lesson time arrives. After all, in most schools, the scheduling of facilities tends to mean that the time to dance is an arbitrary arrangement. If the individual teacher can arrange to have the lesson grow out of the logical development of a project of work, this will be very advantageous. Failing this, it will be necessary for the teacher to provide compelling motivation. The more usual forms of motivation are generally regarded to be stimuli for dance.

In preparing a lesson, the teacher may first select the stimulus to be used, experiment with it and determine what kinds of responses it may elicit. From these expectations the lesson may be planned.

Conversely, the teacher may first determine what experiences should be given to the pupil. Then he must select the stimuli which he hopes will elicit these experiences.

MUSIC is generally considered to be the inevitable partner of dance. Certainly music with a clear or exciting rhythmic emphasis, can inspire rhythmic movement; and, music with a clear emotional content can often elicit movement with a particular quality. For example *In the Hall of the Mountain King** is likely to elicit strong-sustained movement which accelerates into strong-fast movement. However, music can interfere with the movement. For one thing, most children work in very short movement sequences. It is very difficult to find musical selections which are short enough to suit the needs of the dancer. Furthermore, movement has its own rhythm, the accents arising out of its space and effort elements. The child should be free to discover his own rhythmic composition. Indeed, in the early stages, he needs to become aware of his own rhythms. For this reason, he should not have to conform to the structures superimposed by the music. However, there are many times, especially at the beginning of the lesson, when dancing to music is an enlivening experience. The key to success is the careful selection of the music by the teacher.

PERCUSSION INSTRUMENTS are a marvellous help, especially with the primary and junior pupils. However, the teacher must learn how to choose and use them.

The chief requirement should be that they have a good tone. Most of them should be small enough and light enough that they can be carried and played by the dancer as an accent or an accompaniment to his movement. They should also be strong enough to withstand rather vigorous usage.

Children can gain a great deal of experience and become very sensitive to tone and sound variations through making their own instruments.

The teacher needs to build up a collection which will help to develop the effort qualities. Such a collection will probably include:

For sustainment: triangle, a good quality cymbal of 14″-18″ diameter, or a Chinese gong and a good quality lamb's wool beater.

For suddenness: hardwood blocks or rhythm sticks, cymbal, tunable tambour, good quality drum, bells, maracas.

---

* R.C.A. Victor LE 1003 *Adventures in Music,* Grieg, "Peer Gynt Suite No. 1": *In the Hall of the Mountain King.*

For strong actions: drums, tambour, maraca, Chinese gong.

For light action: bells, triangle, Chinese finger cymbals, salt in a box.

For direct actions: hardwood blocks, sticks, tambour, maracas, drums.

For flexible actions: tambourine, bells, maracas.

The teacher and the pupils will have to experiment to discover how the instruments may be played to give the desired effect.

The teacher may play a repetitive phrase, a rhythmic phrase or a sequence of sound to which the pupils respond. This will allow the whole class to work to the same stimulus. Depending upon the problem, they may respond individually or as a group.

The other major use of percussion is for the dancer to carry it with him so that the sound comes as a result of his movement, or the instrument is played as an accent to certain parts of his sequence. For example, bells on wrist bands will give sounds as the arms are used in the dance; but a tambourine may be hit to emphasize the landing or the crest of a jump.

It is also possible for partners to share an instrument and to play for one another, making the transition between the two roles an integral part of the dance sequence. Enlarging upon this idea, a group of four might compose a dance centred about a big tom-tom which remains on the floor and becomes the focal point of their dance. Further exploration will reveal other ways of using percussion instruments. The most important principle to be remembered is that the sound and the movement should be blended together and both should be part of the dance rhythm and shape. There should be no thought of sitting on one side as a member of the orchestra. It would be detrimental to the dance if the task of playing the instrument restricted the full participation of the whole body in the flow of the movement. When the children first use the instruments, they may go through a stage when there is more stress on the playing than the dancing. Teachers should be on the alert for this and encourage free experimentation. For example, how can the instrument be used during a fast twirl which gradually slows and sinks to the ground? What air patterns can be made by a fluttering tambourine? At what points in space can the strikes be placed? What parts of the body can be used to make the strikes? In a similar way, each of the instruments should be explored for sound and movement possibilities.

Sometimes it is difficult to determine whether or not a sound is a stimulus or an accompaniment for the dance. However, if the teacher presents the sound first, it should certainly be the stimulus to the subsequent movement. If the child starts with an instrument of his own and the sound and the movement develop concurrently, it may fulfil either function or it may fluctuate between the two.

If discipline is a matter of concern for the teacher, it may be helpful to guide the work fairly directly at first. For example, it is fun and very effective to play with the idea of starting movement and sound very, very vigorously and gradually slowing the movement and diminishing the sound

Partners sharing percussion equipment in a dance sequence.

into stillness and silence, and then gradually building both up to a climax which is cut off suddenly. There are many alternatives to this idea of increasing and decreasing. It can serve to give vent to the pupil's excitement and energy, but it can also be used to develop a sensitivity to sound and silence. Such experimentation could be followed by work in pairs with one instrument shared between the two. The challenge could be concerned with a "Question and Answer" (Chapter Seven, p. 168) theme. The teacher should have no problem with discipline if the children are given an appropriate challenge and are not frustrated by having to hold the instrument while the work is organized.

THE VOICE can sometimes be used instead of percussion instruments. It has the advantage of added melodic possibilities, though these will be used in a very simple way. The voice can sometimes help sustained actions or very light, fine actions better than any other stimulus. Chants may be made up of one or two words, for example "pit-a-pat," and repeated over and over as an accompaniment to the movement. Hissing, tongue clicks, vowel sounds or single words with the syllables distorted can be used in many ways, but usually by the dancer who creates them as an accompaniment to his movement. This is another aspect of the work which can be explored for the value and richness it can add to the whole experience of dance. It may lead on to the use of other types of sounds which are produced by stamping, clapping, finger-clicking and slapping the body in different ways. Often the slapping can be done on different parts of the body to produce different tone qualities. Dances composed on themes related to natural phenomena often include these kinds of sounds. Music for dances based on such themes as the rain, wind, sea waves, storms or fire is difficult to find, but voice or body clapping and stamping can serve very well, and may be used with or without the addition of percussion instruments.

MOVEMENT IDEAS may be used as the starting point of a dance lesson or a dance study. For example, the theme might be, "Meeting with suddenness and parting with suddenness." The teacher would need to guide the class with verbal cues and would also have to structure the situation. For example, the meeting and parting, a *Relationship* theme, could be focussed upon two parts of the body meeting and parting, or upon partners meeting at high or low levels, or, upon one partner meeting another or several members of a group. The lesson might start with one aspect, develop into another, and finish in the development of a dance study for three participants.

The movement idea used in the above illustration is taken from Laban's four components of movement. (Chapter Four, p. 37) and it includes two of the components, namely, *Relationships* (meeting/parting) and *Effort Qualities* (sudden/sustained). The verbal cues given by the teacher are derived from the two remaining components: *Body Awareness* (*parts* meeting/parting) and *Space* (high/low levels).

When planning the lesson, the teacher must make certain that one component receives the main emphasis but that at least two others are present as subthemes. If only one component is stressed, the movement which develops will be unnatural and there will be an irritation and frustration in the lesson.

Some movement ideas which include more than one component are:
• feet stressed with contrasts of high/low level movements

- partners leading and following with changes of speed
- spreading and shrinking with contrasting tension
- jumps with different body shapes, the jumps being made into varied directions
- partners contrasting stillness with sudden strong actions
- partners moving near to and far from each other with straight or curved floor patterns

IDEAS from life and nature can provide the stimulus for dance. The particular idea is likely to arise from some experience or study in which the pupils have participated as a group and it is especially valuable if the teacher has been part of the original experience also. Thus topics which have originated in science, mathematics, social studies, literature, art or music, may serve as the springboard for dance.

It will be very important for the teacher to guide the selection of the topic into a sphere which has genuine movement possibilities. In addition, the idea adopted must be regarded as merely the starting point and the pupil should feel free to manipulate the idea according to the way the movement seems to dictate. For example, if the moon is being studied in science and it is decided to use it as a theme in dance, there might be several

Vera's picture. The light, joyous running of these children could inspire exciting dance movements. (Grade Three)

characteristics, real or mythical which could inspire a dance study: waxing and waning, changing shape, rising and sinking, serene, sustained, gentle movement, sending out shafts of light, spreading light, casting shadows, creating ghostly shapes. Of course, there are far too many movement ideas to be incorporated in one dance. It would be wise to choose ideas which include at least three of the movement components (Chapter Four, p. 39) and perhaps which offer a contrast in at least one factor. For example, it might be decided that the main theme should be, "Changing group shapes with contrasting effort elements of sustainment and suddenness," the qualities being ascribed to moonlight and darting, dancing moonbeams. The main theme would be shapes, subsidiary themes, group relationships and qualities.

This type of analysis should be done at the lesson-planning stage by the teacher. When the idea is discussed with the children, their suggestions can be substituted or the teacher may guide their thinking towards the themes which seem possible to use. In any case, the teacher should have music and/or percussion instruments at hand in case they are needed and should have a tentative idea of how the theme and subthemes can best be explored. As the teacher becomes more experienced, he will feel more certain of when he should exert his influence and when he can safely leave the ideas with the children.

DANCE FORMS

It is necessary for the teacher to have some knowledge of dance forms in order to help the pupils to develop their movement ideas into a dance rather than leaving them at the movement exploration level. There are two ways of looking at this problem. The first is in terms of the learning process and the second is in terms of the dance forms themselves.

In the course of responding to a stimulus, the child will tend to pass through several stages. There will be the *initial* response. At this stage the pupil is caught up in the flow of movement and his movements are quite diffused, one flowing into another with no apparent phrasing. In the *discovery* phase, the mover begins to sort out what he is doing. This will lead to some sort of phrasing because he discovers that he is "whirling and jumping around in a circle until he slowly stops at the end of a big whirl." During the *refining* phase, he clarifies how he wants to start, what he wants to emphasize and how he wants to finish. Now he has achieved a simple sequence of movement. It is made up of a beginning, an action and an ending, one of which will assume the major importance and each of which is characterized by the appropriate use of effort qualities.

The learning process described above has led to a dance phrase and this in turn may constitute "a dance" in the thinking of a young child. It has a feeling of unity about it for the flow has moved from a recognized beginning into a fully executed action and has terminated in a recognizable ending.

All other dance forms are built upon this initial unit. The other forms which are described are listed without any suggestion as to the order in which they will be used. The stimulus or the purpose of the dancer will determine the form which will be the best type of expression.

- Beginning — first action, second action — Ending.
- Beginning — action, variation(s) of the action — Ending.
- Beginning — action, contrasting action — Conclusion.
- Beginning — (action, reaction) repeated to form a chain of reactions which terminates in some form of conclusion.

There may be a danger of the teacher using these descriptions as formulae to impose some order upon the children's composition. This would spoil their creative freedom. Rather, the teacher may keep these forms in mind and guide the children by appropriate questioning such as: "Do you know how you want to start?"

"What happens now?"

"Which is the most important part of your dance?"

"How many parts do you have?"

"Are all the phrases alike?"

"Do you know how you want to finish?"

STANDARDS

The movement itself can be improved if the teacher will ask the pupils the right questions. The "right" questions are usually pointed toward bringing about a keener awareness of the use of one of the four movement components. For example, the following questions should probably be asked sometime in each lesson.

- "Which part(s) of the body is especially important in your dance?"
- "*How* are you moving? Suddenly? Straight?"
- "*Where* is your movement going? Up? Down? Around?"

The question is usually followed by the admonition to, "Make the answer very clear in your movement."

OBSERVATIONS are a very valuable teaching aid. They should not interrupt the activity of the class very often, but they should be used to increase the variety of movement used, to assist in the mastery of the particular aspect of movement being studied, to give a feeling of achievement and a summary of the level of progress made during the lesson.

The teacher should always set a specific question for the pupils before the movement is observed. In this way, they will know what they are looking for and have some chance of seeing it. Observing and analyzing are difficult processes, and the teacher must appreciate this fact. The observation question will have to be graded according to the ability of the pupils.

If variety is being sought, one half of the class may observe the other half. The observation task is to look at two or three different people to see, for example, how they use their feet. If the answer can be brief, it may be taken orally. For instance, "One used both feet together." If the answer is complicated, some of the more unusual ideas may be observed in isolation. If the answer is simple, no oral discussion need follow and the children may be invited immediately to increase the variety of their own work.

If the awareness of a specific movement or quality is being sought, the teacher may choose for observation two people, one who is already using the desired effort quality while the other is using the contrasting quality. For example, one might be doing *sudden* jumps, the other a *slow* turn. The observation question becomes: "Find the difference in the *way* these two pupils do their movements." The answer may be taken verbally.

If the discovery process (See Chapter Two, p. 18) is being used, the next step is to have everyone try their own work again to find out whether they are using *sudden* or *slow* (sustained) actions. They may then: emphasize their quality; seek further actions which require it; try the effect of the contrasting quality; find movements which will permit the bringing of the contrasts into a phrase of movement.

The most difficult form of observation is to study a movement phrase to determine the significant "intention" behind it. Is he intending to execute a *sudden* jump, or is it a jump for *distance*, or is it really a jump which creates a *body shape* in the air? It is essential that the observer knows exactly what he is attempting to observe. In this case, the observer is not concerned with the jump, or the effort or the space factor, but rather with the *intention* of the dancer. Knowing exactly what one is looking for is just as important to the teacher as to the children when they observe. The *emphasis* of the movement or the *intention* of the mover is a very important category of observation for once it is observed accurately, the performer can be assisted to clarify his movement so that the intention is clearly conveyed.

LESSON PLANNING

It has already been suggested that the lesson be built upon the use of a main theme and two subthemes which are drawn from at least two and preferably three of the four movement components. It has also been pointed out that there will be an initial response to the stimulus. This stage is followed by the discovery phase when the meaning of the movement and the intention of the dancer are grasped. The components selected as subthemes are often added if the first stage of discovery shows them to be neglected. Then there is a refining stage. Once again, the subthemes can be used in the modification and refining process. From here the problem may be enlarged and a dance sequence or study developed. At any point in this process, observation may be used to help the performer to become aware of what he is doing.

The outline of such a plan might include:

---

a. Initial stimulus which will lead to the initial response and the exploratory stage.
b. Challenges and observations leading to discovery.
c. Challenges and observations based on subthemes.
d. Selection of movement phrase or sequence.
e. Refinement and practice — theme and subtheme used as the basis of the refinement or improvement of the movement.
f. Final performance — perhaps for observation and sharing.

Another way to look at the lesson plan is to use a three part plan.

1. *Introductory activity*
   - Use of initial stimulus which brings about vigorous total body activity related to the theme or the subthemes.

2. *Development*
   - Exploration, discovery, tentative selection of movement related to theme and subtheme(s) resulting from the observation of movement arising in the introduction or resulting from the presentation of new stimuli.

3. *Application*
   - Dance making. The material developed earlier may now be adapted to a new situation such as: a group dance; a dance to a given piece of music; a dance based on the use of percussion; a dance based upon a preselected idea.

SUGGESTIONS FOR DANCE THEMES

The teacher will need to select the particular themes which seem best suited to his class at the time. However, children develop in a fairly consistent pattern and, therefore, certain expectations can be made as to the themes which are likely to be most suitable.

Junior Kindergarten (four-year-olds)

These young children should come to dance in the most natural way possible; and there should be no suggestion of a lesson. The teacher may have difficulty distinguishing dance movement from gymnastic movement as done by the four-year-old, but the categorizing of the movement is not important. What is important is that the child be permitted to move and dance when the urge is upon him, always providing the safety and welfare of others are not jeopardized.

The characteristic movements of the age group will be a repetitive jump, and the hitting and pumping of the arms. The jumps will sometimes seem to be an attempt to experience an elevation off the floor. At other times, they will seem to allow for the experience of falling down or of stamping vigorously into the floor. The nursery rhyme, *Ring Around the Rosey,* is an example of this element of dance. The jumps and hits are often accompanied by vocal sounds. This should be encouraged. Forms of loco-motion may be included. Movements will tend to be vigorous, fast and direct. The repetitive element is very important. The method to be used is hardly a method at all, for it is a seemingly casual interest taken by the teacher in the children's activity and the provision of well chosen stimuli. She may provide the latter quite directly by stating that she is going to play the drum for dancing and inviting the children to participate. The beats should be strong, quick and repetitive. Accents and pauses which accom-modate falls or stamps will add variety and vitality. Tambourines, maracas and the Chinese gong may be used at different times to increase the range of stimuli. The teacher should feel free to participate quite naturally with the children. She may form their focal point and as she plays the instru-ment, she may rise or stoop, turn, move forward or backward. In all like-lihood the children will rise, stoop and move with her. She may pause in her playing and ask if anyone has a dance step that she can play for. This idea can be expanded to include enquiries for any dances which don't need accompaniment. Sometimes this will lead to "pure dance." At other times, the dance will include the sound of the feet or some sort of vocal accom-paniment.

When dancing has become an accepted activity, the teacher may offer movement stimuli. These may take the form of identifying a dance as a "jumping" dance or a "turning" dance or a "knees" dance. These ideas are likely to expand as the children start thinking about other possibilities.

The teacher may provide a less direct form of stimuli by giving dance a place in the choice of activities available for work periods. The instru-ments may be made available to the pupils and a dancing area may be marked off on the floor with masking tape. Records with vigorous, fast, or repetitive rhythms may be made available to the pupils. The *Listen and Move* records, (Macdonald and Evans (Educational Recordings) Ltd., Lon-don., Green Label No. 1 and No. 2); rhumbas, Scottish country dances, marches, polkas, singing games and favourite records should be available in the "dance corner." Pictures, poems, natural forms which illustrate rhyth-mic phenomena may be collected, discussed and displayed in the dance corner or in other parts of the room.

If a wide and spontaneous interest is cultivated in dance and dance-like movement, the children will benefit because they will be actively dancing and will begin to consciously appreciate that they are indeed doing so.

Senior Kindergarten (five-year-olds)

If the children have been in a Junior Kindergarten in which dance has been an integral part of the curriculum, they will already have some concept of what it means to dance. They will, therefore, move on from this begin-ning.

If the children have not had the benefit of an informal program, the vocabulary, as well as the experiences, will have to be gradually developed.

The need of five-year-olds is for strong, sudden and direct movement. They will also enjoy being flexible (i.e. wiggly) and "not so sudden." The movement will most often involve the whole body although there will be times when special parts of the body such as the feet, knees, elbows or hands will be particularly stressed. Locomotion of different kinds will be evident. The children will generally work alone and they will be quite capable of learning to keep out of each other's way. Their space sense will be developing. They will enjoy changing levels, using different directions and in a limited way making winding or zigzag pathways. Percussion instruments played by the teacher, and movement ideas arising from the other activities of the school day will provide stimuli for dance. The dance corner, as described in the Junior Kindergarten, can be continued with advantage, allowing the children to dance under the impulse of their own initiative. This informal sort of dance may now be supplemented by a more structured lesson.

DANCE THEMES SUITABLE FOR LESSONS

The themes which the teacher uses for the basis of her lessons are related to the spontaneous dance behaviour exhibited by the children. Hence, they can provide the starting point for the pupils' own dances and for an expansion of their ideas about dance.

a. Using the body in different ways — stiff — wiggly — as if made of rubber — jerky — smooth and floaty. Dances making special parts of the body very important — knees, elbows, head, hands, feet, heels.

b. Repetitive, rhythmic jumping. Discovering the sound pattern of their feet, accents provided by "falling down" or crouching or stopping. Concentration on jumping away from the floor, finding how high up they like to go. Concentration on downward jumping, stamping, crouching, falling.

c. Travelling in different ways — on different parts of the body — on the feet — low down — "not" low — making the feet do special tricks — making knees or elbows or different parts important — travelling to music — travelling to percussion sounds — feet or hands making their own sounds.

d. Being low down — different shapes which are possible, ways of moving when staying low — ways of moving downward or upward — growing smaller, growing larger — the speed at which this is done.

e. Moving forward "and other ways" — discovering the names for other ways — discovering the pathways which they make.

f. Discovering actions — jumps, turns, walking, running, skipping, sliding, kicking, stamping, clapping.

g. Listening to simple sound patterns (percussion) and moving in appropriate ways — stopping when the sound stops.

h. Dancing to short pieces of music. Music should be a strong stimulus — very rhythmic or very clear mood music.

i. The beginning of phrasing — choosing a starting position which helps you to get going; stopping when the sound stops; becoming aware of how many parts you have used to make your dance (i.e. how many different actions such as stamping and skipping).

j. Dances inspired by stories or school projects — Hallowe'en; being a scarecrow — floppy arms, head, legs; weird shape; sudden movement which scares the crows; being moved by the wind. Doing a dance which shows these things about your "scarecrow-self."

Primary Levels

The creative dance program for the six-, seven- and eight-year-olds leads on from the work done in the kindergarten. The teaching can be more structured and its preciseness can gradually increase as the child gains more experience and greater maturity. This means that, in lessons for the six-year-olds, the stimulus must be very compelling. The teacher's job is to observe and analyze the spontaneous responses to the stimulus and to help the children to become aware of the aspects of movement which they are using. For example, if a very rhythmic piece of music is being played and the

Ib's picture. A (nine-year-old) boy's reaction to movement is shown in the vigorous runs portrayed in his artwork.

children are skipping, hopping, sliding and so on, the teacher may draw attention to the fact that the feet are being stressed. The children may be led on to find all sorts of nimble foot actions which can be done in time to the music. At a later stage of experience and maturity, as for example, with many eight-year-olds, the teacher may play the music and *ask* for varied foot movements with changes of direction because he knows that the pupils are already aware of what foot patterns and directions are. At this stage, the teacher may concentrate on helping the pupils to become aware of how they are spontaneously changing directions on the accent of the *phrase,* this being their particular level of maturity and need.

The six-year-old will tend to dance alone most of the time, but the eight-year-old will be gaining experience in working in pairs, threes and in groups no larger than five. The younger ones will tend to use strong, direct and quick movements. The older ones will be capable of using sustainment, flexibility and fine touch as well as the other three effort qualities. The older ones will also be able to use double elements such as strong and sudden, strong and sustained and so on. The young ones will not generally show clear starting and finishing positions, but the older ones should. The older ones will also show clearer body shapes. The six-year-olds will characteristically be active with their whole body. Therefore, the body shape is not very clear and the stressing of various parts of the body such as knees, elbows, toes or hands may be evident, but not always coordinated with the entire body movement. See the chart on page 270 for probable development of dance movement.

LESSON CONTENT OR DANCE THEMES

The teacher should keep in mind the natural development of primary children as it is shown in the chart on page 270. It is recommended that stimuli should be used to elicit the initial response, which, for very young or inexperienced pupils, is likely to be one of those in the left-hand column. During the lesson the teacher should help the pupil to recognize his own choice of action. As members of the class spontaneously use responses which show new appreciations and awarenesses, the teacher can draw attention to these new developments. Gradually individuals and the class in general will move towards the concepts listed in the right hand column. This progress can occur for some pupils within a given lesson; for others over the course of a series of lessons.

When the pupil becomes aware that his movement is, for example, stressing a low level, he may or may not become interested in the concept of the *level.* He may be more interested in the rolling he is doing. The fact that it is done at a low level may be of no particular interest to him at that time. However, with the recognition of the fact that some dance actions can be done at a low level, there will come, at some time, a use of the new knowledge. Thus progress is gradually achieved.

Themes which are related to the early development of the dance move-

CHART OF PROBABLE DEVELOPMENT OF DANCE MOVEMENT

	From	Towards
Effort Qualities:	a) strong b) direct c) sudden	a) fine touch b) flexible c) sustained
Relationships:	a) dancing alone and also, whole class responding to the teacher as a leader.	a) dancing with a partner, in threes, or in small groups.
Body Awareness:	a) whole body action b) symmetrical use of body c) actions — running, jumping, turning. d) body shapes — curled or elongated	a) parts of the body stressed. b) asymmetrical use of body c) step patterns — e.g. step-hop d) body shapes — more clearly defined — increased sense of the extension of the body.
Space Awareness:	a) low level b) forward direction c) general space in concrete concepts e.g. reaching toward the ceiling.	a) distinguishing the three levels b) distinguishing different directions c) some appreciation of personal orientation e.g. reaching outward, folding inward.
General:	a) dance regarded as physical movement such as locomotion and turning b) a sense of movement as a folding and unfolding of self c) sense of keeping going	a) locomotion, jumps, turns, continue to be regarded as "my dance" b) gestures of trunk and, perhaps, limbs c) sense of phrasing: beginning, actions, ending

ment summarized in the above chart are listed and expanded somewhat and offered as some concrete illustrations of how children may respond to an ongoing program of dance. However, no attempt has been made to indicate a priority or sequential order.

1. Locomotor actions: discovering different ways of travelling;
   e.g. jumping, running, twirling.

2. Parts of the body dancing:
   a. making a part of you important in the dance.
   b. discovering different ways of stressing the use of a particular body part, e.g. *feet* — stamping in different ways; feet jumping in different ways (two feet, one foot, high, turns); feet doing special steps (their own ideas of this); using different parts of the feet (heels, toes).
   hands — clapping (together, floor, on the body), hands shaking, hands doing special things (chopping, punching, pressing; waving, pointing; on hips, head).
   knees — bending, lifting, straightening.
   heads — nodding, shaking, turning.
3. Dancing on one spot (jumping, stamping, clapping, crouching).
4. Using the effort qualities:
   a. very fast (locomotion or parts of the body), suddenness (stops, starts), making a movement last a long time (sinking, rising, making yourself big, making yourself small, creeping forward).
   b. strong — gripping strongly in towards the centre of the body, hard stamps, loud claps, kicking feet, hammering hands or feet, big strong jumps, strong walking, proud marching, strong lifting, jerking, vigorous shaking.
   c. fine touch — light running, light bouncy jumps, quiet landings, tapping, clapping softly.
   d. wiggling and twisting — tied in knots; straight, sharp, wooden man.
   e. continuous flow — banking and gliding, decelerating gradually, accelerating gradually.
   f. intermittent flow — repetitive jumps, up and down, stopping, starting and stopping.
5. Awareness of space: going forward, turning around, other directions; being low; reaching to the ceiling, to the walls; making yourself fill up a big space, squeeze into a narrow space, disappear into a tiny creature; moving percussion into different positions around the body.
6. Relationships:
   a. *To People:* dancing by yourself; "all" going counterclockwise; "all" into the middle; "all" rising up, "all" dropping down; partners; taking turns, dancing near each other.
   b. *To Things:* reacting to stimuli; dancing with percussion; getting close to or far away from the floor.
7. Dance forms: *Sequences:* getting ready to start, stopping when the sound stops, doing two things in my dance, repeating my dance exactly, choosing a starting position, holding a finishing position, choosing contrasting parts to a dance.
8. Dramatic stimuli for dance.
   Hallowe'en: Witches: twisted, ugly movements of different parts of the

---

Reacting to percussion stimuli.

body; strong, jerky movements; flying, jumping, sudden arrivals; actions such as stirring witches' brew, walking with a cane.

Ghosts: What kinds? Shapeless, noiseless, floating ghosts; human skeletons, all knees and elbows with clanky, swinging bones and no muscles; movements swing, clomp, walk grotesquely; happy ghosts out on their one day of freedom, etc.

Scarecrows: Loose, wobbly heads, arms, bodies; movements — sudden flappings; long stillness, changes of shape, etc.

Cats: with wind in their tails; fast runs, sudden jumps, sustained crawling; sometimes low, sometimes jumping high; shapes — arched back, long, low and slinky; actions — scratching, clawing, spitting.

Autumn: Leaves:

    a. beautiful shapes, bright joyous colours, dance lightly, hopping, fluttering, skipping on the tree.

    b. drop off and are chased by the wind, here and there, in a group, all alone, in a straight path, in a circle, hopping in the air, sliding along the grass, come to rest in a big pile.

Wind: Mischievous, playful; runs, hops, twirls, jumps, rolls; grows stronger and stronger, then fades away; blows this way and that way.

The analysis of the movement possibilities contained in some dramatic ideas which may appeal to children of the first three grades is given here as a reminder that it is necessary to discover what movement factors may be of significance in the topic. The teacher, having considered the movement possibilities, may then lead the children's discussion into aspects of the topic which may be richly developed in movement. The discussion relative to the use of *ideas* as stimuli to dance is given on p. 261 of this chapter.

Other topics which may be useful are: Christmas Toys; A Fireworks Display including roman candles, cartwheels, sparklers, etc.; Santa Claus parade; animals in Noah's Ark; storms, wind, rain, thunder, lightning.

9. Music Stimuli for Dance: The *Listen and Move* series of Green Label records, published by Macdonald and Evans (Educational Recordings) Ltd., London, England, have been especially made to provide stimuli for dance. The teacher may guide the response, but the records are carefully constructed to elicit a rather specific initial response. With six-year-olds, the teacher may allow them to listen with eyes closed, ask them to think of ways in which they would like to move. He should play the music often enough to allow them to become acquainted with it. Then they should be allowed to try out their ideas by dancing to the music. Ask them if they have a starting position and at the end of the piece urge them to hold their finishing position. The teacher may offer praise and encouragement and play the piece several times, allowing the pupils to move easily to it. At his discretion it could be used for subsequent lessons with the expectation of further variety being developed. With the seven- and eight-year-olds, the initial response could be individual and exploratory. After several replays, the teacher and class could plan a "dance," paying attention to spatial factors such as directions and levels, and to relationships such as groupings. The dances could then evolve through trying out simple ideas and adapting them as needed.

The records, particularly useful for primary classes, are:
Listen and Move: Green Label No. 1. Percussion including Drumming Rhythm, Continuity and Stop, Ding Dong.

Green Label No. 2. Percussion and Music including Jolly Little Tune, Clitter Clatter, Quiet Mood.

SAMPLE LESSON PLANS

SAMPLE LESSON PLAN ONE

GRADE: One, in its simplest form
Two or Three, with elaborations

THEME: Body Awareness — feet and other part stressed

SUBTHEMES: 1. Response to percussion instruments
Quality — Drums — strong and quick beats

— maracas — light and quick beats with strong accents.

2. Pathways.

INTRODUCTION:

Play: Jimmie Shand's *Teviot Brig.* *

Challenge: "Listen and clap. How could you move to that music? Think for a minute — and away you go! Spread out. Find a big space."

Teacher praises as many children as possible and chooses two or three to be observed because their footwork is particularly significant.

Observation: "Watch these people dance and find out in what ways they use their feet." (Both feet at once, one foot always in front, one foot at a time, or foot actions, such as skipping.)

DEVELOPMENT:

Challenge: "When the music goes again, you may make your feet dance too."

Teacher praises their use of feet and perhaps identifies verbally some of the foot actions or the different uses of the feet.

Challenge: "If there is no music, can you still dance with your feet?"

Teacher coaches: "Where will they go? When will they stop? What are they doing?"

Praise. "Very good. You had some lovely dances."

Observation: (Used only if a child is showing a marked awareness of pathways or stopping.)

Challenge: "You dance again and I will try to play the drum for you. You may have to change your dance to fit the drum sound. Use some interesting pathways. Be ready to stop when the sound stops. Start to dance now."

(Use the drum to provide an interesting rhythm, preferably the one that suits most of the children. Use short phrases. Encourage an awareness of stopping.)

Challenge: "Now we will have a new sound. Listen and think how you can dance to it." (Maraca — it may be played with a long shower of sound, starting softly and getting as loud as possible, and followed by three sharp claps into the palm of the hand. Repeat often.)

Children respond.

* Capital 10014, *My Scotland*, Jimmy Shand, "Teviot Brig."

Observation: "What part of the body is important?" (e.g. the trunk); or, "Where do these people do their dance?" (e.g. on the spot/travelling.)

Challenge: Use the sound again. "Where is your dance done? What part of you is important?"

CULMINATION:
Planning: "Let's do a two-part dance. The first part will be with the drum. The second part will be with the maracas. Decide where you want to do each part."

(This may be left to the individual decisions, or it can be group planning. It can be structured into a simple group dance, worked out in pairs for older children, or left as an individual two-part dance.)

Note that the stimulus for this lesson was chiefly a movement idea. Also note that the feet are "important" in some dances.

The stimulus for the next dance is Hallowe'en and, in particular, witches.

SAMPLE LESSON PLAN TWO

GRADE: One to Three depending upon the amount of elaboration used

THEME: Witches' Dance: Ugly, weird use of the body and its parts

SUBTHEMES: 1. Response to changes of moods in music
2. Strong, sudden effort quality: lighter, smoother effort quality.

INTRODUCTION:
Free response to music related to the subsequent parts of the lesson. For example: *Accordion Hambo,* (Folk Dancer 2004) which may encourage the use of jumps, runs, pounces, peculiar gestures of different parts of the body. The pupils may already know that they will be doing Witches' Dance later and, therefore, be experimenting with suitable movement. Or, they may be responding quite freely to the Hambo.

The teacher will judge whether any observations are to be made or whether freedom and variety of movement with evidence of a good listening response is what is required.

DEVELOPMENT:
Short discussion of Hallowe'en witches, "What are they like? How do they move? What might they do?"

The teacher has at least two options.

Challenge:
Option I — Pupils experiment without music; trying out some of the ideas brought out in the discussion. For example: they may try ways of moving in

an ugly fashion, ways of frightening imaginary people (pouncing, stopping suddenly in a horrible shape); ways of riding a broom.

Challenge:
Option II — Listen to the chosen music, e.g. Leap Frog.* "Can you find music for a particularly ugly, frightening witch? Can you find some quiet, smooth music? What could the witch be doing at these different times?"

Several suggestions should be received from the class, but very soon the music should be played so that the pupils actually develop their ideas in movement. For example, perhaps the witch is on the ground frightening people for one part and in the air riding a broomstick for the other part.

Observation: Observe two or more dancers who have good ideas for one or both parts of the music.

Challenge: "Practise again so that everyone can make their movements quite clear."

The teacher may need to ask them to decide how they start their dance. "How does it end? What happens to the witches at the end?"

Depending on the maturity of the pupils, the dancers can be quite independent of one another; or, a few pupils might be objects attacked by a band of witches.

CULMINATION:
Observation: Have a sharing session. Perhaps a quarter of the class could do their dance for the others. Thus four groups would show their work.

Challenge: "Finish with a happy skip, moving in your own pathways to the Western Polka." (Folk Dancer 2004)

"Find your own spot. Relax. Bend lower and lower. Lie on your backs. Go limp."

"Quietly get up and return to the classroom."

As was mentioned earlier, the above lesson is centred around the idea of the character, mood and actions of witches. Both the previous lessons have started with a rather free response to music of a highly rhythmic quality. The third lesson is an attempt to show how the Listen and Move records, which are designed and tested to be a stimulus for creative or modern dance, may be used. The selection chosen is Ponderous, (Green Label No. 3).

---

* R.C.A. Victor LE 1000 Adventures in Music, Bizet "Children's Games": Leap Frog.

SAMPLE LESSON PLAN THREE

GRADE: Three, or Two with a good dance background

THEME: Dimension or Size of Movement

SUBTHEMES: 1. Different parts of the body stressed
2. Changes of Levels

INTRODUCTION:
Challenge: "Start by travelling all over the room. See if you can visit every part of it." (Using the room in large dimensions).

Challenge: "Now change so that you seem to keep yourself very busy moving but you don't really go anywhere at all in the room." (Using the room in small dimensions).

Observation: Two or three people show how they can "keep very busy" and move a lot without going anywhere.

Challenge: "All try again and see what ways you can find to do this."

DEVELOPMENT:
Challenge: "Could you do these two things so that sometimes you go everywhere and sometimes you move a great deal but get nowhere?"

Observation: All watch two or three interesting solutions (optional).

Observation: Observe (if possible) someone who uses large movements and someone who uses minute movements. (See if the class can distinguish between large and small movements by observation.)

Challenge: "Experiment with your own kinds of large and small movements."

Observation: Observe (optional) different parts of the body which are used for large and small movements. Follow this up with a chance to experiment with these relationships.

CULMINATION:
Ponderous (Listen and Move, Green Label No. 3). "Sit and listen to this music. Try to decide if there is music for large movements, and some for small movements."
Replay it. "Think of the parts of the body which would be best to use." Probably, no discussion would be needed.

Challenge: "Take a starting position. When the music is played see if ur ideas will work to the music."

Teacher may replay the music several times, giving some encouragement, but very little coaching. An observation may be made to show a contrast in levels if it has occurred spontaneously.

Observation: The lesson would likely conclude with four different groups showing their dances. Some discussion might follow with reference to what kind of dance they felt they were doing, and perhaps some suggestions of a name for one's own dance.

Challenge: "To finish, do your own dance to the music."

Junior Levels

The children of these grades are likely to bring to bear a more decisive outlook to their dance composition. The shape of the movement becomes clearer. The effort content becomes more clearly defined and there should be a fuller study of the effort elements and the eight effort actions. There is likely to be more continuity in the movement phrases with clearer starting and finishing positions. Children of this age can concentrate the movement in specific parts of the body. Alternatively they can involve the whole body in the action. Therefore, gestures, in the technical sense, become a significant part of their dance. The teacher should now encourage them to give the centre part of the body, including the spine, an appropriate part in the movement.

Methods may now include a more structured approach to the study and understanding of dance movement. Analysis should be part of the learning process, but it should be applied to the movements which the children have discovered for themselves. This may mean that the whole class may analyze movement which has been discovered by individual members of the group. It will be possible and profitable for partners to mirror each other's movements exactly as a test of their own analysis and control. These children are capable of practising, refining and perfecting their dance sequences, and the form of their dances will tend to become increasingly well defined. This will probably mean that the accents, contrasts, emphases and logical flow from one movement into another will begin to receive some consideration.

SUITABLE LESSON CONTENT OR DANCE THEMES

The teacher should feel free to use any of the themes suggested for use in the primary grades if it is felt that the pupils of Grades Four, Five and Six need the experience. However, generally speaking, these children have matured and now have a different outlook and put their bodies to new uses.

Therefore, the deficiencies in their background should probably be remedied within the lessons which are drawn from their own themes.

SUGGESTED THEMES (to be used in any order as deemed suitable):

1. Locomotion: actions; combinations; foot patterns; jumping with turns; running with rising and falling; skips with turns, etc.
2. Parts of the body: a. leading into rising, turning, jumping, stepping.
     b. meeting and parting — arms gathering and scattering; legs gathering and scattering; knees opening; hands meeting knees or feet, etc.
     c. gestures which lead away from or towards the centre of the body.
3. Weightbearing: a. balances — high on the balls of the feet; on one leg; in body arches and extensions
     b. transference — bringing the body weight down from a high elevation; falls as a dramatic expression; rolls as a dramatic expression or as a means of maintaining a continuity of flow.
4. Effort Qualities of Movement: combining two elements — *strong and sudden*: sudden gripping and slow releasing repeated as a phrase of movement; sudden, isolated, energetic jumps; sudden downward jumps or stamps; sudden strong kicks or jabs of feet, knees, fists, elbows.

Strong! Sustained?

strong and sustained: pulling different parts of the body strongly and slowly apart; strongly pushing slowly upward from the floor or downward into the floor; slowly pressing one part of the body against another.

sudden and fine touch: sudden movements done lightly, often with a small part of the body; darting lightly and hastily about the room; jumps, turns, rushes, falls done with a surprise or the shock of the unexpected, but done lightly. Maracas may be needed to help. Vocal expressions may be used by the teacher as a form of accompaniment.

sustained with fine touch: slow, gentle rising or turning; quiet, slow walking to sneak forward; balance walking slowly along a narrow line; slow and gentle opening and closing gestures of the arms, legs and body.

Pupils discover that they can combine space elements with time or weight elements:

direct and sudden: sudden gestures of arms, knees, elbows directly forward, upward, backward, etc., using straight pathways; sudden jumps or pounces of the body directly upward or downward.

direct and sustained: slowly moving the limbs straight down, up, sideways, etc.; moving the whole body slowly and in straight pathways into space.

sudden and flexible: sudden wriggles and squirms while lying on the floor, or standing; short whips by the limbs.

sustained and flexible: slowly winding, dipping and floating in curving pathways and floor patterns.

The other combinations of two effort elements are briefly described on p. 284 in Chapter Seven. The vocabulary which the teacher uses in setting the problem will be very important in providing suitable stimuli. Similarly, if the teacher is using percussion as the stimulus, it will be necessary that the sound is suited to the two elements. For example, the drumming can be a sudden and loud accent followed by a series of six light beats played at extended intervals.

5. Effort actions: select any of the ideas given in Chapter Seven, p. 159 to p. 165. It is likely that one or two of the vigorous efforts, *thrusting, wringing, pressing* or *slashing*, might be used in the first attempts with their opposite efforts; *floating, dabbing, flicking, gliding* being used as compensatory or resting efforts.

6. Relationships: To *people* — question and answer, action and reaction to partners; small groups — meeting and mingling, changing shapes, dispersing and reforming, cooperating in working actions, e.g. sailors swabbing the deck.

7. Occupational rhythms such as sweeping, chopping, digging, pulling a rope.

8. Machine rhythms such as wheels turning, pendulums, pistons, machine hammers, conveyor belts, gears turning, capping bottles and jars. (Always regular repetitive phrases. Pathways must be kept mechanical.)

9. Statues: movements leading into and out of the chosen statue shape; kinds

of shapes used, such as: pin, ball, wall, screw or twisted; awareness of the dimension of the statue.

10. Space: being aware of the direction of the movement, movements using high level or using contrasting levels; movements going outward from the centre of the body or being drawn into the centre of the body.

11. Dance forms: Sequences — clear starting and finishing positions; using contrasts within the sequence, e.g. a travelling section contrasted with movement in one place; building up to a climax and including an ending.

12. Use of percussion: dancing with your own instrument; sharing an instrument with a partner; a group dance based on the use of one instrument; responding to the teacher's instrument.

13. Dance ideas and dance stimuli:

    a. Music: *Listen and Move* (see p. 266, 273) Green Label No. 1 and No. 2 can very well be used again. New responses and greater sensitivity to the stimuli may be expected. Green Label No. 3, No. 4 and No. 5 will probably be very useful.

Short excerpts from the classics may be helpful. For example, R.C.A. Victor LE 1000 and LE 1001 *Adventures in Music* series contain some useful pieces. Sometimes folk dance records can be helpful as can currently popular pieces.

14. Dance Ideas: (Think in terms of: "The Dance of the —")

    1. An Indian Village at Early Morning.

        a. The braves
        b. The squaws   "What would they be doing in the early morning?"
        c. The children

    2. Partner Dance: "Anything You Can Do, I Can Do Better."

    3. Building Noah's Ark:

        a. Cutting the trees — "The Tree-cutters' Dance."
        b. Sawing and Carrying the Logs — "The Sawyers' Dance."
        c. Constructing the Ark — "The Ark Builders' Dance."
        d. Celebration.

    4. Jimmie's Train:

        a. In the station — yard — engine coupling the cars
        b. On a winding track
        c. The milk-stop run
        d. Coming in on time

    5. Two Cats:

        a. Friends — "The Dance of the Friendly Cats."
        b. Enemies — "The Cat Fight."
        c. Two alone — "The Dance of the Two Lonely Cats."

    6. The Valley of Dry Bones*

---

* *Movement Speaks*, Education Committee, School Museum Service, The County Council of the West Riding of Yorkshire, black and white, 16mm, 18 minutes, 1961.

a. A view of the valley — heaps of bones of different shapes
    b. The wind of change — rushing, blowing and moving the bones
    c. Life renewed limb by limb
    d. Procession to the new land.
7. The Cave of Mystery: (Develop as five mini-dances or as five episodes of the "Dance of Adventure.")
    a. Enter through a long, dark tunnel
    b. Into the light: the treasure cave — jewels of all shapes and sizes, glittering and dancing in the light
    c. Into dimness: mysterious and frightening shapes
    d. Into the caves of sound: sighs, moans, clicks, scratches
    e. The trip back: flight, pursuit, escape; or the parade of treasures.
8. Nature Themes: "Trilogy of Water"
    a. Water into ice; ice shapes; the melting
    b. Water surging around rocks (Theme and variation)
    c. The underwater world.

SAMPLE LESSON PLAN ONE

GRADE: Five or Six

THEME: Action and reaction between partners

SUBTHEMES: 1. Use of percussion
            2. Space or effort patterns

INTRODUCTION:
    Challenge: "Dance about the room filling up all the spaces, using your own movement ideas in response to the playing of the tambourine."
    Teacher plays a phrase which includes shaking and beating. The phrase is repeated often.

    Observation: One half watches the other half of the class to see what responses are made to the shaking as compared to the beating of the tambourine.

    Challenge: "All work again, trying to achieve a clear contrast in the two responses."

DEVELOPMENT:
    Challenge: "Listen carefully as you dance and show by your movements that you are listening."

The teacher plays the same phrase, but accelerates or decelerates it, or plays it lightly or vigorously.

This may be done as a little game based on responding to sound, or the teacher may bring it into a short composition wherein the class is formed into two groups and one group dances to the first phrase and the second group responds to the second phrase.

Challenge: Partners, one with an instrument held fairly close to the other's feet, knees, head, one elbow or hand. "Use the instrument as a magic power to lead your partner into movement. Partner, allow yourself to be inspired by the instrument."

Observation: Two pairs may be watched. Observe:
1. The action-reaction of the instrument and the dancer.
2. The kind of dancing the instrument player does.

Challenge: "Experiment some more. Try to have both partners dancing. You may try to decide what kind of inspiration the instrument can give."

Observation: Watch one couple whose dance is based on changing rhythms and another whose dance is based on the instrument leading the partner into different space patterns.

CULMINATION:
Dance Making: The challenge is to compose a short dance for three about "Influence". Each group may use one instrument.

"Decide on a starting position. Will you be close together or spread apart? Will someone have the instrument or will it be on the floor? When you are ready, get into your starting positions and begin."

The teacher may have to urge some to terminate verbal planning, to assume a starting position, and to let the dance evolve.

As the groups work, the teacher should alternate between taking an overview of the progress of the different groups and visiting individual groups to encourage them or help them by asking questions. An observation of one or two groups to show different starting positions and the composition of the first phrase may be helpful. It is usually necessary to advise the groups to keep the dance short and to decide how it will end. As the groups work on refining their original idea, the teacher can help them by reminding them: to make one part of the dance a climax; to provide contrasts; to clarify where they are in space and how fast or how energetically they are moving; to start and finish in very clear positions of stillness.

Observation: Half the groups could show the other half their dances as the conclusion to the lesson. If the group has a title for their dance, it should be mentioned.

The tambourine is the stimulus for a dance study for five boys.

SAMPLE LESSON PLAN TWO

GRADE: Four, Five, or Six with little experience

THEME: Effort elements — strong and sudden; strong and sustained

SUBTHEMES: 1. Compensating effort element — fine touch
2. Relationships — four individuals meeting and parting

INTRODUCTION:
Challenge: 1. "Dance to this music (*Baby Elephant Walk* by Henry Mancini) quite freely bringing out the cheerful, cheeky, jaunty spirit of the music," or
2. "Sit and listen to the music. Clap the rhythm."
The teacher should discuss briefly the spirit of the music and help the pupils to think of the kinds of movement that would be suitable, and what parts of the body might be stressed. Immediately the pupils should be allowed to try out their ideas moving freely about the room to the music.

Observation: (Optional) One half may watch the other half of the class to see what responses are made to the music noting the stress given to different parts of the body and the general carriage. Note the general expression of the movement.

Challenge: "All work again, trying to keep the movement gay."

Observation: One half observes the other half of the class noting how the dancers pass each other and interweave.

Challenge: "Work again, trying to meet and pass several different people. How do you react to these people?"

DEVELOPMENT:
Challenge: "Sit and listen to the music, *The Comedians.** What is the spirit of the music? Where does it seem to suggest strong, sustained movements?"

Challenge: "This time, work by yourself. Experiment with movements which are as big and strong as the music seems to require. You may find that your body shapes are big and queer also."
This may be a difficult challenge and the teacher may replay the music for further exploration.

Observation: Some pupils may be observed for: i) strong actions or; ii) large shapes; or iii) floor patterns.

CULMINATION:
Discussion — sit in a close group. Exchange a few ideas as to what the music and movement reminded them of. Recall the quality of strength with slowness, also the possibility of large movements and floor patterns.

Challenge: "Make up a dance for four. The requirements are that you must start in a position which allows you to meet at least once in the dance. Try to show the quality of the music in your movements."
Arrange groups and starting positions. Play the music for experimental work.
The teacher must judge how many replays are necessary for the exploratory stage. He must remind groups of the requirements: 1. meeting at least once; 2. quality of movement. He must regulate the use of the time, indicating when the dancers must select the movements which they want to use. He must control the interval between the replaying of the music, thus influencing the amount of verbal planning which is used.

Observation: Use an observation of a group even while the dance is

* R.C.A. Victor LE 1000 *Adventures in Music,* Kabalevsky, "The Comedians": *Pantomime.*

unfinished and somewhat confused. If this is done, it will be for the purpose of helping the class on a specific point. For example, one group may start far apart working as individuals, but when they meet they may remain together. Another group may meet and pass each other dancing as individuals throughout the composition.

The teacher should coach the dancers to be aware of the ending. "What meaning does it give to the dance?"

CONCLUSION:
Challenge: "Practise once more before you show your dance to us." Each group should be warned of the last practice.

Observation: If possible, each group should dance for the rest of the class. If a title can be given to the dance, it tends to give satisfaction. Some word of praise should be found for each group's work.

The lessons illustrated above indicate ways of handling individual, partner and small group situations. The teacher may need to cultivate some skills in developing a lesson in which the whole class is participating in a single composition. Such a situation might arise in the dance The Valley of the Dry Bones (see page 281). This particular composition may be prefaced by the reading of the scriptures[1] as the stimulus to dance-making.

In discussing how the story might be expressed in dance, the teacher should help the pupils identify significant acts or scenes in the story. Possibilities are suggested on page 282.

SAMPLE LESSON PLAN THREE

GRADE: Five or Six. Especially suitable for an all-boys class

THEME: The flow of movement into isolated parts of the body
Contrasting movement of living bodies and movement of skeletons

SUBTHEMES: 1. Group shapes
2. Locomotion — varied by the effort qualities emphasized

INTRODUCTION:
Challenge: "Warm up by working on locomotion which could represent the Wind of Change: rushing with utmost speed; changes in the way the wind blows — with increasing (decreasing) speed and/or force; changes of direction (in a direct path, rising, down-draft, whirls and turns)."

DEVELOPMENT:
a. Skeletons: crumpled individual shapes — stillness, distortion. Succes-

[1] Book of Ezekiel, The Holy Bible, King James version, Chapter 37.

sive enlivening of one part of the body after another. Expression of incredulity upon the discovery that life powers are restored (testing partial movements, joyous utilization of powers of movement).

b. Group shapes: size of groups (three, four, five, six to a group); forming a group shape with some slight contact with others (use of levels): changing the group shape without verbal planning, but rather by being sensitive to the movement of others and adjusting oneself to contribute to the emerging shape.

c. Group discussion: i) characters required — some for the wind — perhaps breezes which merely cause the bones to stir and a North Wind which re-initiates life — a decision on the number who will act as the wind; ii) order of the scenes; iii) the use of the space, including the starting positions; iv) forms of accompaniment — vocal phrases for breeze and/or wind — creaks for bones as they move — sounds of life returning.

(None of these ideas need to be settled, but some will be tentatively accepted as starting points).

CULMINATION:
a. "Take starting positions as planned and proceed with the plan as far as it will develop under reasonable control."

b. "Stop and assess." Accept suggestions for parts which are basically workable. Accept suggestions for change.

c. "Repeat a. and b. several times." The teacher may need to remind pupils of what they want to express. Check on the quality of the movement; the phrasing, including the length of time required to develop each movement idea. Check the usefulness of the vocal accompaniments and the appropriateness of the spatial balance.

d. The teacher should time the cut-off point so that the pupils feel that they have accomplished something fairly satisfactory upon which to build the next day.

e. "Finish with a final 'run-through' of the dance as it has so far developed."

f. A final discussion will often result in the pupils planning privately so that they come to the next lesson with ideas for enrichment of the current work.

SAMPLE LESSON PLAN FOUR

GRADE: Four, Five, Six

THEME: Action and Stillness

SUBTHEMES: 1. Direct and flexible use of space
2. Relationships. Threes (possibly taking turns)

INTRODUCTION:

Challenge: "Scatter about the room. Listen to what I am going to play for you on the maracas. Take a starting position from which you can quickly move to another spot. Go and stop with the sound."

The teacher plays three short phrases, each ending strongly. A long pause is held between the phrases.

DEVELOPMENT:

Challenge: "Start either very low down or very high up. Start turning as you change your level. Interrupt your movement with a sudden freezing which you hold for quite a long time. Do this in several stages and finally travel for a long time and then finish in the same position as you started."

Observation: Watch two or three individuals. "Notice that a sudden stop seems to become a surprise. Notice the 'statue' body shape it makes."

Challenge: "All try to improve the sudden stillness."

Challenge: "Start in a semi-crouched shape. Choose a part of the body to make three sudden jabs outward from the body. Explore to find different parts of the body which can be moved away from the centre of the body in jabs."

Observation: "Find people who use elbows, knees, legs, arms, heads, and hips for jabbing outward. Notice how straight the jabs are."

Challenge: "Try again. Do three straight jabs and then do a shower of shaking and wiggling movements that go all over in the space."

Challenge: "Listen to this music and begin to imagine how you could dance to it." Play *Intent.** "Take a starting position and try out your ideas."

Observation: "What sort of surprises does the music have for her? How is she showing them? Do you know how many parts the music has?"

Challenge: "See if you can decide how many parts it has. Show your answer in your movement."

CULMINATION: Dance-making in threes:
1. A moment of preliminary planning.
2. A starting position.

* Macdonald and Evans (Educational Recordings) Ltd., Green Label No. 3, Stephenson, *Listen and Move*, (d) "Intent."

3. Exploration while the music is played.
4. Group consultation.
5. Repetition with revision or exploration to the music. This will be repeated as often as the teacher thinks necessary.
6. Final practice to get the dance ready for showing.
7. Dances for the purpose of sharing with the class. The teacher may want to identify one particularly good feature in each dance.

Note: The teacher may make himself available at stages 4, 5 and 6. He may visit groups which appear to be having difficulty. He may pose a question or offer some alternative to the pupils' plans or he may identify what they may not be able to recognize for themselves.

Intermediate Levels — Girls

The boys and girls are usually in separated classes for physical education when they reach Grade Seven, Eight and Nine. Therefore, the creative dance can cater to the interests of the girls or the boys as the case may be.

Adjustments will have to be made to accommodate the past dance experience of the girls. Those who are starting it for the first time may be somewhat hesitant and shy. The girls may have marked individual likes and dislikes, but most of them can be accommodated by a program which gives them choices and a voice in the planning.

The theory of movement can now be explored with intellectual understanding being a guiding force behind the movement. The forms of dances may be understood and compositions may be planned according to a specific form. The girls will have ideas which they will want to work out in dance. Conversely, after they have started a dance, they may find that they have to consider what they want to say. For example, one group may want to use the music "Born Free" but soon find that they don't know what they wanted to say about "freedom." This is a challenge which they can enjoy if they can achieve some success.

At this age, they are beginning to become involved in the moods which are created by combinations of efforts. They continue to enjoy working with others and if they have had a good program in the earlier grades, they will be able to do some good work in groups of fives or sevens, or even larger groups.

They will take an interest in the music chosen for their dances. Many of the currently popular pieces will be requested by them. The teacher should work with them to establish criteria for selecting music. Such considerations as: the effort qualities; the contrasts within the form of the work; and the length of the piece, should be evaluated.

The teacher should know the recommended curriculum for the earlier grades, but should avoid "starting the girls at the beginning." The thirteen-year-old needs to acquire the skills for her own projects in the context which is compatible with her stage of development.

Partner relationships (enclosing — penetrating) and spatial elements (rising — sinking) used as themes for dance.

SUGGESTED THEMES:

1. Spatial patterns:

   a. straight lines   I X L

      rounded lines   O C S ∿

      twisted lines   8 𝒶 𝒮

   explored and contrasted.

   b. Using different parts of the body to lead the movements.
   c. Placing the movements as air patterns in different locations in space: in front of the body, over the head, down one side.
   d. Developing them as floor patterns.

2. Link suitable rhythms with spatial forms:

   a. angular movements   L ∨ N 7

   making the change of direction the point of emphasis.

   b. circular movements characterized by continuity, acceleration and deceleration.
   c. twisting movements characterized by acceleration and deceleration — with an ongoing flow in the rounded parts and a restricting of flow in the changes of direction.

3. Using the arms or upper body to lead the body into rounded, angular, or twisted movements which are echoed by floor patterns which are also rounded, angular, or twisted.

4. Contrasting the size of the patterns, either in the air, or on the floor.

5. Starting a small movement in one part of the body and allowing it to grow large enough to encompass the whole body, perhaps in a jump or a travelling through space.

6. Starting a movement shape and passing it along to a partner who finishes it, adds to it or repeats it in a different size.

7. Exploring movements which are created by changing the body shape, using the rounded, elongated, spreading or twisted shapes as the basic ones.

8. Extending these movements by including locomotion in the course of changing the body shape.

9. Experimenting with movements and rhythms which will arise when a body shape is basically retained and variations of movements are adapted to it.

10. Effort transitions:
   a. changing one element only such as *Thrust* → *Press* by decelerating the time element.
   b. changing two elements such as *Thrust* → *Glide* by decelerating and lightening the tension.
   c. change all three elements such as *Thrust* → *Float* by decelerating and lightening the tension and changing from directness to flexibility.

11. Dance of changing moods achieved through transition of efforts. For example, slashing rage, changing to tormented doubt (wringing), changing to hopefulness (floating) and calm preparation (gliding); moving into gathering determination (pressing) and a final attack (thrusting).

12. Abstract dances using transitions of efforts to suitable music. "Fernando's Hideaway" from *The Pajama Game*; "Just You Wait" from *My Fair Lady*; "These Boots Are Made For Walkin' "" might be helpful for a dance which stresses strong efforts. "The Ascot Gavotte" from *My Fair Lady*; Gluck's *Air Gai**; Massenet's *Aragonaise*† could be used for transitions from flicks and dabs.

13. Percussion work in three's or four's. Each dancer should have a different type of instrument. (See p. 257 of this chapter for descriptions.) The dance form of chorus and successive soloists could be used or the form of question-and-answer, or verse and chorus might develop. The stress should be on a transition between efforts.

* R.C.A. Victor LE 1000 *Adventures in Music*, Gluck "Iphigénie in Aulis": Air Gai.
† R.C.A. Victor LE 1000 *Adventures in Music*, Massenet, "Le Cid": Aragonaisé.

14. Exploration of movements which arise out of the use of the dimensional cross including central and peripheral transitions.

15. Exploration of movements in the diagonals.

16. Linking efforts with the dimensional and diagonal crosses.

17. Exploration of jumping:
    a. five basic uses of feet (pp. 106-107)
    b. different parts of the body leading the jump,
    c. feeling of freedom and lightness, and lessening of tension while in the air,
    d. kinds of jumps — turning, travelling, repetitive jumps on the spot.

18. Dance forms:
    a. Sequence with a clear beginning, the movement(s) and a clear ending,
    b. Theme and variation(s),
    c. Verse and Chorus,
    d. Contrasts in an ABA form,
    e. Narrative form of A→B→C→D.

SUGGESTIONS AND SAMPLE LESSON PLANS FOR SPECIAL SITUATIONS

GIRLS OF GRADES SEVEN, EIGHT OR NINE WITH LITTLE OR NO EXPERIENCE

The need here may be to use contemporary music and to have subject matter which is meaningful to the teenager's life. For example, *Hard to Find* on Liberty Label (1967) by Gary Lewis and The Playboys may be suitable.

The discussion can deal with "What is hard to find?" They may suggest: a boyfriend; a friend you can trust; a job; yourself and how you want to dress and wear your hair, etc. The lesson may be worked out as a workshop with very little decision making from the teacher. However, the teacher will probably have to help the girls decide how *Hard to Find* can be worked out in movement. For example,

1) a *soloist* can use floor patterns with changes of direction, "dead end" pathways; various forms of searching
2) *partners* could use a separation in space; a persistent difficulty of the searcher to see the partner's face; a difficulty at arriving at the same location at precisely the same time.
3) a *group* might divide into characters: the searcher; the barriers; the one to be sought
4) the pupils may make further suggestions.

SAMPLE LESSON PLAN ONE: Girls with little or no experience

GRADE: Seven, Eight, Nine

THEME: The idea "Hard to Find"

SUBTHEMES: 1. Response to music
2a. Interaction between partners, or the group and individuals, or
2b. Spatial concepts

INTRODUCTION:
Challenge: "Warm up to the music Hard to Find, finding different ways of moving with a stress on changes of direction. Try to give the impression of searching. Allow the body movement to be quite free, developing step patterns and special gestures of the arms, head and legs."

DEVELOPMENT:
Let them move into the groups which they wish to use for the dance. Allow a very short period of discussion to decide the main form that the dance will take.

Challenge: "Take a good starting position and improvise to a fairly short segment of the music."
The teacher should make herself available for reference but should not superimpose her ideas on the group. Allow a short time for verbal assessment and planning and then call for starting positions and a repetition of the dance using the same amount of music again.

Challenge: "Now choose the movements you want to use. Practise to get them under control. Do them several times to the music."

Challenge: "Now improvise to the next part of the music." At this stage warn the dancers that the music will start at the beginning and will be kept on through the next reasonable segment of time. The dancers should be prepared to add the next part of the dance as a form of improvisation.
This general pattern can be followed: discussion; exploration; evaluation; revision and practice; next stage of the dance handled in a similar way.
The music may be too long for the content of the dance. If so, it should be terminated at a suitable place. The teacher should urge the dancers to consider the ending. If possible, bring about a conclusion (either the sought-for is found; or the searcher is defeated).

CULMINATION:
The different groups should perform for their peers. Praise for a specific good point and perhaps one suggestion for improvement might be offered.

GIRLS OF GRADES SEVEN, EIGHT OR NINE WITH A REASONABLE BACK-GROUND OF EXPERIENCE.

This type of class can appreciate the value of becoming familiar with a variety of dance themes. For this reason, the main theme of the lesson can be chosen from those suggested earlier. The dance which follows the preliminary movement study will, in most cases, be based on the main theme and may also incorporate the material suggested for the subtheme. The lesson usually begins with a review of some aspect of movement which has been studied in earlier lessons.

SAMPLE LESSON PLAN TWO: Girls with reasonable background

GRADE: Seven, Eight, Nine

THEME: Curved air patterns

SUBTHEMES: 1. Part of the body leading a movement
                2. Rhythmic flow from one shape to another

INTRODUCTION:
    Challenge: "Warm up by combining a jump, a turn and a run into a rhythmic phrase which gives major importance to one of these movements."

DEVELOPMENT:
    Observation: Examine one or two of the above sequences to see what shape patterns (in the air) have arisen spontaneously. (Circular pattern for the turn, and possibly straight lines or angles for run and jump.)

    Challenge: "Do your own again and see if you have air patterns in your work, or could bring them out by making slight adaptations."

    Challenge: "Choose a rounded letter and explore ways of making it. Try to give it a rhythm and flow so that it becomes a dance movement rather than an air drawing."

    Observation:
        a. how one person has experimented with different parts of the body used to describe the shape
        b. how another person has been conscious of placing the shape in the space around herself
        c. how another has linked one completed shape with the next variation of it.

    Challenge: "Keep these ideas in mind, but stress particularly a change in the part of the body leading into the shape."

CULMINATION:
A short excerpt from *Waltz No. 1* from Gounod's "Faust."* "Listen and note the introduction, the length of the excerpt."

Challenge: "Compose a solo or couple dance to this music based on circles and rounded air patterns supported by whatever foot patterns and floor patterns are needed."

A MIXED CLASS OF GRADES SEVEN, EIGHT, OR NINE, OR A CLASS OF INTERMEDIATE GIRLS.

When a dance lesson is given to a class of boys and girls of one of these grades, it is usual to choose material which is of interest to the boys because they are likely to have had less experience than the girls. Furthermore, it is important to plan material which is suited to the masculine image as well as being adaptable to the girls. This is especially important if the teacher is a woman. Dances which have a rhythmic stress; or which require contrasts of the efforts or the effort actions; or which stress body actions such as runs, leaps, and turns; and those which have such clear action-and-reaction sequences as to be dance dramas, are very suitable for a mixed class. They will permit the boys and girls to adopt contrasting roles. They can, of course, be quite acceptable to an all girls' or an all boys' class.

SAMPLE LESSON PLAN THREE: Girls or mixed class

GRADE: Seven, Eight, Nine

THEME: Effort Transitions: Press to Thrust; Float to Flick

SUBTHEMES: 1. Rhythm — acceleration
2. Body Parts used

INTRODUCTION:
Challenge: "Warm up by using phrases of runs which start very slowly and gradually build up speed and stop suddenly. Give some attention to floor pattern. Develop the rhythm and flow so that it becomes a dance rather than a gymnastic warm up."

DEVELOPMENT:
Observation: Study one person's work, the class trying to provide a sound accompaniment by means of claps or vocal improvisation.

* R.C.A. Victor LE 1002, *Adventures in Music*, Gounod's "Faust" Ballet Music: *Waltz No. 1*.

Challenge: Teacher (or pupil) will retain this sound accompaniment on a drum. "Everyone, try to use the sound as a stimulus."

Challenge: "Try to discover the effort action of the slow steps (sustained, strong, direct which is *press*) and the effort action of the fast runs (fast, strong, direct which is *thrust*) and the sudden stop (sudden, strong, direct)."

Observation: Observe, discuss, and experience this change of effort. Note that only one element (*time*) has been changed.

Challenge: "Improvise other pressing actions using other parts of the body. Accelerate the press changing it to a thrust."

Challenge: "Change now to a slow, undulating creeping which causes you to weave in and out of one another without touching so that there is a gentle stirring going on. Increase the speed of the undulations but keep the movement very light so that it becomes a gay, light flicking. Heels, fingers, wrists, elbows, heads lightly tossing and twisting quickly."

Observation: One half of the class studies the other half. Note the change in quality from floating accelerating into flicking with only the time element being changed.

CULMINATION:
Partners. "Compose a dance of contrasts which are based on the strong efforts (press, thrust) and the fine touch efforts (float and flick). Stress acceleration."
Discuss ideas: a. A dance of characters; one strong and dominant, the other gay and frivolous. (The Owl and the Pussycat; Father and Daughter; The Boss and the Secretary; December and May.)
b. Abstract dance based on contrasts:
i) bring out the contrast as a change in rhythms resulting from efforts used. The ABCD dance form may be organized in different ways.
ii) bring out the contrast in the parts of the body used.
iii) bring out the contrast as a change of moods.
Percussion could be made available at the discretion of the teacher.

GIRLS OF GRADE EIGHT OR NINE WITH A GOOD BACKGROUND

These classes should be provided with interesting and challenging dance lessons. The teacher may choose any of the themes suggested and expect a higher standard of work than would be required of a less experienced class. The themes dealing with space study, dance forms, and group relationships (five or more in the group) are likely to be very appropriate choices.

SAMPLE LESSON PLAN FOUR: Girls with a good background

GRADE: Eight, Nine

THEME: Dimensional Cross. Up-Down Dimension

SUBTHEMES: 1. Body awareness — curl and stretch
               2. Group work for five

INTRODUCTION:
    Challenge: "Warm up by improvising dance movements arising out of contrasting body stretches with body curls. Try to shape your movements into a phrase which may include locomotion."

    Observation: Study one or two persons' work. The teacher should select at least one student who uses a vertical transition from stretch to curl or vice versa. Observers should be asked to identify the lines of transition between the stretches and curls (the Up-Down Dimension).

DEVELOPMENT:
    Challenge: "Repeat your own work and try to identify the pathway used to move from curl to stretch, or vice versa."

    Challenge: "Explore ways of moving vertically from the highest point possible to the lowest point possible."

    Observation: a. partners observe each other
                     b. teacher selects three or four variations for the whole class to watch:
                         i)   jumping and landing in crouch
                         ii) stretching high with a hand, and leading low with an elbow
                         iii) using a flexible pathway downward
                         iv) seeming to be reluctant to abandon the high point.

    Challenge: "Explore ways of moving from a point on the floor to the highest point possible. Use what you have learned from the observations to broaden your ideas."

CULMINATION:
    Dance for Five.
    Challenge: "Using the idea of moving from the high to the low points, or vice versa, as your main motif, compose a short group dance for five. Feel free to use locomotion, turns or other movements as long as the main motif is clear."

At the present time, few classes of boys continue their creative dance work beyond Grade Six. The boys are usually separated from the girls for physical education in Grade Seven. This can give the teacher an excellent opportunity to take the movement training into topics which are especially suited to boys of this age. In some school districts there may be resistance to the idea of boys dancing. One solution is to call it "Movement Training" or perhaps "Dramatic Movement." Schools which sponsor an extensive activity program are likely to have groups of boys engaged in orchestra, choir and dramatic work. "Movement Training" or "Dramatic Movement" can well take its place alongside these activities. Since the work pursued in Grade Seven, Eight and Nine should emphasize the control of the eight basic efforts and the transitions between them, plus a command of the spatial orientation of movements and the control of jumps and landings, the "Movement" classes should provide valuable training for sports and occupational skills. The name of the course is unimportant but the skill background that the students acquire is very important indeed.

SUGGESTED THEMES

1. *Straight air patterns.* Moving through air patterns with the body or a specific body part I X L ▢ △ N V

   Use right and left sides of the body equally. Make the largest possible form, using the highest jump, the lowest landing, and the widest stretch possible. Start the figure sometimes from the top, sometimes from the bottom. Relate body control and exercise with the execution of the spatial pattern.

2. *Angular movements* V L M 7 Z

   Stress the abrupt change of direction. Use the first line for a preparation, i.e. unaccented, and emphasize the second line. Involve the whole body in the reach, bend and stretch.

3. *Round air patterns:* circles arcs, pendulums. Use different parts of the body — arms, legs, trunk, head, hands, forearms, feet, lower leg. Place the movement: in front, at each side, overhead, parallel to the floor. Stress the continuity inherent in round forms. Accelerate and decelerate the speed used. S ∞ ◎

4. *Twisted air patterns:*

   Bring the movement from one side of the body to the other. Bring it from the upper to the lower part of the body. Involve elbows, knees, waist, head and spine. Show the contrast between the ease of flow on the rounded sections with the restricted flow in the sections where the directions change.

---

5. *Floor patterns.* Different types of locomotion used in a variety of floor patterns: zigzag, straight lines, circles, figure-eight weaving. Individuals, pairs, and threes may create these patterns.

6. Contrasting the size of patterns in the body, the air or on the floor.

7. Exploring movements which are created by changing the body shape, using the rounded, elongated, spreading and twisted shapes as the basic ones.

8. Extending these movements by including locomotion in the course of changing the body shape.

9. Adding a body shape to the flight of a jump.

10. Effort transitions: a. changing one element only such as *Slash* → *Thrust* by changing from flexible to straight spatial patterns.

    b. changing two elements such as *Slash* → *Press* by decelerating and changing to straight line spatial patterns

    c. changing three elements such as *Slash* → *Glide* by decelerating and lightening, and moving into a straight line spatial pattern.

11. Dramatic mimes of changing moods achieved by the transition of efforts. For example, a reasonable cycle might be a smooth (gliding) existence, violently (thrust) interrupted by great doubts (wring), pressing on until irritated (flicking) into a slashing attack and a jaunty (dabbing) exit.

12. Movement conversations with a partner, for example, a series of dabbing jumps answered by a slashing turn; a pressing advance answered by a floating evasion.

13. Dramatic mime on creatures of the moon: writhing reptiles, birds of prey, slow ponderous beasts, supermen who have a full range of effort qualities and are master creatures.

14. Dance mime: two ape-men investigate a drum.

15. Movement study inspired by a percussion instrument and including effort and space patterns.

16. Exploration of movements which arise out of the use of the dimensional cross
    a. close fist leading into the direction as contrasted to the palm of the hand pressing into the direction
    b. the head moving into each direction
    c. leg, knee, foot leading into the six directions
    d. jumps, falls, strides to move the whole body into the directions.

17. After the above movements have been experienced compose a mime (to electronic music) on the theme of "The Robot."*

18. Working with a partner develop a sequence on the theme of "Opposition." (Dimensional Cross).

19. A group of six could build a large machine and work out a rhythm for

---

* Westminster XWN-18962, *Electronics*, Sala "Five Improvisations on Magnetic Tape."

pistons and levers each working into a particular series of spatial directions.*

20. Explore ways of reaching from one point to another without approaching the centre of the body.
    a. Finding all triangles possible
    b. linking right-to-up with a jump and finding the other three jumps
    c. linking forward-to-down to produce a collapse and finding three other collapses
    d. linking right-to-forward to produce a turn and finding other turns.
21. Exploration of jumping
    a. five basic uses of feet (pp. 106-107)
    b. different parts of the body leading upward
    c. kinds of jumps — turning, travelling — repetitive jumps on the spot
    d. combining jumps with runs and floor patterns.
22. Mime studies with percussion or music accompaniment
    a. The workers: (i) harvesters (ii) builders (iii) sailors
    b. Street gangs: (i) walk by (ii) Rival gangs (iii) ''Rumble''
    c. Cowboys (i) The riders (ii) The ropers (iii) The shooters
    d. Negro Spirituals — *Joshua Fit the Battle of Jericho*
    e. Architectural Tableaux: (i) High Rise (ii) Town Houses (iii) Split Levels (iv) Demolition (in changing groupings)
    f. *Girl Watchers Theme*: (i) Lounging (ii) Comments (iii) Reactions
    g. The Shape of Things to Come — a surrealistic happening
    h. *Oliver!* The Gang of Pick Pockets
    i. History (i) The Death of a President (ii) Louis Riel (iii) The Plague of London.

SUGGESTIONS AND SAMPLE LESSON PLANS FOR SPECIAL SITUATIONS

BOYS OF GRADE EIGHT OR NINE (OR SEVEN WITH A GOOD BACKGROUND)

Boys of this age need to work hard physically in a dance lesson. They also strive for good control of their movement. Their background in music may be weak. If this is the case, the use of percussion instruments, first by the teacher and then by the dancers themselves may be helpful. They need to work with a partner or in a small group.

SAMPLE LESSON PLAN ONE:

GRADE: Eight, Nine, (or Seven with a good background)

THEME: Deceleration of strong actions: *Thrust* → *Press; Slash* → *Wring*

---

* Macdonald and Evans (Educational Recordings) Ltd., Green Label No. 4, Stephenson ''Machine Rhythms.''

SUBTHEMES: 1. Straight-line floor patterns
  2. Action and reaction in two's

INTRODUCTION:

1. "Warm up by practising a hop for a distance followed by one step leading into a high stretch with both hands overhead, fists clenched. Slowly collapse to the ground and roll over sideways and stand. Repeat starting off in another direction. At the end of four repetitions a square floor pattern could have been described."

2. "Add a series of vibratory shakes which start in the hands and spread into shoulders, head, spine and knees. Terminate with a sudden freeze."

DEVELOPMENT:

1. Repeat these two phrases to a rhythm supplied by the teacher on the drum (Phrase 1) and a pupil with a maraca (Phrase 2). "Practise until rhythm control and floor pattern are clear. Find out how the collapse and roll can be done as an extension of the movement along the side of the square. Make the turn into the next side sudden and surprising. Notice that in the vibrations, the performer has no responsibility for the shape of the movement but must concentrate on strength and speed."

2. "Experiment with a jab (strong, *sudden*, straight) and then a press (strong, *slow*, straight). Use the feet the same way — a stabbing downward jump followed by a slow downward press. Note these experiments are two related movements but they do not merge. Try to merge two related actions by means of decelerating. Start with two fists clenched high. Stab them strongly downward, and, while keeping the strong downward pressure, slow the action into a press."

CULMINATION:

Partners: "Work out a stabbing scene in which the initial stab changes to a slow penetration. The victim tries to change a sharp resistance to a slow and decreasing resistance. The scene may include preliminaries to the stabbing."

BOYS OF GRADE SEVEN OR EIGHT

These boys need a strenuous lesson. They need a mental challenge and they should be required to produce a high standard of bodily control. The dances which they improvise should be related to movement ideas which are of particular interest to them. They usually work better in two's or three's than in large groups.

SAMPLE LESSON PLAN TWO:

GRADE: Seven, Eight

THEME: The six dimensional points of orientation

SUBTHEMES: 1. Floor patterning with rhythmic patterns
2. Body awareness — controlled walks, runs, jumps

INTRODUCTION:
"Scatter formation all facing the front wall. Run the side of the hand down the nose, gullet, breast-bone, and navel with the realization that this is the centre line of the body."

Challenge: "Find out all the ways of walking and running and jumping that can be done while keeping the centre line always facing the front wall."

Observation: Watch two or three boys to determine the floor patterns used: forward and back ⇄; squares and circles; and elevations ↑ ↓.

Challenge: "Improve your own work by choosing your own floor patterns to suit the movement."

Observation: "Assess the skill of the running, walking, jumping. Observe the speed, the elevations used, the control of the sideways, backward and upward movements as well as the control of the landing."

Challenge: "Improve the finish and control of your own work."

DEVELOPMENT:
Observation: "Analyze a sequence to determine the different directions used: up; down; forward; backward; sideways right; sideways left."

Challenge: "These six directions form the "compass" orientation for human movement. They can be felt in the body if they are practised with concentration. Using the closed fist of the right hand to lead the movement, find where each of these six points of orientation are for you."

TEACHER'S CUES:
"Keep the centre line of the body facing the front wall all the time. Use movements of the feet to help you reach, (but keep the front of the body facing the front wall). Do it vigorously. The closed fist implies a punch."
Observation: "Notice what happens when the right fist goes left. (The body gets in the way. The arm folds across it). Notice what happens when the right fist goes back. (It is difficult. The right leg steps back. The trunk is pulled almost horizontal. The left leg and arm work as counterbalances.)"
"Notice that 'up', 'forward' and 'right' are quite easy. 'Right' opens the front of the chest."

"Notice that 'down' is fairly difficult, the knees usually bend and the fist settles on the floor between the feet."

Challenge: "Practise again. Get the feel of the easy and awkward directions when the right arm leads. Find the easy and awkward ones when the left arm leads. Add a finger snap when the fist arrives at the farthest spot."

Challenge: "Do them again and add jumps, steps and runs where they fit in best. Do one set with the right fist and another set with the left fist."

CULMINATION:
Groups of three's.
Challenge: "Build a robot or a machine with pistons or levers that can go to some or all of the points of orientation. Work out the robot's movement program. Some parts may have locomotor possibilities. Sound effects may be added."

BOYS OF GRADE EIGHT OR NINE WITH A GOOD BACKGROUND

Boys of these grades can do interesting work in the area of dramatic dance which includes a characterization made evident through movement rather than by means of the spoken word. It is possible that their sense of humour will add some comedy to their work; but this will be incidental to the development of characterizations. Comedy, as a main theme, is very difficult to deal with.

SAMPLE LESSON PLAN THREE:

GRADE: Eight, Nine

THEME: Body Shapes suited to cowboys' actions

SUBTHEMES: 1. Actions (mime): riding; sauntering; lounging; taking cover
2. Floor patterns
Pre-class planning: Look for pictures of cowboys on horseback, and on foot. Bring hats, belts, boots, guns. Bring folk records.
Music: R.C.A. Victor LE 1009 Adventures in Music, Copeland "Billy The Kid Ballet Suite": Street in a Frontier Town.

INTRODUCTION:
Challenge: "Warm up by running low and dropping flat and freezing, as if running under the cover of sagebrush. Do it with urgency and conviction."
Put music on for background. Encourage them to react quite freely to the music as they run, fall and freeze.

Challenge: "Walk like a cowboy. Explore the shape of the body, the rhythm, the swagger." (This may include: thumbs in belt; hand on holster; bow-legged walk; nonchalant swagger.) "Group and regroup.in two's, three's, four's and five's."

Challenge: "Explore some different patterns of groups of cowboys. Try to achieve varied group shapes by having some sitting and some standing." Play music. Let them experiment with changing the positions and changing from one group to another. "Loners" could join a group. Others could leave the group. One or two "loners" could move down the street.

Challenge: "Riders: Body shape — legs astride, knees bent, one hand on the reins, bodies erect

Actions — bend and stretch legs as for trot, as for gallop on the spot

— foot patterns of travelling in astride position

— other ways of using legs — gallop, trot, high step, paw, slide to a halt, buck, rear, jump."

Play music. "Experiment with movements which will fit in. Work out groupings — for example, groups of cowboys might form a posse."

"Explore the possibilities of floor patterns; galloping forward, halting side by side in a line, following the leader, surrounding some imaginary object, spreading or converging while riding the range."

"Use the various foot patterns discovered earlier."

Play the music and have them organize their ideas to fit the music.

CULMINATION:

Groups of six, with or without music

Challenge: "Work out your own frontier scene wherein the cowboys are at one time on foot and another time on horseback."

Note: Students may either be left to work out their own dance, or the teacher and class may plan together:

Scene I — Main Street
Scene II — Race to mount: Posse rides the range
Scene III — The fight
Scene IV — Posse returns

In the latter case, they may agree to use music and the teacher may guide them to select suitable sections of the music for the four scenes.

FOLK DANCE

THE VALUE OF FOLK DANCE

Folk dance offers some benefits which are not offered by other forms of dance. One of the most important benefits of these is that folk dance gives

---

us a firsthand acquaintance with the heritage of our past. The elements of the dances which have remained through the years are rooted in the fundamental nature of the society of which they are a part. For example, the control and preciseness of the English country dances as compared with the lively, exuberant, noisy square dances of North America are each a reflection of the society from which they stem. Children who participate in these dances, executing them in the mode of the originals, benefit by understanding a little of the influences which have molded their heritage.

By the same token, children can become acquainted in some degree with peoples of other lands. Furthermore, folk dances were part of the social intercourse of the people who danced them. People participated because dance was a way of enjoying themselves. It can be used for the same reason by the pupils. It can also contribute to wholesome social relationships between boys and girls, and between the teacher and the children.

RETENTION OF THE ETHNIC CHARACTERISTICS

If the benefits mentioned above are to be realized, it will be necessary to make every effort to execute the different folk dances in as authentic a way as possible. The music chosen can facilitate this authenticity, especially since there are some excellent recordings available. The culture of the people can be made evident by studying pictures and artifacts, by using the costumes, foods, and musical instruments, by learning the customs of the people and by attempting to understand the influence they would have upon the dance. For example, if the costumes are heavy, the spirit of the dance may be somewhat restricted. If the shoes are clumsy, the footwork will not resemble the precision characteristic of the Scottish sword dances. Many dances are done in the spirit of fun and teasing; others are dignified and ceremonial. These special features are very important and should be preserved as far as possible.

Attendance of pupils and teachers at the performance of the folkloric ballets which tour the main cities of the country can be a source of information. Similarly, many communities have ethnic groups who dance on a regular basis and who are generous with their advice and assistance.

AN ANALYSIS OF THE CONTENT OF A FOLK DANCE CURRICULUM

In all grade levels and in all ethnic forms, folk dances will draw upon and utilize the skills related to the four components of movement which were outlined in Chapter Four, page 39. The basics required in folk dances can be associated with the movement principles which the pupils have used in creative dance and even in gymnastics classes. In folk dance, however, body awareness will be directed towards a stress on footwork and the body carriage and sometimes to a particular use of special parts of the body. The effort quality of the movement will require skill in using the subtleties of strong or light actions, sudden or sustained, flexible or direct movements. Spatial awareness will be directed towards placing a particular stress on floor patterns, and relationships with partners and other members of the group will be of paramount importance.

Primary Grades (One, Two, Three)

The early grades should be presented with dances which are simple in terms of footwork, floor patterns and partner relationships.

1. *Simple footwork* includes dances based on: runs, walks, skips, slides and gallops.
2. *Accents* may be provided by: stamps, claps, bows and simple turns.
3. *Formations* may be: single circles, lines which move forward and back.
4. *Relationships.* The youngest children should be able to dance alone or they may all join hands and do a unison movement like walking clockwise. Partners side-by-side with inside hands joined, or partners face-to-face are formations which can be used by seven- and eight-year-olds.

Junior Grades (Four, Five, Six)

1. *Footwork*
    a. Even rhythm patterns: walking, running, hopping, step-hop, running schottische, basic schottische, side schottische, Bleking step
    b. Uneven rhythm patterns: skipping, slip-step or sliding, gallop, polka
    c. Special steps: buzz step turn, etc.
2. *Accents* may be provided by: claps, stamps, bows, turns, swings, knee bends, distinct changes of direction on the first beat of a phrase.
3. *Formations*: single circles, lines facing each other, double circles, squares, weaving patterns, moving through arches.
4. *Relationships*: unison movement, all hands joined or hands unjoined; partners side-by-side — inside hands joined, two hands crossed, open dance position, promenade position; partners facing — hands on own hips, two hands joined, shoulder-waist grips; two partners facing another couple; four couples in a square.
5. *Rhythm Patterns*: Israeli, Slovanic, Northern European.

Intermediate Grades (Seven, Eight, Nine)

1. *Footwork*
    a. all foot patterns suitable for Junior Grades
    b. uneven rhythm: two-step
    c. even rhythm: waltz
    d. special steps: free choice to suit ability of the class.
2. *Accents*: may be provided by: claps, stamps, bows, turns, swing, knee bends, distinct changes of direction on the first beat of a phrase.
3. *Formations*: single circles, lines facing each other, double circles, squares, weaving patterns, moving through arches.

Paul and His Chickens is a dance based on the running schottische and the step-hop.

4. *Relationships*: unison movement, all hands joined or hands unjoined; partners side-by-side — inside hands joined, two hands crossed, open dance position, promenade position; partners facing — hands on own hips, two hands joined, shoulder-waist grips; two partners facing another couple; four couples in a square. Partners in closed ballroom dance position.
5. *Rhythm Patterns*: Greek and Slovonic, Israeli, Mexican, American western square dance rhythms.
6. Dances which relate to the adult dance club situation.

SUGGESTED DANCES

Recommendations for dances which are suited to the various grade levels are offered in many textbooks and courses of studies. The location of the school and the ethnic background of the pupils will have a bearing on the dances which are chosen for specific classes. Also, the knowledge and ability of the teacher tends to influence his choice of dances. Further, the availability of good music and simple directions are of practical importance.

The lists of dances suggested here are in keeping with the principles of child growth and development and are compatible with the progress expected in the use of movement principles as outlined in the other facets of physical education described in this book. The lists are not exhaustive but should provide a good working base. The directions are not included because the record companies are now providing them with the records or albums.

Kindergarten — Junior and Senior

1. *Singing Games* such as:
Ring Around the Rosie	Folkcraft 1199
London Bridge	
Farmer in the Dell	Folkcraft 1182
The Mulberry Bush	Folkcraft 1183
Looby Loo	Folkcraft 1181
Bluebird	Folkcraft 1184

Primary Grades (One, Two, Three)

1. *Singing Games* such as:
Go Round and Round the Village	Folkcraft 1191
A Hunting We Will Go	Folkcraft 1191
Pussy Cat, Pussy Cat	Folkcraft 1199
The Grand Old Duke of York	
Oats, Peas, Beans	Folkcraft 1182
Did You Ever See A Lassie?	Folkcraft 1183

2. *Folk Dances*
Chimes of Dunkirk	World of Fun M105
Swedish Clap Dance	Folkcraft 1188
Shoemaker's Dance	Folkcraft 1187
Rig A Gig Gig	Folkcraft 1199
Jingle Bells	Folkcraft 1180
Danish Dance of Greeting	Folkcraft 1187
Children's Polka	Folkcraft 1187
Pop Goes the Weasel	Victor 6180
Jump Jim Crow	Folkcraft 1180
Hansel and Gretel (Let Your Feet Go Tap)	Folkcraft 1184
Carrousel	Folkcraft 1183
Paw, Paw Patch	Folkcraft 1181

Junior Grades (Four, Five, Six)

1. *Easy Dances*:
Czebogar — slip-step; Hungarian turn	Folkcraft 1196

Tropanka — run	Folk Dancer 1020
Durham Reel — slip, skip	Folkcraft 1142
(Use *A Hundred Pipers*)	
Troika — waltz run	World of Fun M105
	Folkcraft 1170
Gustav's Skol — walk, skip	Folkcraft 1175
Crested Hen — step-hop	Victor 45-6176
Seven Jumps — step-hop	Victor 45-6176
Napoleon — slip-step, running schottische	Folk Dancer 1054
Military Schottische —	McGregor 400
running schottische, step-hop	
Paul and His Chickens —	Folk Dancer 2001
running schottische, step-hop	
The Waves of Tory — running	Folk Dancer MH 1075

2. *More Difficult Dances*

Thady You Gander — walk, skip	Folkcraft 1167
Man in the Hay — skip, slip-step, buzz step	Folk Dancer 1057
Cherkessia — Israeli — stepping	Kismet 130
Dance Lightly — walk, run	World of Fun M114
Patch Tanz — Israeli — stepping	Folk Dancer 1092
Virginia Reel — walk, slip-step, reel	Capitol C40028 (with calls) RCA, EPA 4138 (no calls) or "Circassian Circle" on Folkcraft 1167
Danish Schottische — schottische	World of Fun M102
Rheinlander for Three — schottische	Folk Dancer 1050
Horah-Israeli — schottische, step-hop	Folkcraft 1110
Alfelder — walking	World of Fun M115
Mayim-Israeli — run, hop	World of Fun 119
Tampet — walk, slip-step	World of Fun M114
Ace of Diamonds — polka, bleking-step	World of Fun M102
Heel and Toe Polka — polka	McGregor 400
Clap Dance — heel-toe polka	Victor 45:6171
Tantoli — heel-toe polka, step-hop	Victor 45:6183
Kalvelis — polka, clapping	Folkcraft 1051

Intermediate (Seven, Eight, Nine)

1. *Folk Dances*
   a. Based on the schottische

Weggis (Swiss)	Folkcraft 1160
Korobushka (Russian)	Folkcraft 1170
Hora (Israeli)	Folkcraft 1122
Rumunjsko Kolo (Yugoslav)	Folkcraft 1402

b. Based on the polka
    Granny Polka (American)   Folk Dancer 2001
    Feder Mikkel (Danish)   Folk Craft 1098
    Norwegian Polka   Folk Dancer MH2001

c. Based on Two-Step
    Czardas — draw, Hungarian turn   Burns Album B344
    The Roberts — draw, two-step   Folkcraft 1161
    Teton Mountain Stomp   Windsor A753
    Boston Two-Step   Folkcraft 1158

d. Based on the Waltz
    Norwegian (or Danish) Mountain March   Victor 6173 (45 RPM)
    Masquerade (Scandinavian)   Folkcraft 1097
    Veleta (American)   Imperial 1045
    Waltz of Bells (American)   Windsor A7S4 or
                                    Lloyd Shaw 109

    Little Man in a Fix (Danish)   Folk Dancer 1054 or
                                    Victor 20449

    To Ting — waltz, pivot turn   Folk Dancer 1018

e. American Couple Dances
    Mexican Waltz   Folkcraft 1093
    Cotton-Eyed Joe   Folkcraft 1255
    Rye Waltz   Folkcraft 1103
    Black Hawk Waltz   Folkcraft 1103

f. Mixers
    Bingo
    Patty Cake Polka Mixer   Folk Dancer MH1501
    Little Shoemaker   Windsor 4141
    Spanish Circle Waltz   World of Fun M105
    Oklahoma Mixer   McGregor 4005
    Promenade by Threes   Folk Dancer MH1506

2. *American Square Dances*
    a) Easy
    Head Two Gents Cross Over (Ocean Wave)* Ford, p. 54
    Little Brown Jug — i.e. swing at the centre Ford, p. 60
    Form a star with the right hand crossed†   Shaw, p. 63
    Pop Goes the Weasel   Ford, p. 62
    Adam and Eve   Shaw, p. 228
    b) Easy — but using Allemande Left, Grand Right and Left
    The Girl I Left Behind Me   Ford, p. 55
    Irish Washerwoman   Ford, p. 57
    Hinky-Dinky, Parlee Voo   Ford, p. 64

---

* Ford, Henry, *Good Morning*, Dearborn, Michigan, 1943.
† Shaw, Lloyd, *Cowboy Dances,* Caxton Printers Ltd., Caldwell, Idaho, 1947.

| Spanish Cavaliers | Ford, p. 65 |
| Red River Valley | Ford, p. 74 |

c) More Difficult — figures involving more dancers

Nellie Bly	Ford, p. 75
My Old Kentucky Home	Ford, p. 68
Buffalo Girl	Ford, p. 56
Grapevine Twist	Shaw, p. 276
Forward Up Six	Shaw, p. 258
Promenade Your Corners Round	Shaw, p. 249

3. *Utilitarian Records*: (For use in establishing skills of: schottische, step-hop, skip, slide, gallop, polka, two-step.)

1. Norwegian Polka	Folk Dancer 2001
Telemark Schottische	
2. Circassian Circle	Folkcraft 1167
(reel — Little Brown Jug)	
Thady You Gander (skipping —	
Scottish skip, change-of-step)	
3. Polka Zu Drien	Folk Dancer 1050
4. Heel and Toe Polka (polka)	McGregor 400
5. Hundred Pipers (skip, Virginia Reel)	Folkcraft 1142
6. Totur (two-step)	Folk Dancer 1021
Sextur (polka, skip)	

DEVELOPING THE DANCE STEPS

The Fundamental Steps

The walk, run, hop and jump are basic locomotor actions (p. 106) and most children are able to execute them in some fashion by the time they begin their schooling. However, each of these types of steps can be done in many different ways. A great deal of practice should be given to these basic actions in all the grades of the school. Much of the practice should be done to different kinds of music and a good deal of attention should be given to exploring different styles of dancing them. For example, the walking shuffle of western American square dance is quite different from the marching walk of the Gustaf's Skoal. The fascination of the dance is as much in the styling as in the steps or figures and therefore, proper attention needs to be given to the way these simple steps are done.

The Basic Dance Steps

1. The skip, slide or slip-step and the gallop are the uneven rhythm steps and they also generally develop in a spontaneous way as the child matures. Their development can be facilitated by encouraging the children to respond quite freely to lively ⁶⁄₈ music. The practice can be done alone, with a partner with hands joined, or with hands joined in a circle. Quite

often a child can absorb the rhythm from his partner, always providing that no stress or tension is built up. "Teaching" in the ordinary sense is not very helpful. A complete participation in the flow of the rhythm is required and this can best be achieved by clapping the rhythm, moving freely to it, observing others who are using the steps easily and by participating with others. However, the style of execution can be improved by a teacher who draws attention to lightness, ways of using the legs, feet, arms, head, and to the pathways of the movement.

2. The traditional dance steps. The step-hop, schottische, polka, two-step and waltz require careful teaching. A very effective way of helping someone to learn these steps is to work through the rhythm and flow pattern. The appropriate music must be selected for each step, the rhythm pattern tapped out, and a time for free movement response provided. It is very important that all the exploration and practice should be done to music. After the pupils are moving on the beat and without tension, the teacher should then direct the foot pattern. Music should be used. Counting should be avoided. The teacher may help by cueing the steps verbally, for example "Hop-and-change, Hop-and-change."

3. *Step-hop*. Use ¾ or ⁴⁄₄ even rhythms. Any schottische record is suitable

- clap the beat
- move to the beat, individual exploration
- hop on the spot: *8 hops right foot: 8 hops left foot
  - 4 hops   4 hops
  - hop-and-change   hop-and-change
- "hop-and-change" is the step-hop and may be practised in many situations to the music. Useful situations are: circling to the right, into the centre and out, turning yourself around, side-by-side with a partner
- learn folk dances based on the step-hop.

4. *Schottische I*. Use ⁴⁄₄ even rhythm. Most schottische records are suitable.

- clap the beat
- move freely to the beat, individual exploration
- *run* on the beat. Use varied situations — circles, partners, alone: forward, turning
- clap every other beat
- *step-hop* review. Move freely
- clap the schottische rhythm, ⁴⁄₄

$$\frac{4}{4} \quad \downarrow \quad \downarrow \quad \downarrow \quad \xi \quad |$$

clap, clap, clap, throw-away

* Each phrase may be repeated as often as required to establish it well before a shorter one is used.

- chant and clap: run, run, run, hop
- *running schottische*: run, run, run, hop
- practise it in many situations
- learn a folk dance based on the running schottische, e.g. Napoleon.

5. *Schottische and Step-hop*

- combine two schottisches and four step-hops *without* counting. Clap out the phrases

R R R H   R R R H   S-H S-H   S-H S-H

- practise it in many situations: single circles; partners side-by-side and moving forward
- explore different ways of doing these steps; e.g. two schottisches *forward*, four step-hops turning
- learn dances based on this combination

The step-hop may be practised in many situations.

6. *Schottische II*. Use ¼ even rhythm. Most slow schottische records are suitable

- clap the schottische rhythm pattern: clap, clap, clap, hold
- review the *running schottische*
    - change the running schottische to:
      step — diagonally forward right
      close — left to right
      step — diagonally forward right
      hop — hop right, and swing the left foot diagonally
        forward right
- cueing chant is: right close right hop or step close step hop

$$\frac{4}{4} \quad \text{♩} \quad \text{♩} \quad \text{♩} \quad \text{𝄽} \quad | \quad \text{♩} \quad \text{♩} \quad \text{♩} \quad \text{𝄽} \quad |$$

right close right hop   or   step close step hop

- learn a dance based on Schottische II such as the Danish
  Schottische

One way to turn a partner while using the step-hop.

7. *Polka*   Use ⁶⁄₈ or ²⁄₄ uneven rhythm
   Method I

- clap the beat
- move freely to the music
- practise the slide or slip-step sideways in a single circle
- partners facing — slide counterclockwise
- continue counterclockwise but change from face-to-face and back-to-back
- cueing chant: (Hop)* face-to-face, (Hop) back-to-back

Method II

- clap the beat
- move freely to the music
- practise the gallop
- partners gallop side-by-side with the outside foot leading
- partners explore the idea of changing the lead foot after every *four* gallops, then after every *two* gallops, and finally after *every* gallop. This will be the polka
- learn a dance based on a polka such as *Ace of Diamonds*
- practise with a partner, face-to-face and back-to-back polka; side-by-side travelling forward, facing forward; facing each other in shoulder-waist grasp so that one travels backward and the other forward; same position but turning as they travel. *Note,* this is made easier if the partners pull slightly away from each other.
- learn folk dances based on a polka and danced with a partner, such as *Heel and Toe Polka*

8. *Two-Step.* Use ²⁄₄ uneven rhythm

- clap the beat
- move freely to the music
- clap and chant: "step-close-step and, step-close-step and," etc.
- partners side-by-side, inside hands joined, starting with the outside foot, move forward swinging face-to-face and back-to-back very smoothly so that the hop used in the polka is eliminated

step close step   step close step
    (and)   (and)

* The hop permits a quick change of facing and produces the polka foot pattern which is: hop, step, close, step; hop, step, close, step.

hop step step: step   step   hop step step: step   step
     close   hop   close   close   hop   close

- practise in different situations such as those suggested for the polka
- learn dances based on the two-step such as *The Boston Two-Step*.

9. *Waltz*. ¾ even rhythm
   - clap beat, accenting first beat of the bar
   - move freely to the music
   - run to the music accenting the first beat by a slight stamp, a slight knee bend, or a slight leap
   - learn a dance based on a waltz run. *Norwegian Mountain March* is good.

10. *Waltz Balance* — explore ways of keeping the rhythm without travelling. Small step on right foot, rise on right toe, lower right heel, (done with the right foot while the left taps, swings, brushes or closes on the rising beat). The left foot then takes over with a step, rise, fall.

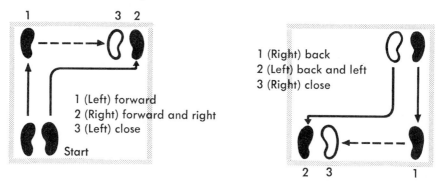

Right: Left:
  step rise fall   step rise fall

Waltz Walk — mark the accent with a slightly larger step.
   - Clap and chant: "large, small, small; large, small, small," etc.
   - practise walking to that rhythm
   - combine: two balances and two phrases of walks. Cue: (balance) *right,* up, down; *left,* up, down; (walk) large, small, small; large, small, small
   - practise this combination in different situations such as a single circle; partners facing with one or two hands joined
   - learn several dances based on the waltz balance and waltz walk.

11. *Box Waltz*
   - explore, probably without music, to determine the spatial relationship of the feet in the box.

1   3   2

1 (Left) forward
2 (Right) forward and right
3 (Left) close

Start

1 (Right) back
2 (Left) back and left
3 (Right) close

2   3   1

   - practise to slow waltz. Cue: *forward,* side, close; *back,* side, close

- practise in various situations including partners facing and using shoulder-waist grasp
- learn dances based on the box waltz such as *The Black Hawk Waltz.**

SAMPLE LESSON PLAN

GRADE: Five

THEME: The Danish folk dance *Paul and His Chickens* featuring running schottisches and step-hops

SUBTHEMES: 1. Floor patterns
2. Groups of four, retaining and breaking contact

INTRODUCTION: (Review)
Challenge: "Listen to this music (*Telemark Schottische*). Softly clap a schottische rhythm pattern to it" (see p. 313). "Move in your own pathway, practising the schottische. Make a pattern of your own on the floor."

Challenge: "Listen again. Softly clap a step-hop rhythm" (see p. 312). "Make a little pattern of your own using the step-hop."

Challenge: "Listen again. Clap this pattern: run, run, run, hop; run, run, run, hop; step-hop, step-hop, step-hop, step-hop." (The teacher may chant the step pattern; the pupils may clap it, or vice versa.)

Challenge: "Use the music to make up a little dance using that step pattern."

Observation: "Watch these two people. Try to decide what they stress in their patterns," (one is based on directional patterns such as forward and turning; the other is based on travelling during the schottische and remaining on the spot during the step-hops).

DEVELOPMENT:
Challenge: "Find a partner. Try out some dance patterns based on schottisches and step-hops. Decide how the partners will relate to each other. Choose a starting position: Will you hold hands or not? Will you face your partner or both face the same way? Place yourselves and be ready. When the music begins experiment with your ideas."

* Imperial 1006A, *The Black Hawk Waltz*, Mary E. Walsh.

The teacher may encourage them by remarking upon some good ideas which are being tried. The music may be stopped after a reasonable interval.

Challenge: "This time select the figures you like best. Choose two. Try to have a good contrast between the two figures. Take a moment to plan. Decide on your starting position. Ready! Here is the music."
The teacher should probably stop the music after two figures have been done. He may indicate to the pupils that this is the amount of music available for the two figures.

Challenge: "Try several times more. I'll stop the music at the proper place each time."

Observation: "Let's watch several dances and enjoy the variety that is shown." (Probably a quarter of the class can show their dances at one time.)

CULMINATION:
The dance *Paul and His Chickens*.
Challenge: "Form groups of four with one set of partners leading and

the other set following (e.g.   ). Hold your partner's hand. Give your free hand to the other pair. See if your group can stay together while you all run forward with schottisches and step-hops (two schottisches and four step-hops). Leaders, travel in an interesting pathway."

Observation: "Watch these three groups. Notice the interesting pathways they use. See how they travel a long way on the schottisches and travel very little on the step-hops."

Challenge: "All try again." (The teacher should stop the music after the pattern has been done twice. He should make it clear that this is the first figure of a Danish dance called *Paul and His Chickens*.)

Challenge: "Which groups can discover how to do Figure Two? When the music starts, do the schottische running forward as you did for Figure One. But when you do the step-hops, find a way for the leaders to change places with the followers. You can release hands in one place only, and must join them again when everyone is in the new position."
The teacher should regulate the music. He should watch the groups. If they stop when they get into the new positions, the teacher should restart the music after challenging the new leaders to carry on until all are back where they

started. The solution:

Observation: "Watch these solutions." (The teacher should show any good ideas, and then state which one is required for the dance.)

Challenge: "All groups try Figure Two."

Challenge: "See if you can do Figure One and Two. Remember, each one is done twice."

Challenge: "Now can you discover how to do Figure Three? The schottisches are the same. The couples change places on the step-hops, but *without* releasing hands! Here is the music."
The teacher must be prepared for quite an entanglement in the initial stage of experimentation. If the music is left on, one or two groups usually manage to solve the problem. If not, the teacher may give a clue, "Would it help to go through an arch?" He may have to ask how many arches they have to go under to unwind their arms.

Observation: "Watch how these people solved their problem. Who went under the arch first?" (There are several solutions. The correct one requires the head couple to back through the arch made by the rear couple as they advance into the lead position. They will have to turn under their own arms to

untangle themselves. ( go under own arms).

Challenge: "All try with the music. Take several repetitions."
The teacher may need to visit several groups to cue them. If the music is left on, they will gradually get back on beat, especially if the teacher helps by clapping the pattern (p. 312) as they dance.

Challenge: "Now can you manage the whole dance? Remember, each figure is repeated." The teacher may cue:

Figure One: "step-hop *forward*"
              Repeat
Figure Two: *Change* — around the outside
              Repeat
Figure Three: *Change* — through the arches
              Repeat
The whole dance may be repeated several times.

Challenge: "We can finish with one of your favourite dances. Which one today?"

QUIET ENDING: Music: A waltz
"Scatter. Stay in one place. Move gently to the music. Lift one arm slowly,

until it is as high as possible. Watch it all the time. Lower it slowly. Keep watching it. Do the same movement with the other arm. Then raise both arms while you rise up on your toes. Look upward. Now, slowly come downward until you are sitting and quiet."

THE TEACHING OF SQUARE DANCES

The styles of movements, rhythms and callers vary quite markedly between various parts of the country. The teacher may want to confine the program to the locally popular styles, or may wish to extend the pupils' appreciations to styles and rhythms new to them. The choice of records used in the program will exert a major influence on the style. A study of square dancing can be extended beyond the mere learning of a few dances to include an appreciation of style, rhythm and the basic elements of this type of dancing, and may bring about an awareness of the modern and ongoing changes which are characteristic of the present programs of the clubs and associations which currently exist throughout Canada and the United States. The art of calling may also be incorporated into the program. Indeed, dancing to a caller, rather than to records which include the calls, sets up an entirely unique experience. Dancing to a 'live" caller depends upon an interplay between dancers and caller, with the former necessarily having to be prepared to respond to spontaneous changes of pattern. Conversely, the caller must be able to judge the extent of the challenge he presents and be able to assure a successful response. This is a quite different experience from that which arises when dances are learned as a memory response to a fore-known call.

Fundamentals of Square Dances

The components of movement as outlined in Chapter Four can be used to advantage in the following situations.

a. The basic step: a light, gliding dance walk with weight largely on the ball of the foot so that changes of directions can be readily executed. The body is held tall and erect. Most "old-timers" acquire a slight jauntiness or swagger.

Alternatives: a skip-change-of-step such as is used in Scottish country dancing, is used in some districts; skipping is often used by young children. However, it makes quick changes of figures difficult to execute and is rarely used by experienced dancers.

b. The swing: partners turn one another. The basic hold is that used for ballroom dancing, except that the partners move so that the right sides are touching. The most sophisticated swing uses the basic gliding walk for two complete revolutions. The secret is for the partners to lean away from each other, especially with the head and shoulders, and to make use of centrifugal force to create a neat rotation.

Alternatives: There are other ways of holding a partner; the more usual one being the shoulder-waist grasp; a less usual one being the two-hand grasp. There is another important step pattern called the "buzz step." In this step, the weight is kept mainly on the right foot while the left pushes as when using a scooter. The outward lean to create centrifugal force is just as important in this style of swing as it is in the other forms.

c. The promenade: partners dance forward in a side by side position with the lady on the gentleman's right-hand side. The steps used may be any of the basic steps described above. The way the partners hold one another varies with the style being used or the district from which the dance comes. The main positions are: skating position with hands crossed in front of the body, the girl's right held in the boy's right (left in left); "varsovienne" position with the hands right-to-right — left-to-left, but the boy's right arm is behind the girl's shoulder.

d. The grand right and left: this is a weaving pattern usually done simultaneously by all eight dancers. It is started by the partners of each couple facing one another and grasping right hands. This causes all the men to face counterclockwise (ladies — clockwise). The dancers all move in the direction thus established using the basic step(s) described above. They alternate hands starting by giving the right to their partners and the left to the next dancer they meet. This pattern continues. In some calls, the phrase "Grand Chain" is used to indicate the same pattern. The chain may continue until all the dancers' arrive back at their home position ("Grand chain all the way round"). Or, it may continue until they meet their partners ("Grand Chain halfway round"). It is usually combined in different ways with the swing and the promenade.

e. The allemande left: partners are in place (side-by-side facing the centre of the square). For the allemande left, each dancer turns his (her) back on his (her) partner and turns the corner dancer once around by joining left hands. The figure is finished when all have returned to the home position. However, "allemande left" is usually followed by a variety of alternatives such as "swing your partner" or "grand chain." Note: it may be necessary to foreshorten the arm (bend the elbow) and pull against the other dancer to turn quickly enough to stay "on phrase with the music."

The Basic Format of Square Dances

Most square dances are arranged in a four-part pattern which includes an Introduction, the main Figure, which may be interrupted by a Break and then repeated with another couple leading. The alternation of Figure and Break continues until all the couples have had a turn to lead. The dance is then usually closed with an Ending which may be somewhat like the Break but more elaborate.

Sample Format

1. Introduction:
   Bow, swing, promenade around the ring
2. Figure — Head couple – – –   (to indicate a figure following)
3. Break   — Swing your corner
            Swing your partner
            Promenade your lady around and home
4. Figure — Second couple – – –
5. Break   — as above
6. Figure — Third Couple – – –
7. Break   — as above
8. Figure — Fourth Couple – – –
9. Ending — Swing your corner; Swing your own,
            Allemande left on the corners all,
            Grand right and left around the hall,
            Meet your partner and promenade home.
            When you're home, swing your own,
            Bow, my friend, and that's the end.

Difficulties

Whenever the dancers work with anyone other than their partners, there is a likelihood of beginners getting lost. Therefore, when the dances are first introduced, most of the beginnings, breaks and endings should be designed to be done with the dancers' own partners. The swings should be timed to allow only two revolutions. The home position of each couple should be clearly established. The beginnings, breaks and endings can be practised to music several times before the figure is introduced and, while this is being done, a feeling for the phrasing in the music should be cultivated.

The Figures

There are many kinds of figures, ranging from those in which the first couple visits each of the others in turn, to those figures in which all four couples are active simultaneously. For a detailed analysis and description of the different types, the reader is referred to "Cowboy Dances".*

Programing

An evening program usually starts with a mixer and then alternates two square dances with one couple dance, finishing with a home waltz. A school lesson could gradually achieve similar variety (in miniature) as more dances become familiar and can be performed without requiring much time for instruction. One new dance could receive the major emphasis in the lesson.

* Shaw, Lloyd, *Cowboy Dances*, Caxton Printers Ltd., Caldwell, Idaho, 1947.

APPENDIX

APPARATUS FOR GYMNASTICS

Three categories of materials are used for gymnastics, namely, the small manipulative pieces, the portable items, and the installed units. There should be a sufficient number and variety of small pieces to allow each child to work on his own. The portable and installed pieces should be numerous enough to allow the groups to work in fours. It is advantageous to combine different pieces of apparatus so that the movement involved corresponds to the theme of the lesson. Encouragement is given to developing phrases of movement which flow together as a result of moving from one piece of apparatus to another, as well as from different movements which arise from a repeated use of one unit before going on to the next. Prior to installation, consideration should be given to the relationship of one unit to the other. For example, proper location of the vertical ropes may permit a transition from ropes to climber. The horizontal ladder may facilitate a flow of movement from one frame of the climber to the other. The floor should be considered an important part of the working unit.

School authorities usually make provision for the in-service instruction of their teachers when the large apparatus is installed.

KINDS OF APPARATUS

1. SMALL MANIPULATIVE EQUIPMENT. These include hoops, ropes, canes, blocks, clubs, staves, cones and individual mats. (See p. 208)

2. PORTABLE APPARATUS. The following items are in wide use: tumbling mats, balance benches fitted with clips (p. 207), balance beams, vaulting boxes — sides may be solid, barred (p. 131), or omitted (p. 238), beat boards, portable climbers including "A" frames which can be used in a variety of ways (p. 215), utility boxes, and vaulting bucks.

Using simple apparatus.

3. INSTALLED APPARATUS. The fold-away climbers are available in different designs and sizes and include such units as window ladders, Swedish wall bars, balance beams, horizontal ropes and ladders, vertical climbing ropes and rope ladders, vertical rope scrambling nets.

Some types of installed apparatus which fold against the wall when not in use.

SOME SAMPLE ARRANGEMENTS

1. TO ELICIT THE FOLLOWING: going over/under or landing on a target, working close to apparatus, near to/far from the apparatus, sequences of several movements related to one piece of apparatus, weight on body part and the floor (avoiding the obstacle), shape of body stressed, balances related to apparatus, twisting or arches related to apparatus. See See Figure 1. on page 326.

2. TO ELICIT THE FOLLOWING EXPERIENCES: practising landings or using flight, meeting the floor in different ways, on-and-off relationships, using different heights of apparatus, or joining movements to create a sequence. See Figure 2. on page 327.

3. TO PROVIDE THE FOLLOWING EXPERIENCES: mounting-dismounting, sequence building, varied forms of locomotion, travelling along pathways. See Figure 3. on page 328.

Figure 1.

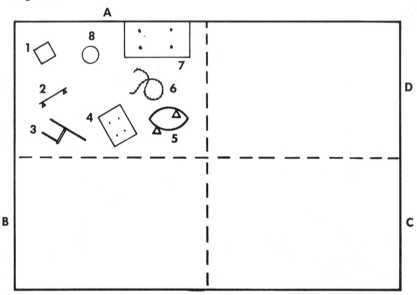

1 Agility box	Sections B, C, D can be supplied with similar items, or portable units, or installed apparatus.
2 Wand on two cones	
3 Chair tipped up	
4 Individual mat	
5 Hoop on two cones	
6 Rope (shaped) on floor	
7 Mat against wall	
8 Hoop on floor	

Figure 2.

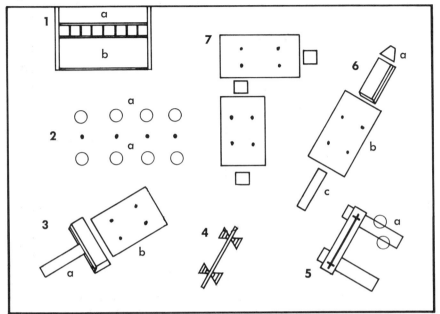

1 Climber with
   a) horizontal ladder
   b) balance beam

2 Climbing ropes with
   a) two hoops on the floor

3 Vaulting box with
   a) inclined bench clipped
      on bar
   b) mat

4 Two "A" frames with a pole

5 Two balance benches
   supporting a bench with
   balance beam up and
   a) two hoops inclined to the
      floor

6 Vaulting box with
   a) beat board
   b) mat
   c) balance bench

7 Two mats with three agility
   boxes

Figure 3.

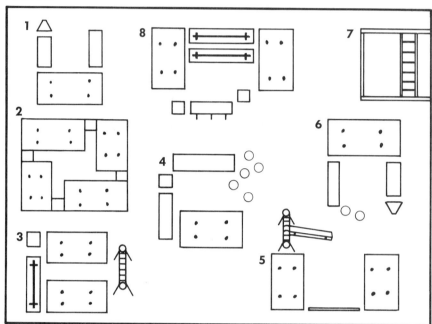

1 Beat board, vaulting box, mat, bench, floor.

2 Four mats, four agility boxes alternated.

3 Agility box, bench (beam up), mat, ladder on two "A" frames, mat.

4 Agility box, bench, mat, hoops, bench.

5 Inclined bench on "A" frame, tumbling mat, balance beam, mat.

6 Beat board, vaulting box, mat, bench, hoops.

7 Climber with horizontal ladder and beam.

8 Mat, agility box, bench, agility box, mat, two benches (beams up).

BIBLIOGRAPHY

A. Bilbrough and P. Jones, *Physical Education in the Primary School,* University of London Press Ltd., London, 1964.

Marion R. Broer, *Efficiency of Human Movement,* W. B. Saunders Company, Philadelphia, 1961.

Camille Brown and Rosalind Cassidy, *Theory in Physical Education — A Guide to Program Change,* Lea and Febiger, Philadelphia, 1963.

John W. Bunn, *Scientific Principles of Coaching,* Prentice-Hall Inc., Englewood Cliffs, N.J., 1955.

W. McD. Cameron and Peggy Pleasance, *Education in Movement—School Gymnastics,* Basil Blackwell, Oxford, 1964.

Mr. and Mrs. Henry Ford, *"Good Morning,"* Dearborn, Michigan, 1943.

Alice Gates, *A New Look at Movement,* Burgess Publishing Co., Minneapolis, Minnesota, 1968.

Alma M. Hawkins, *Creating through dance,* Prentice-Hall Inc., Englewood Cliffs, N.J. 1964.

Doris Humphrey, *The Art of Making Dances,* Rinehart and Company, Inc., New York, 1959.

Ann Hutchinson, *Labanotation,* New Directions Books, James Laughlin, New York, 1961.

Newell C. Kephart, *The Slow Learner in the Classroom,* Chas. E. Merrill Books, Inc., Columbus, Ohio, 1965.

B. Knapp, *Skill in Sport,* Routledge and Kegan Paul, London, 1966.

Rudolf Laban, *Modern Educational Dance,* Macdonald and Evans Ltd., London, 1948.

Rudolf Laban, *The Mastery of Movement,* Second Edition, Revised by Lisa Ullmann, Macdonald and Evans Ltd., London, 1960.

Rudolf Laban, *Choreutics,* Annotated and Edited by Lisa Ullmann, Macdonald and Evans Ltd., London, 1966.

Rudolf Laban and F. C. Lawrence, *Effort,* Macdonald and Evans Ltd., London, 1947.

Warren Lamb, *Posture and Gesture,* Gerald Duckworth and Co. Ltd., London, 1965.

London County Council, *Educational Gymnastics,* London, 1963.

London County Council, *Movement Education for Infants,* London, 1964.

E. Mauldon and J. Layson, *Teaching Gymnastics,* Macdonald and Evans Ltd., London, 1965.

Eleanor Metheny, *Movement and Meaning,* McGraw-Hill Book Company, New York, 1968.

Ruth Morison, *Educational Gymnastics,* Speirs and Gledsdale Ltd., Liverpool, 1956. (Obtainable: Ling Book Shop, 10 Nottingham Place, London W.1.)

G. Doreen Pallett, *Modern Educational Gymnastics,* Pergamon Press Ltd., Oxford, 1965.

Donald S. Purdy, *Basic Physical Skills,* The Copp Clark Publishing Co., Toronto, 1953.

Valerie Preston, *A Handbook For Modern Educational Dance*, Macdonald and Evans Ltd., London, 1963.

Joan Russell, *Creative Dance In The Primary School,* Macdonald and Evans Ltd., London, 1965.

Joan Russell, *Modern Dance in Education,* Macdonald and Evans Ltd., London, 1958.

Curt Sachs, *World History of the Dance,* W. W. Norton and Company Inc., New York, (The Norton Library Edition) 1963.

Lloyd Shaw, *Cowboy Dances,* The Caxton Printers Ltd., Caldwell, Idaho, 1947.

Lloyd Shaw, *The Round Dance Book,* The Caxton Printers Ltd., Caldwell, Idaho, 1948.

Peter Slade, *Child Drama,* University of London Press Ltd., London, 1954.

Hope M. Smith, *Introduction to Human Movement,* Addison-Wesley Publishing Co. Inc., Reading, Mass., 1968.

John M. Stephens, *The Psychology of Classroom Learning,* Holt, Rinehart and Winston Inc., New York, 1966.

D. K. Stanley and I. F. Waglow et al, *Physical Education Activity Handbook for Men and Women,* Allyn and Bacon Inc., Boston, 1966.

Margery J. Turner, *Dance Handbook,* Prentice-Hall Inc., Englewood Cliffs, N.J., 1959.

Peggy J. Woodeson and Denis C. V. Watts, *Schoolgirl Athletics,* Stanley Paul, London, 1966.